Film, Philosophy, and Reality

D0144628

Film, Philosophy, and Reality: Ancient Greece to Godard is an original contribution to film-philosophy that shows how thinking about movies can lead us into a richer appreciation and understanding of both reality and the nature of human experience. Focused on the question of the relationship between how things seem to us and how they really are, it is at once an introduction to philosophy through film and an introduction to film through philosophy.

The book is divided into three parts. The first is an introduction to philosophy and film, designed for the reader with little background in one or the other subject. The second examines the philosophical importance of the distinction between appearance and reality, and shows that reflection upon this distinction is naturally provoked by the experience of watching movies. The final part takes a close and careful look at the style and techniques of Jean-Luc Godard's groundbreaking film *Breathless* in order to illustrate how such themes can be explored cinematically.

The book addresses topics such as:

- Film: what it is and how to understand it
- The methods and concerns of philosophy
- The nature of cinematic appearances
- The history of metaphysics
- The relationship between cinema and life
- The philosophical relevance of film techniques.

With a glossary of key thinkers, terms, and concepts, as well as sections on suggested films and further reading, this textbook will appeal to lecturers and students in undergraduate philosophy and film courses, and in courses focused on Philosophy of Film, Philosophy and Film, or Film-Philosophy.

Nathan Andersen teaches philosophy and film studies at Eckerd College in Saint Petersburg, Florida, USA. He programs an award-winning cinema series and is the co-director of the "Visions of Nature/Voices of Nature," Environmental Film Festival. He is the author of *Shadow Philosophy: Plato's Cave and Cinema* (2014, Routledge), and has published on the history of philosophy, environmental philosophy, and film.

Film, Philosophy, and Reality

Ancient Greece to Godard

Nathan Andersen

Routledge
Taylor & Francis Group

LONDON AND NEW YORK

First published 2019
by Routledge
2 Park Square, Milton Park, Abingdon, Oxon OX14 4RN

and by Routledge
52 Vanderbilt Avenue, New York, NY 10017

Routledge is an imprint of the Taylor & Francis Group, an informa business

© 2019 Nathan Andersen

The right of Nathan Andersen to be identified as author of this work has been asserted by him in accordance with sections 77 and 78 of the Copyright, Designs and Patents Act 1988.

All rights reserved. No part of this book may be reprinted or reproduced or utilised in any form or by any electronic, mechanical, or other means, now known or hereafter invented, including photocopying and recording, or in any information storage or retrieval system, without permission in writing from the publishers.

Trademark notice: Product or corporate names may be trademarks or registered trademarks, and are used only for identification and explanation without intent to infringe.

British Library Cataloguing-in-Publication Data
A catalogue record for this book is available from the British Library

Library of Congress Cataloging-in-Publication Data
A catalog record has been requested for this book

ISBN: 978-0-415-74211-5 (hbk)
ISBN: 978-0-415-74212-2 (pbk)
ISBN: 978-1-315-81488-9 (ebk)

Typeset in Sabon
by Deanta Global Publishing Services, Chennai, India

Contents

Preface

Many books and articles have been written with the aim of introducing philosophy through film. Many others draw upon highly specialized and technical insights of philosophy in order to examine some of the challenging issues that arise when we take film seriously. This book aims to show why film has such a deep affinity with philosophy, and to do this in a way that is accessible for a non-specialist audience. Films can help us think about a range of questions important to philosophy, regarding such topics as knowledge, art, ethics, politics, gender, identity, embodiment, desire, to name a few. Arguably, however, it is film's capacity to deliver an appearance that seems to be real while we know it isn't that makes it such a potent source of philosophical reflection. Film is capable of provoking philosophical questions so powerfully because the situations it allows us to perceive can grip our imaginations as if they were real. When a film works we consider what it shows us to be intuitively plausible or at least in principle possible. Film thus has the capacity to give us insight into the nature of our insight. It can show us what we are willing to accept as real or valid or valuable, and encourage us to reflect upon why. Such reflection upon what we think and why, and on what we ought to think, form the basis of philosophy. The book as a whole, then, is intended at once as an introduction to philosophy through film and an introduction to film through philosophy.

The first part is entirely introductory, aimed at the reader interested in ideas and in film, but who may not have a background in either film studies or philosophy. It provides enough background and vocabulary for such a reader to appreciate the second and third parts, where I aim to say something original about both film and philosophy and the relationship between them. One might consider the first part as if it were a short introductory textbook. The second functions somewhat more like an extended essay or monograph. Its primary contentions are that film occupies a special position in relation to the history of philosophy, and that film has the natural capacity to orient its audience towards a post-Kantian understanding of the relationship between appearances and reality. The final part examines a single film, Jean-Luc Godard's *Breathless*, to show how the ideas developed in the second part can help to make sense both of its stylistic features and its content. Readers who have a background in film and philosophy should feel free to jump directly to the second part. There are suggestions for further reading at the end of the book, but what is covered in the first part should be enough to prepare any reader to appreciate the arguments of the second and third parts.

While this book was written as a companion (perhaps even as an introduction) to my previous book *Shadow Philosophy: Plato's Cave and Cinema*, both can be read independently. *Shadow Philosophy* examines the often mentioned, but rarely explored, analogy between Plato's allegory of the cave and the experience of watching films. To introduce this analogy, the book compares Plato's account of the cave in *The Republic* with the scene in Stanley Kubrick's *A Clockwork Orange* during which a fierce young criminal is forced to watch violent films as a part of his "rehabilitation." The book as a whole aims to show that films can function like philosophical texts, provoking the reader to ask questions and supplying the reader with vivid examples that help orient the direction of their insights. It also aims to show that the themes explored in certain films can be brought into conversation with the ideas of some of the great works of philosophy. Specifically, the film *A Clockwork Orange* was shown to provoke questions that could be profitably considered in connection to those suggested by Plato's dialogue, *The Republic*. Socrates, the main character of that dialogue, encourages his interlocutors to imagine an ideal city, a utopia, in order to reflect on the nature of justice; they deem it necessary that for the city to function well its spirited youth should be given a very precise education, ensuring that they put the good of the city higher than their own ambitions. In Kubrick's film audiences are given a vivid depiction of a dystopia and encouraged to reflect on why its own spirited youth run wild, and whether it might be moral to force their reformation. Both the dialogue and the film – which was withdrawn from circulation for a time in Britain due to its supposedly bad influence – encourage us to consider the legitimacy of censorship, the relation between art and morality, as well as that between citizens and state, the importance of education, the character of philosophy, and the nature of freedom.

Of course, Stanley Kubrick's film is distinctive. One might say it is obviously philosophical, without being any less cinematic. So while it may seem natural to bring it into conversation with *The Republic*, this might appear to be a special case. One still might consider that there is not, in general, any special affinity between film and philosophy. This book was written to address that question. It goes into much more detail regarding the metaphysical questions raised by the comparison between Plato's cave and cinema than was possible in *Shadow Philosophy*. In particular, *Film, Philosophy, and Reality: Ancient Greeks to Godard* aims to develop the implications of the analogy between our experience of watching films and between human experience generally. It examines the history of philosophy more deeply, beyond just the work of Plato, and develops ideas that apply to film more broadly. It aims to show that film is naturally philosophical insofar as it invites reflection upon the distinction between appearance and reality. Whether it succeeds in these aims is left to the judgment of its readers.

Acknowledgments

I could not have written this without Jim Goetsch, Jared Stark, Christina Petersen, Sorella Andersen, Ryan Conrath, Evgenia Chrysochoou, the students in my Film and Philosophy classes, and the anonymous reviewers for Routledge, all of whom read all or parts of the manuscript and provided invaluable feedback. Thanks to Stephen Mulhall. I've never met him but his groundbreaking and essential book *On Film* first got me thinking about film's philosophical potential. Thanks also to Dan Shaw, Robert Sinnerbrink, Hunter Vaughan, Matt Zoller Seitz, Thorsten Botz-Bornstein, and John Mullarkey for their inspiring work and encouragement. Thanks to John Russon for his ongoing support and to the participants in his Toronto Philosophy Seminars, which have been extremely valuable for my own continuing philosophical education. I would also like to thank a few of the other friends and colleagues whose thoughts in conversation have helped to shape my own: Dave Ciavatta, Kym Maclaren, Dan Spoth, Cathy Griggs, Louise Daoust, Shannon Hoff, Greg Recco, Scott Marratto, Pete Costello, Eric Sanday, Patricia Fagan, Susan Bredlau, Laura McMahon, Kirsten Jacobson, Greg Kirk, Laura McMahon, Ömer Aygun, and Ollie Wiitala. Thanks to Eckerd College and to Dean Suzan Harrison for encouraging and supporting my work. Finally, and above all, thank you to Andrea for watching so many movies with me – even the obscure ones, with unhappy endings that we enjoyed discussing afterwards. Thank you for sharing laughs over lighthearted and silly films we didn't really need to talk about, but kept us smiling on the way back to the car. Thank you for tolerating my absence when I was in my office or in a coffee shop working on this book. Thank you for sharing a life with me, and for all you've done for me and for our children, Sorella, Isaac, Kate, and Joel.

Introduction

We are moved at the movies. Films make us feel. They lead us to care about lives at a distance from our own. They entertain, excite, frighten, and arouse. Some films, perhaps the best ones, also manage to make us think. They challenge our prejudices. They pose puzzles we may solve. Films broaden our horizons, letting us see and begin to understand matters we had never considered. Sometimes they challenge us to think about some of the very basic questions that traditionally belong to the domain of philosophy. What is real? How do we arrive at knowledge? How should we act? What is art, and what is beauty?

In fact, all films pose such questions to some degree or other. Films are naturally and spontaneously philosophical. Some manage to highlight and intensify such questions, but all films provoke them. All films, for example, can provoke reflections on reality. They each depict a world, a reality, both like and unlike the real world outside of the theater. We are aware that the world imaged on screen is not real, but it feels like it is. Our awareness of a difference between reality and its moving image leads us naturally, as we reflect on the experience of watching films, to consider just what it means to be real. How, we might ask, does reality relate to its appearances, images, and representations? Such questions belong traditionally to metaphysics, one of the four central themes of traditional philosophy, and the primary focus of this book. Metaphysics has sometimes also been called "first philosophy," because, arguably, pursuits of any other philosophical questions depend on how we construe the character of reality.

One could, with equal justification, focus on any of the other primary areas of philosophical concern: epistemology, the investigation into the nature of knowledge; ethics, which considers what is morally right and wrong and why; and aesthetics, which studies art and beauty. Films pose ethical questions insofar as they lead us to sympathize with characters who behave in ways we might consider immoral or inappropriate, or insofar as they encourage us to rethink our moral positions. Films require interpretation, and to consider whether we've interpreted them correctly is to consider the question there are correct interpretations and how we could know for sure. These are concerns of epistemology, another central arena of philosophical investigation. Finally, films are, or can be, works of art. To consider them as art requires, at least, that we have some conception of what it means to call something "art." We might also reflect on the characteristic features of different kinds of art, such as painting, sculpture, poetry, literature, and theater, and wonder how the modern arts of photography and film relate to and differ from these more traditional art forms. These questions form part of aesthetics.

The decision to focus on metaphysics draws upon the fact that one of the most distinctive features of cinema, as an art form, is its capacity to immerse its audiences into an experience that seems to be real but that they know is not. Indeed, some of the earliest and most influential theoretical discussions of the newly emerging art of cinema questioned whether its distinctive artistic contribution was to capture reality as it is or to transform it through artistry. Either way presumes some conception of what it means to be real. The aim of this book is to show that thinking about film requires careful and critical reflection upon questions regarding the relation between reality and appearances. At the same time, because some films manage to highlight and explore such themes, reflection upon such films can offer a valuable and distinctive contribution to philosophical thought. There are, however, difficulties that face any approach to bring film and philosophy together.

Challenges and rewards of connecting philosophy with film

Films have been around since the turn of the twentieth century. Philosophy goes back much further, to at least the sixth century BCE, with the Greek sage Thales who aimed to make sense of the underlying nature of reality through his proclamation that "all is water." In the case of both philosophy and film we can say more or less how and where they got started, but the stories are complicated. Long before the invention of movie cameras and projectors there were motion picture entertainments and technologies, and developments in other arts that predate and anticipate cinema. Before it explicitly emerged in ancient Greece, and in other traditions and other cultures than those in the West which inherited the Greek philosophical tradition, there were thinkers engaged in the kinds of practices we would now identify as "philosophical."

Two basic difficulties face beginners in both film studies and philosophy. They are at once both too obscure and too familiar. It seems you have to learn a lot to say anything intelligent at all about either one and yet most of us tend to think we know all we need to know about both. On the one hand, they are academic disciplines with wide-ranging, complex subject matters, and long, detailed histories of debate and scholarship. On the other hand, their subjects may seem obvious. Most of us watch movies, television, and video online all the time. All of us, at least sometimes, speculate on the nature of reality, on the meaning of life, on what is right and wrong and just and unjust, on the extent of our knowledge and the nature of ignorance, and on the value of art.

So either we come to the study of film and of philosophy thinking we know all we need to know or we are overwhelmed when we find out just how much more there is to know. It's better to think that we always must start somewhere, and a little time, thought, and practice can take us much further, helping us better understand what was familiar but unclear and underdeveloped to begin with. The aim of the first part of this book is to help clarify some of the basic vocabulary and methods in both philosophy and film studies. These can then be put into practice in the following parts of the book as we consider the implications that reflections upon the character of cinematic appearances can have for considering the metaphysical question of the relation between reality and appearances more generally.

One motivation for connecting film and philosophy is the assumption that the former is exciting, familiar, and timely, and the latter boring, obscure, and irrelevant. The idea is to make philosophy seem relevant and vital by linking it with popular culture. Film is, as it were, the sugar coating that makes the bitter pill of thinking easy to swallow. There is some justification for this, since more people watch movies than study philosophy, and films and popular culture generate a lot of enthusiasm. On the whole, though, this outlook is mistaken. Academic philosophy can become very technical and difficult to follow, but its central concerns are quite basic and approachable. We can't help but care about such basic concerns. For those who see their importance, the more apparently obvious assumptions regarding everyday life suddenly seem less obvious and more open to question. Moreover, the ease with which we access films obscures the fact that many don't consider how films work – or how they work upon us – to make us think and feel as they do. There are many rewarding insights to be gained from film studies, even when it comes to understanding movies that seem to be easily accessible. For many, though, the most memorable movies are those that not only excite but engage us in thinking, and push us to think differently. While such films can often be appreciated without careful study, they reward repeated viewing and analysis, revealing riches unglimpsed on an initial encounter.

A further challenge facing any effort to link film and philosophy is that of finding the right balance. Focus too much on the film, according to the methods of traditional film criticism and analysis, and the depth and rigor of philosophical discussion may suffer. Where philosophy dominates, films can end up serving a merely illustrative role. Plot descriptions, stripped bare of cinematic detail, function as examples, clarified by appeal to philosophical concepts originating elsewhere. What is overlooked in such contexts is the possibility that cinema has its own philosophical and conceptual resources, and that films themselves might have "something to say" about both the philosophical problems they raise and the import of the examples they provide.

The approach taken in this book works at the intersection of film and philosophy, focusing on some of the most basic philosophical concerns that arise naturally in connection with cinema. The general issues should be somewhat familiar to anyone who has seen a lot of movies, even for those who may have never reflected on them explicitly. Our exploration of these issues will require some introduction of technical terms, important thinkers, and themes from the history of philosophy. Yet nothing that follows presupposes that readers have any prior familiarity with the subject. In order to describe and consider the importance of the specific films that will be discussed here, some of the ideas, vocabulary, and methods of film studies will be introduced as well. The primary method is, however, simply to pay close attention to the specifics of story, image, and sound, as these work together to create an experience whose significance can then be discussed. The focus will be to consider the ways in which films are able to provoke and examine philosophical questions for their viewers.

Connecting film with philosophy

There are several ways that film and philosophy can be brought together, or that film can be approached philosophically. The most popular – sometimes described simply as the conjunction of "film *and* philosophy" or as "philosophy *through* film" or as a subset of "philosophy and popular culture" – focuses on films that illustrate or serve as test cases of established philosophical concerns. Because films depict scenarios from everyday life vividly, and because philosophy has something to say about a variety of themes from everyday life, discussing specific films in connection with this or that philosophical theme often manages both to illuminate the movie and bring philosophy to life. Where films depict fantastic or futuristic situations, their differences from what we ordinarily consider to be real or possible can serve as a convenient starting point for introducing philosophical questions regarding what is possibly and actually real.

So a film that shows a "decent" man responsible for murder, such as Judah Rosenthal in Woody Allen's *Crimes and Misdemeanors* (1989), can highlight the importance of thinking along with Aristotle about what makes a man decent, or with Kant and Mill regarding what is wrong with murder. A less realistic film like Spike Jonze's *Being John Malkovich* (1999) can be considered along with traditional philosophical ideas regarding the nature of identity. The film's conceit that one could "be" (or become) John Malkovich by sliding into a portal "metaphysically" linked to his brain naturally provokes the question what it means to "be" someone in the first place. At its best, this approach provides a new and compelling critical look at the film and a vivid illustration of philosophical themes. Less helpful are accounts that provide little more than a synopsis of the film, and treat this as a segue to the introduction of some relevant philosophical position without considering how the details of the film might contribute to – or complicate – our thinking on the issues.

Film theory, which has a long and varied history, also tends to be philosophical. The earliest sustained theoretical investigations of film and its potential focused on whether it could be considered a new art form. Such questions overlap with the traditional concerns of philosophical aesthetics. Many held that the best movies were those that focused on what was distinctive to film as opposed to other artistic media. Some of the most influential early film theorists, such as Sergei Eisenstein and Jean Epstein, also made movies that illustrated (more or less) the ideals they argued for in their writings. Increasing academic interest led to a renewal of theoretical approaches to film. In the 1940s and 1950s in France, for example, there was an interdisciplinary movement for the study of the character and impact of cinema known as "filmology." This was followed – in the wake of the rising importance of structuralism and semiotics in French universities in the 1950s and the 1960s – with investigations into film's connection with language. Subsequent theories of film examined how film impacts its viewers, how it serves to communicate and reinforce dominant ideologies such as those of capitalism and patriarchy, and how particular approaches to filmmaking might help viewers overcome indoctrination.

Some film scholars in the 1980s considered the latest film theoretical approaches too obscure and too detached from actual film analysis. They urged a more empirically grounded approach to film studies that would take its cue from interdisciplinary research into the nature of thinking known as cognitive studies. At the same time, motivated by similar concerns, the philosophy of film emerged as a branch of aesthetics, whose conceptual investigations into film included the revisiting of questions regarding the unique characteristics of cinema that had concerned the earliest film theorists. One such question asks what is distinctive to film, and whether that is relevant to assessments of a film's aesthetic worth. Is there an "essence" of cinema and how is it defined? If, as early film theorists contended, films can do something no other art form can, is it right to say that the best films are those that best demonstrate its unique capabilities?

While film theory and the philosophy of film tend to treat film as an object of study — focusing on the themes, structures, and concepts employed in film criticism and analysis — another approach to film and its significance considers that films themselves contribute to the discourse about them. Film-philosophy, inspired by the cinema books of the French philosopher Gilles Deleuze and the American philosopher Stanley Cavell, considers that films do more than merely provide a subject matter for philosophical investigation, but are themselves capable of contributing to philosophical thought.

Films not only provide situations to be considered from a philosophical perspective, but also provoke the viewer to reflect upon what they reveal, and are structured in ways that guide philosophical thought. Film-philosophy often focuses carefully on the details of specific films, and describes the impact of these details on considerations of the philosophical questions provoked by these films. Film-philosophical studies often read like rigorous film-criticism, whose interpretive and analytical accounts are focused on the recognizably philosophical issues raised explicitly or implicitly by the story and structure of the films they describe.

This book draws upon the methods and assumptions of film-philosophy, while developing the general claim that film by its very nature engages us with some of the basic concerns of philosophy. Films present us with the appearance of something that isn't real. They present us with situations that appear to be real but aren't. The situations they present us with make sense to us, in roughly the same way as situations from everyday life. Yet it is at the same time obvious to viewers that those situations are not real, but are merely appearances. Specifically, they are appearances through which the very nature of appearance becomes apparent. To consider rigorously the nature of film requires us to examine one of the most basic questions of philosophy, one that is arguably the core question of metaphysics from the time of the ancient Greeks up until at least the time of Kant, and which has remained central to at least the post-Kantian tradition of Continental philosophy. It is the question of the relation between appearance and reality, which is closely related to the relation between the subject of experience and the object of experience. All films engage us at some level with the question of what we consider to be real and how we can distinguish that from what merely appears to be real. At the same time, because this is a concern that arises naturally when thinking about film, it is only natural that some filmmakers address and explore this theme explicitly within their works, and that the best filmmakers and the best films are likely to contribute meaningfully to our thinking about it.

The first part of the book is introductory, intended primarily for readers without an extensive background in either philosophy or film studies. In the first chapter, we'll consider some of the range of philosophy's concepts, methods, and concerns, with a special focus on the kinds of concerns that film naturally evokes. The second chapter, on film, will go into greater detail, because it aims to provide an overview of some of the basic concepts essential to interpreting and evaluating cinema. Part Two of the book combines film and philosophy to develop the core argument, which is that our experience of watching films can help us to make sense of the relation between experience and reality more generally. The third chapter examines the nature of film as an appearance through which we seem to see something real. The fourth chapter traces the development of the theme of the relation between appearance and reality throughout the history of philosophy. The two chapters of Part Three examine a single film, Jean-Luc Godard's *Breathless*, to show how that groundbreaking work of French New Wave cinema both draws upon and complicates some of the insights into the relation between appearance and reality that can be gleaned from a more general analysis of the nature of cinematic appearances. The final chapter looks at the philosophical potential of film techniques, focusing on the way Godard's uses of jump cuts and tracking shots in *Breathless* highlight the connection between moral issues and the metaphysical themes that are the focus of this book.

Part I
Philosophy and film

1 What is philosophy?

Philosophy is the art of asking questions. Not just any questions. Most philosophical questions cannot be answered conclusively, and yet every conclusive answer to any other kind of question presumes that they are settled: questions about the way things are, what is of worth, what counts as knowledge, how we can arrive at it, and what we should do about it. The aim of asking questions is to clarify our ideas regarding themes such as reality, knowledge, ethics, and beauty – notions at the heart of everything we do and experience. The clearer our ideas become, the more it becomes clear that these are subject matters open to question. To think about them is to enter into an open-ended conversation that has been going on for centuries.

Philosophical questions

"What is that?" a child might ask. "A fish." But what is a fish? There are easy (and obvious) answers, both everyday and scientific, and any good answer designates the fish as a kind of living thing. If we ask, though, what is life and what is a thing, we begin to move into philosophical terrain where the answers aren't so easy (or obvious). Much of the work of biology, for example, can proceed under the assumption that what "life" means is well understood. Yet in special moments of discovery – say, of an unusual substance on another planet or deep in the ocean – the question whether something should be considered a life form may very well arise. In such moments the investigating biologist or chemist or marine geologist is compelled to operate as a "philosopher of nature": to raise anew the question just what it is to be alive, to ask where precisely to mark the division between the living and the non-living. For philosophical questions, moreover, it is not enough just to ask; it is necessary to highlight the difficulties that make the questions inevitable, which is to say, to show the conflicts and contradictions in our ideas and practices that require working through. Such discoveries signal the need for an inquiry in which there are no easy answers, but in which new answers can help us see things differently, illuminating connections we hadn't suspected.

The question about "things" may seem like a silly one. We know about all kinds of things: animals, people, movies, rocks, and less tangible things like emotions and ideas. We rarely (if ever) consider what makes a thing a thing, or what these very different kinds of "things" have in common. It is this question, however, that formed the primary subject matter of one of the foundational texts of Western philosophy, Aristotle's *Metaphysics*. He considers there what it means to say something is a "substance," which he defines as a thing whose reality does not depend on anything else.

He shows that we can distinguish between a substance and its properties, as well as between a substance and its activities and movements. Emotions, then, are not substances. They are not real things. Instead, they are ways in which substances – including human beings – can be affected. Ideas are more complicated. Some seem like they don't exist apart from the individual substances (people) who think about them. Other ideas, such as the idea of a number, seem to have properties that are independent of whatever anyone happens to think about them, and so seem to be real all by themselves. They aren't just thought up. They're discovered. Indeed, one of the basic and persistent philosophical questions is whether ideas are real in their own right or whether their existence derives from the individual realities (or substances) they refer to and describe. Do concepts exist independently of thinkers? Do they exist apart from the things they refer to? These seem to have been subjects about which Aristotle disagreed with his famous teacher Plato.

To illustrate some of the issues, we might consider briefly whether a film can be considered a substance. A film is certainly something, but it isn't immediately obvious what kind of thing it is. Take, for example, the film *Jurassic Park* (1993), directed by Steven Spielberg. It isn't a natural thing. It's made. It is a specific thing, with features that make it different not only from other kinds of things, like fish and chairs, but from other things of the same kind, such as other films. At the same time it doesn't seem to be just a single thing, like a specific fish or a chair, because there can be many different copies of it – the original negatives, the 35mm prints from which it was originally projected, DCP drives that might be sent out to modern theaters for digital screenings, Blu-Rays and DVDs for home screening, online streaming files, etc. – and each one might be said to be the film *Jurassic Park*. It isn't just the total group of these copies either, because you could destroy all but one of them without destroying the film.

We might, perhaps, consider films to be analogous to animal species, such as, for example, the Tyrannosaurus Rex. Aristotle considered species to be secondary substances, where the individual members of a species were primary, which means they

Figure 1.1 Steven Spielberg's *Jurassic Park* (1993).

exemplify more fully what it is to be a substance. Still, while there can't be a species unless there are at least some individual members, the reality of the species is more enduring. As long as at least some individual T-Rexes existed, the species still existed. Yet the species is not just the sum total of living individuals. Even now, when there are no such individuals, we can still talk about the species, and can say we know roughly what it would be like for something to be a T-Rex. There is still something it is to be a Tyrannosaurus Rex, and it is this fact that makes it possible to conceive that some future technology might allow us to bring them back. That is, after all, the premise of the film *Jurassic Park*. The current non-existence of living individual T-Rexes may not mean that the species has ceased to exist. What it is to be a T-Rex – the defining conception that allows us to think about them, to recognize them in images and descriptions, to make movies about them even after their extinction, and, at least in principle, to bring them back using advanced cloning techniques – that is at least partly what Plato had in mind when he held that ideas (or forms) transcend their instances.

Still, it is not just the defining conception that allowed dinosaurs to come back in *Jurassic Park*. John Hammond and his team of scientists needed dino-DNA. They needed not only the information coded in the DNA, but a mechanism for inserting that information into modified frog DNA, initiating the causal sequence that would allow them to hatch dinosaurs in the laboratory. Similarly, it would not be enough just to have the idea of the film *Jurassic Park*. In the absence of a negative, or a film print, or a digital file, *Jurassic Park,* the film, would cease to exist. It would, like some of the lost works of great philosophers, exist at most in memory and historical records. The most one could do is create a remake based on the original script, and that would be a markedly different thing. The performances wouldn't be the same, and neither would the moving images, even if some portions could be duplicated. So while the film *Jurassic Park* is not identical with the sum total of existing copies, it couldn't exist unless at least one of them exists or enough parts of it exist somewhere to enable a complete restoration.

Even that might not be enough. In a future world, perhaps so far into the future that the existence of human beings could only be inferred from our remains in the way that we have learned about the dinosaurs, even if it happened somehow that a DVD or a digital file of *Jurassic Park* still existed, it wouldn't make sense to say the film itself existed unless there was also the technology to play it and beings capable of watching it. Without some way of reading the data and translating it into the moving images that make up the film, these "copies" would be useless. It wouldn't be clear what they were copies of. Similarly, dinosaur DNA, trapped inside of a mosquito trapped in fossilized amber, is not the same as a dinosaur. It is among the material conditions that make it possible for dinosaurs to exist, but it isn't a dinosaur until it takes on the form of a dinosaur. We might think about this in terms of the distinction between potentiality and actuality that Aristotle sometimes employs in his *Metaphysics* to discuss the nature of substance. Dinosaur DNA may have the potential to become a dinosaur, but it is actually just a complex molecular structure that won't produce anything unless this potential is actualized through the fertilization of an egg. Even a fertilized dinosaur egg is only potentially a dinosaur, and it isn't substantially a T-Rex until it actualizes that potential and hatches. Only after hatching is it capable of acting as we expect baby T-Rexes to act and, furthermore, of then growing up into a mature dinosaur. Only then would it fully exemplify the kind of independent being – the kind of substantial reality – we associate with T-Rexes. Likewise, we might say, a DVD or a digital file of a film is only potentially a film. It is actually a film only when this potential is actualized, when the film is played using the appropriate equipment and screened for an audience. If this is so, though, it seems we were wrong to think of the film as a kind of substance. It is not something that can exist on its own. It exists to be shown, and can only be the film that it is and tell the story we associate with *Jurassic Park* when it is screened for an audience capable of perceiving it. Still, if it is not a substance, it is not nothing. It is at least something real.

Whatever it is, it is clearly not the same as the material stuff that makes it possible to watch it. Perhaps the reality of the film is best characterized as a process, that of screening the film for an audience. Only as that process is realized is it truly the film, only then does it exhibit the distinctive qualities we associate with this film. The many copies of *Jurassic Park* that exist around the world in various forms are not really the film itself, any more than the fossilized DNA of a dinosaur is the dinosaur itself. You can't have the film without some copies, just as you can't have a dinosaur without dinosaur DNA. But the film itself is the reality that unfolds for an audience each time it is screened. Arguably, while the audiences may respond differently, and the conditions of each screening will vary, it is the same film they are watching each time. So, if the movie *Jurassic Park* is just one thing, it is the thing that audiences get to watch every time it is screened. We'll examine much more closely just what kind of thing that is in the third chapter. For now, though, we can say that even while it may not make sense to speak of a process that unfolds over time as if it were a substance, this doesn't make film all that different from entities that on Aristotle's terms are clearly substances, such as dinosaurs. The being of a dinosaur is not something that exists all at once in its entirety. It is something that unfolds over time, from the moment that the egg hatches to the moment that the dinosaur dies. Moreover, the dinosaur's existence at any given moment is not static. It is and can only be the dinosaur that it is by engaging in characteristic activities such as hunting, feeding, and sleeping. These activities, moreover, are only made possible by the ongoing mechanical, chemical, and biological processes taking place inside the organism. Similarly, a film like *Jurassic Park* can be what it is only as a result of technical processes that make its screening possible. Its reality depends upon these processes. Moreover, it is not something that can simply exist only for a moment, or even forever. It is a finite reality that takes up space and occupies time. It exists – it *is* the film it is — only in the time it takes to screen it, and in a suitable place it can be screened; and since each screening is roughly the same, each person who sits through it can say that they've seen *Jurassic Park*.

Metaphysics, the inquiry into the nature of reality and into the question what is ultimately real, is one of the basic subject matters of philosophy. Each of philosophy's primary subjects — metaphysics, epistemology, ethics, and aesthetics – is defined not by a body of information or teachings, but by a set of questions and a (historically developing) series of (increasingly sophisticated) concepts in terms of which answers can be explored. What makes these subjects primary (and perennial), and what makes the questions philosophical, is that they are at the heart of every other inquiry. To answer any other questions requires that we take answers to these questions for granted. Any inquiry into what is real, or into why things are the way they are, presumes an acceptance that there is a reality and that we can somehow make sense of it. It supposes a rudimentary grasp of the nature of things, of the nature of change, and of what counts as explanation. Claims to know (or even believe) anything rest on some grasp of the nature of belief and of criteria for knowledge. To make moral judgments is to presume that people are free to choose what they do. It would be unreasonable to say that someone had done wrong if they were not capable of acting otherwise. To claim that someone has done wrong also presumes that there are standards for action, and that these standards can be justified. It would be unreasonable to expect someone to adhere to a moral standard that they were not aware of or didn't accept, or that, at the very least, could not be defended and justified with reasons that they could endorse. Finally, our experiences of art and beauty and our assessments of their worth presume at least some rudimentary notion of what art is, and some sense for a difference between what is and isn't beautiful. The assumptions needn't be (and often aren't) fully spelled out or thought through. Still, everything we do or say rests on some assumptions regarding, among many other things, existence, causality, truth, knowledge, right and wrong, art, and beauty. To do philosophy is to consider all of these assumptions, to examine whether there are good reasons to accept them, to determine whether they are consistent, and to explore the implications of other ways they might be spelled out.

The point of all this effort is to figure out and clarify how we really ought to think about the way things are and ought to be. We think all kinds of things, and our actions imply a number of assumptions about the world. For the most part, however, we haven't thought things through. We inherit the assumptions we use to make sense of the world. Even those working in established disciplines – whether in the natural or social sciences, or in the humanities, or in business – operate with established methods and work from ideas and theories about how things work and why. Such methods and ideas may have stood the test of time, but they aren't timeless or inevitable. They could be challenged, and often are. When the notions we've inherited no longer serve to make sense of what we experience, whether in our everyday lives or in our highly refined expert practices, it is time to let go of established assumptions, ask new questions, and sort things out differently. That is what philosophy is all about – except that philosophy does not wait for the crisis, when our concepts and assumptions no longer match our experience. Philosophy aims to show that the core assumptions at the heart of our experience are always open to question.

So philosophy begins by asking open-ended questions. To explore these questions requires that we make distinctions. Of course, to make distinctions also involves drawing connections between apparently disparate things, things that share a distinction in common. We have so far distinguished between philosophical and non-philosophical questions, and have distinguished between the four primary philosophical subjects, and at the same time shown that these diverse themes are connected. They are all focused on what we might call "fundamental questions," questions at the heart of all inquiry and action, whose answers are presupposed by both theories and practices.

Philosophy, myth, and religion

Traditionally, myth and religion have provided answers to these fundamental questions. Stories about the gods and sacred writings taught about reality; temples and sculptures of deities and other religious works of art provided inspiration; songs and ritual practices motivated and instructed peoples how to act. Yet stories of the gods still require interpretation and explanation. Philosophy begins when the answers provided by religion and myth are treated as a starting point for new questions. That a god – or God – laid down this or that decree begs the question what it means and why it should be followed, and who or what is God, and how can we know his will or that he is at all (or that God is a "he")? A ritual begs the question what is its purpose and value? To ask such questions is not to reject religion, or to reject the importance of the stories people tell to make sense of things they cannot fully understand, and the rituals and practices they employ in order to orient their lives around what they consider to be of ultimate importance. It is, rather, to see that religion, myth, stories, images, and rituals are of worth, at least in part, precisely because they provide groups of people with beliefs and practices that contribute to their identities, and shared cultures they care about, and can thereby demonstrate the importance of sorting out what it means and why.

The first major Greek philosopher we know about was Thales of Miletus. He is most famous for his proclamation that "all is water." The claim is not as absurd as it might seem to be at first. Water is, after all, ubiquitous. The lands the Greeks inhabited were dwarfed by vast and uncharted oceans. He had postulated, as well, that earthquakes resulted from the fact that the Earth floats upon water. There are waters in the heavens that pour down in the form of rain, and water vapors can be observed to condense from the air. All living things, moreover, depend upon water. Water, like film, takes on an almost endless variety of forms and is always in flux.

Yet Thales also proclaimed, cryptically, that "all things are full of gods." That may suggest he is not so far from myth, that he considers changes taking place in nature to result from supernatural forces, or divine intervention. The point may also be more subtle, however, since if things themselves are full of gods we needn't look elsewhere, as to Mount Olympus, for an explanation of their activities. It suggests that the explanation of their movements is contained within things themselves, right there in front of us, and that to understand their nature requires that we observe and study nature, rather than wait upon muses or soothsayers to reveal the hidden will of gods.

Many other Greek sages in the aftermath of Thales sought also to understand the natural world without a direct appeal to gods. They considered what underlies and causes natural changes, reflected upon the nature and possibility of change, and sought to identify those things that do not change. Their inquiries were, fundamentally, attempts to identify principles, the most basic and core truths or realities that help explain and make sense of everything else. Socrates came in their wake. He grew up in Athens, in the fifth century BCE when it was arguably the heart of Western civilization. He applied the same method of searching for principles as his predecessors, but he was less interested in nature and more interested in truths regarding human experience and the social world. Socrates spent his days in Athens asking questions of elderly statesmen, celebrated poets and speakers, skilled artisans, and promising youth. He saw how they lived, and sought to draw out from them the assumptions that informed their attitudes and practices, and then assisted them in subjecting these assumptions to scrutiny. He showed, inevitably, that their assumptions were flawed, and that they hadn't given them much thought. They, like most of us, operated with a whole range of unexamined notions, all inherited from parents, teachers, and peers, and he argued that the beginning of wisdom is to recognize the limitations of one's own conceptions.

Socrates comes to life in the writings of Plato, his most famous pupil. Rather than expound teachings in philosophical treatises, Plato wrote dialogues featuring a variety of characters engaged in discussion on important topics. They usually featured Socrates pushing and prodding his interlocutors to define the values they claimed to live by, such as justice, courage, love, and knowledge. When their ideas were shown to be inconsistent or otherwise flawed, he insisted they search, together, for new and better ones. The assumption of all of this is that the quest is not futile, that there are better answers to be found, and that the way to find them is to see what is wrong with the opinions one begins with. If there is a difference between the views of Socrates and Plato, it is that while Socrates assumes there are better and worse answers and that overcoming the worse answers through dialogue is the route to the better ones, Plato used his own written dialogues to explore the question what it would mean to suppose that true answers exist, and that their truth is independent of any particular opinions about them. The so-called "theory of the forms" attributed to Plato represents an attempt by his interpreters to collect the considerations scattered throughout his dialogues into a systematic account of the ultimate nature of reality.

Subsequent thinkers only rarely followed Plato's example of writing their philosophy in the form of dramatic conversations. His impact can be seen in the fact that all great philosophers after Plato acknowledge, by responding implicitly or explicitly to their predecessors, that their own thinking contributes to an ongoing conversation regarding the origins and nature of the cosmos, the extent of what can be known, how to live the best life, and the nature and importance of values such as beauty, goodness, and truth. The methods adopted in their inquiries and the results they obtained vary widely, yet for the most part their works can still be read profitably. While they may not answer every question, and may sometimes be misguided, each contributes something valuable to the understanding of the topics they pursued.

In some ways, one might argue, to study the history of philosophy is to enter into an apprenticeship in thinking. It is to learn how to think along with those whose thinking has stood the test of time, but with the aim, in the end, of thinking for oneself about the problems of one's own time. The task, when approaching a new philosophical text, is never just to figure out what some great philosopher thought. It is to think along with them, and to learn thereby what can reasonably be thought about the subjects they address. We, who come later, also have the advantage that we can consider the ways in which each great philosophy is challenged by subsequent thinkers. We can also see how changes in politics and history show the limitations of philosophical insights bound to a particular time and place, and how throughout its history philosophy has responded to developments in other domains of inquiry such as science and art.

The ancient quarrel

In Plato's *Republic*, Socrates claims there is an "ancient quarrel" between philosophy and poetry. Poetry and the other arts are dangerous, he suggested, because they both affect the character of their audiences and lead people to believe things that aren't true. While others throughout the history of philosophy have shared Plato's skeptical appraisal, not all considered art to be dangerous. Plato's student, Aristotle, held that art can be beneficial because artworks such as Greek tragedies allow audiences both to appreciate and reconcile themselves to certain hard truths regarding the nature of human experience. Appraisals of the nature and value of art have varied widely throughout the history of philosophy. Hegel, the great nineteenth-century German philosopher, considered that art, religion, and philosophy all aimed at the same thing, but in fundamentally different ways. They were all concerned with what he called "the Absolute," with what is ultimately real, the matter of ultimate concern. While religion calls the absolute God, and philosophy searches for truth, art attempts to create beauty, which Hegel defined as the sensuous presentation of the absolute. Artists from various ages aimed to clarify for themselves and their communities what they considered to be holy or divine in their sculptures, paintings, poetry, and music. In the modern age, of course, the turn towards purely human subjects in art signals that what Hegel's own contemporaries considered to be of ultimate importance was inseparable from (or perhaps identical with) human life and activity.

Subsequent philosophers and artists have been less willing to identify the aims of art with the creation of beauty. When Marcel Duchamp submitted a urinal (signed "R. Mutt" and with the title of *Fountain*) to an art exhibition in 1917, he hardly intended it to be seen as beautiful. One might, of course, consider that its symmetry and appropriateness to its function are aesthetic qualities, but the real point of the work was to challenge traditional understandings of art and of aesthetics, to break down the distinction between ordinary objects and artworks, and to encourage its audience to see and think about art differently. Modern art is incredibly diverse, and contemporary philosophical interpretations of art vary widely, but if there is some consensus it is around the idea that what art can and ought to do is provoke feelings and thoughts, encouraging those who encounter it to notice certain things, to ask questions about what they see, to wonder whether their habitual assumptions or their accepted values hold firm. While science aims at understanding, sorting out how things work with mathematical precision, art aims at illumination, in the sense of showing how things can be thought about and felt differently and more expansively. Where science aims to explain the what and how of nature, art aims to provoke a sense of wonder as to why and what it all means, and stimulates a refusal to respond to these questions with ready-made answers.

Good philosophy draws both upon the scientific demand for conceptual clarity that comes from making careful distinctions and is also, like art, unwilling to reduce questions of meaning to measurements. There is a difference between the kind of accuracy that can be achieved by the use of mathematics, and the kind of insight into the significance of complex situations that can be gained when they are described in new ways, as when we ask new kinds of questions and apply new concepts to those situations. Art, which at its best manages to depict things that are familiar in new ways, is in this sense an ally to philosophy because it can stimulate wonder. Both art and philosophy provoke questions and suggest new possibilities for thinking.

Film, the most popular and influential art form of at least the twentieth century, is an obvious example. Film may be said to have a special affinity with philosophy, because it naturally provokes thought regarding the most fundamental questions. Variations on the questions that define philosophy's primary subject matters – what is reality, what is knowledge, what is ethics, what is art – arise naturally when thinking about film, and there are a variety of film techniques that can be understood only by drawing upon our familiarity with concepts whose exploration belongs to philosophy.

The question of film's relation to reality naturally comes up because films present to us scenarios we consider could be real but that we know are not. They do not merely describe such scenarios but allow us to observe them as if we were there. Films present us with perceptual evidence that we must interpret, and that can be interpreted in various ways. So they confront us with the epistemological question of how we ought to make sense of things. They show us characters behaving in ways we might consider wrong, and thus confront us with the problem of how to appraise action morally. They are works of art, and can sometimes be quite beautiful, and other times repulsive, and thereby confront us naturally with the challenge of aesthetic appraisal.

Part of what is involved, then, in understanding film as a medium, and part of what is involved in understanding any particular film, is some reflection upon film's relation to reality, some consideration of film significance, and some assessment of the moral and aesthetic impact and import of film. All of these questions have been central to film theory and criticism since film was invented, and at the same time, each of these questions connects directly with the primary topics of philosophical inquiry. Because these questions are central to the self-definition of film as a medium, it is not surprising that many films address such questions, either directly by incorporating such questions into the narrative of the film, or indirectly by employing a style or exploring a subject matter that can best be understood in relation to metaphysical, epistemological, ethical and aesthetic themes.

Ethical considerations can be provoked by the common narrative device in cinema of marshaling sympathy for a particular character by juxtaposing that character with another whose portrayal is unsympathetic. Romantic comedies, for example, often encourage audiences to root for one character to "hook up" with another, by implying in a variety of ways that their current partner is unsuitable. Most films put audiences in a position to understand best a particular character, who becomes the protagonist, and often portray another character as antagonistic to her aims. Because they know less about the antagonist, or because what they know about him is not enough for them to understand or sympathize with his actions, audiences come to prefer the protagonist and favor her actions. When the audience sympathizes with specific characters, they tend to want them to succeed, and sometimes want them to succeed in actions that they might otherwise consider to be wrong or unethical. That puts audiences in a peculiar position where their immediate sympathies are in conflict with moral assumptions, and can provoke them to reflect upon those assumptions, on what they consider to be right and wrong and why.

A film technique that evokes metaphysical considerations is when a film shows us something happening that later on we realize didn't happen, or didn't happen in the way it was presented. This can be very explicit, as in the dream sequence on Mars at the beginning of Paul Verhoeven's film *Total Recall* (1990), which ends with Douglas Quaid (Arnold Schwarzenegger) waking up startled in bed next to his wife Lori (Sharon Stone). Or it can be much more subtle, as in the film *Memento* (2000). Towards the end of the film the viewer begins to realize that the memory-impaired Leonard Shelby (Guy Pearce), who is pursuing a quixotic quest to avenge the death of his wife, is not nearly as innocent and well-meaning as he himself thinks he is. In any such case, the viewer can make sense of what happened only by making a distinction between appearance and reality, between the way things seem to be and really are, and noting that in this case, the very distinction between appearance and reality appears within a film, which is itself an appearance.

Why and how to do philosophy – a brief historical overview

Philosophers ask questions about subjects that lie at the heart of what we do, and know, and care about. They ask about reality, knowledge, ethics, politics, and art. They consider puzzles that arise from our conflicting intuitions about the way things are and ought to be. We are, on the one hand, bodies, subject to physical laws. We are, on the other hand, conscious beings, aware of ourselves and of our bodies, and it is hard to see how a mere body could become aware of itself. Philosophers ask about the relationship between the mind and the body, between the brain and consciousness. They consider whether our experience of freedom can be reconciled with our scientific understanding of the world. In addition to such questions about the world and our relationship to it, philosophers also ask about the nature of philosophy itself. They consider, for example, whether the methods appropriate to understanding the world are adequate to the task of understanding our capacity for understanding. In what follows, we'll consider briefly some of what has been said throughout the history of philosophy about both the value of philosophical inquiry as well as the proper methods and tools for pursuing it.

Philosophy begins in wonder, according to Socrates, in Plato's dialogue *Theaetetus*. Plato's student Aristotle says something similar in his *Metaphysics*, adding that we seek to understand how and why things are as they are only after our basic needs have been satisfied. The latter point might be taken in two different ways. On the one hand, it could mean that philosophy has nothing to do with our practical concerns. While it may satisfy curiosity regarding ultimate questions, it has no further utility. On the other hand, it might suggest that the satisfaction of our basic needs is insufficient for a fully human life. Aristotle insisted in his *Nicomachean Ethics* that our lives would be incomplete, and we could not be happy, without engaging in inquiry for its own sake, going beyond what is merely useful. Socrates also famously stated that "the unexamined life is not worth living" and held that philosophy is the way to arrive at the wisdom that acknowledges the limits of human understanding. He considered, further, that such wisdom had a practical purpose. Socrates tells the man Meno, in the dialogue named after him, that

> I would contend at all costs both in word and deed as far as I could that we will be better men, braver and less idle, if we believe that one must search for the things one does not know, rather than if we believe that it is not possible to find out what we do not know and that we must not look for it.
>
> (Plato, Meno 86b–c)

The pursuit of wisdom, he insists, makes us better people.

These two ways of interpreting what Aristotle wrote about its origins signal two distinct conceptions of philosophy. Some have considered that philosophy is the pursuit of wisdom for its own sake, a pursuit that might occupy one's free time but needn't otherwise impact how one lives one's life. Others consider philosophy itself to be a way of life, where the wisdom sought is insight into living well, and it doesn't count as wisdom unless it is put into practice. The life of Socrates is a good example. He didn't just pursue philosophy as a hobby. He lived as a philosopher. He spent his days (and nights) talking with people about their ideas, challenging them to compare their ideals with their practice, and seeking to draw out from them truths that would correct their prejudices. In the *Theaetetus*, mentioned above, he compares his philosophical practice to that of a midwife, who not only assists her patients in giving birth to what is living inside of them but can also assess the health and independent vitality of what they deliver. He assisted his interlocutors in getting clear about the ideas and ideals that shaped their attitudes and actions, and then considered with them whether those ideas could be defended. His way of life inspired several schools of philosophy, whose central teachings were focused less on the aim of understanding the world as to orienting themselves properly within it.

Philosophy as a way of life

The stoics and the skeptics, for example, were rival philosophical schools. Stoicism got its start in ancient Athens, but its influence spread later from there to Rome and some of the most prominent stoic thinkers were Romans. Stoics held a number of significant philosophical views about the nature of reality and how we could know it. Their logical investigations were highly original and influential. Yet they are most well-known for their ethics. They considered that things in the public, material world are subject to the influence and control of forces outside of them. Since our bodies are part of the material world, they are, naturally, impacted by it. We live best when we accept the way things are and don't seek to change what is out of our control. It is not entirely up to me whether I am healthy or wealthy, for example. What are up to me are my thoughts and my attitudes. To live well, one should focus less on the futile effort to change what we can't and more on changing ourselves by cultivating virtues such as wisdom, justice, courage, and moderation.

While the stoics argued that we live best when we accept the way things are, the skeptics held that we cannot know. Skepticism grew out of Plato's school, the Academy, and the skeptics had been especially impressed by the capacity of Plato's teacher Socrates to show that seemingly solid convictions lose their grip upon us when we examine their foundations. They recognized that there are competing and contradictory ways of viewing the world, and considered that there is no way to decisively overcome the confusion to which this situation gives rise. Since living with doubt can be profoundly unsettling, the solution the skeptics arrived at was to demonstrate the impossibility of deciding between conflicting viewpoints. They showed this by producing equally compelling arguments for either side of a variety of controversies. Their aim: to achieve tranquility by suspending judgment regarding all those beliefs that admit of doubt.

Philosophy as dialogue

While Plato is widely considered to be committed to the controversial theory of forms – about which both the stoics and the skeptics raised serious doubts – many of the most serious objections to the theory had already been raised by him, in the words he attributes to various characters in his dialogues. Plato seems, in fact, to have written in dialogue form precisely because it allowed him to explore the implications of ideas, and engage the reader in the process of discovery. Plato's dialogues, then, don't present Plato's own philosophical convictions, except perhaps indirectly. They present positions, many of which their readers can be presumed to accept, and then proceed to show that these positions are problematic. They examine theories, many of which may seem at first absurd, and show that various common-sense assumptions don't make sense except in relation to them. Then, of course, they show some of the ways that even these theories can be challenged or defended. The attentive reader is led to examine her own preconceptions, is encouraged to consider what else might have been said in defense of the positions explored through conversation. The effect is similar to what the skeptics hoped to achieve by presenting opposing arguments. Except that here the result is not so much suspension of judgment but the engagement of critical thought. Careful readers of Platonic dialogues do not walk away satisfied that the issues have been thoroughly explored, and that the controversies raised are incapable of resolution. They are awakened, instead, to the importance of the questions posed in their pursuit. The enduring power of these questions is demonstrated by the great dialogue that we find enacted throughout the history of philosophy, as new philosophers develop new ways of addressing old questions, and also take up the ideas of their predecessors, both to challenge them and to draw out from them resources for thinking through the challenges of their own time.

Films can also function like philosophical dialogues by evoking ideas, challenging preconceptions, presenting puzzles, and provoking questions. Plato seems to have been led to the format by his recognition of the capacity of Greek tragedies to tell stories through which audiences were led both to feel powerfully and to reflect upon the human condition. Perhaps if he were alive today, Plato would have chosen to make movies instead. In his dialogue *The Republic*, he has Socrates encourage his interlocutors to imagine the formation of an ideal city so that they can see more clearly the nature of justice and injustice. This is not so different from what modern philosophers call "thought experiments," and films are quite effective in assisting us to imagine situations that make our intuitions clearer. The theme of skepticism, for example, is a natural subject for cinematic exploration. Films can present situations that seem to be real, and then present equally compelling evidence to undermine that sense. As we'll see in parts two and three of this book, films also have the power to indicate positively how we ought to think about the world.

Philosophy as logic and argument

Logic, the study of the ways in which thoughts entail other thoughts, is an important tool for philosophical investigation. While the stoics made significant advances in the theory of logic, it was Plato's student Aristotle who, even before them and almost single-handedly, invented the subject. Immanuel Kant, writing roughly two millennia after Aristotle, considered that very little of significance had been said to expand upon the subject in the intervening time. Logicians and philosophers of logic now are unlikely to agree with this assessment, yet it is inarguable that Aristotle and his commentators had done essential work in establishing both the character and the importance of the subject. An indication of the central importance of logic for philosophy is that throughout the middle ages, both in the European countries where Latin was the primary language of philosophy and in the Islamic world, the study of Aristotle's logical works – known as the "Organon" – was central to its introductory curriculum. Even today, a course or two in logic are basic requirements for a philosophy major or concentration at the undergraduate level. Irrespective of the subject matter in which they specialize, many philosophers consider the primary and almost exclusive task of philosophy to be the production, analysis, and assessment of arguments, in which logic plays a central role.

At the heart of Aristotle's logical writings is the theory of deduction, or of the syllogism. According to Aristotle, a syllogism is "a discourse in which, certain things having been supposed, something different from the things supposed results of necessity because these things are so" (*Prior Analytics* 2). In other words, a syllogism is meant to demonstrate that we can make inferences on the basis of certain assumptions. We can call the assumptions premises and the inference we draw from them the conclusion. Both the premises and the conclusion in a syllogism combine a subject and a predicate. Put more simply: each of these statements say something about something.

Each is about some subject, and what is said about that subject is its predicate. Take, for example, the claim "Tom Cruise is an actor." The subject is Tom Cruise and the predicate is "actor." While the subject is an individual in that case, the subject can also be a class or type of thing, as in assertions such as "some action films cost more than 100 million dollars to make," and "the *Mission Impossible* films are action films," and "no romantic comedies cost more than 100 million dollars to make." Sometimes when two different assertions share a term between them, either as a subject or a predicate, we can draw a conclusion linking the terms that they don't share. Such assertions may or may not be true, but what matters for a syllogism is that if the premises are true the conclusion should follow. If "some of the *Mission Impossible* films cost more than 100 million dollars to make" and "all of the *Mission Impossible* films star Tom Cruise," then it follows, necessarily, that "some films starring Tom Cruise cost more than 100 million dollars to make." Aristotle's logic shows when such inferences are legitimate (or valid), which is to say when the premises do in fact guarantee the conclusion.

Throughout the medieval period, when a background in Aristotle's logical theory formed the basis for further philosophical training, the subject matters explored using syllogisms varied widely. It might seem, though, that apart from the fact that syllogisms can be used to talk about films, the theory of syllogisms has no special relevance to the subject of cinema. In fact many of the inferences we make while watching movies, that allow us to make sense of what we are seeing, are arguably syllogistic in form. While the abstract analysis of syllogisms can get technical, it is aimed at elucidating the basic inferential structure of ordinary thinking. We identify something as qualified in some way, or as belonging to a group of things. If we associate that group or quality with certain characteristics, we infer that the thing we'd previously identified must have those characteristics. Even when, as is often the case, we are mistaken in the associations that form our assertions, the general syllogistic form (A is B, B is C, so A is C) helps us to see what it was we were *thinking*. I might, for example, see a dog and back away, reasoning that dogs are vicious so this one is. This dog could turn out to be gentle, but I would have backed away based on reasoning from a false premise.

Syllogistic inferences can be contrasted with inductive inferences, which are often the source of the premises we employ in our deductions. Inductive inferences include making generalizations based on a few observations, reasoning by analogy, and even the process of drawing upon various bits of evidence to build a case for a claim. Inductive arguments are often used to predict a film's commercial performance, for example: "The last science fiction film with a similar budget to open over the summer was a big box office success, so this one will be too." The core difference between deduction and induction is that the conclusions of deductive arguments seem to follow necessarily from their premises, where inductive arguments only seem to make the conclusion likely. In the case of good deductive arguments, or valid syllogisms, the conclusion doesn't only seem to follow necessarily but in fact does.

We usually come to any given film having seen many other films. That is to say, we come to any given film already having arrived (inductively) at some generalizations regarding how they work. Filmmakers presume this. They don't tend to reinvent everything. They draw upon familiar patterns, they employ clichés in order to automatically indicate what is distinctive to the story they are telling. We see a shot of a person talking, and then another shot of a person listening. Even if we don't know the technical vocabulary to describe this shot (as a "shot-reverse shot," for example) we recognize the kind of shot it is, and know what that entails. Upon seeing the second shot we conclude that the person it depicts is listening to the person speaking in the first shot. There needn't be a shot that shows both people together. We see that it is a shot-reverse shot. We know that shot-reverse shots link the perspective shown in the first shot with the perspective shown in the second shot. We conclude that the person spoken to in the first shot is the person shown in the second. Additionally, films often rely upon stereotypes and other generalizations to communicate quickly details about characters without needing to make them explicit. A shot opens on the face of Tom Cruise, for example. We know Tom Cruise primarily for his leading roles in action films, where he plays tough and heroic but vulnerable characters. We conclude that the character will be a tough but vulnerable action hero. Some such associations are less innocuous. Films can draw upon our prejudices about race, sexuality, and gender. Hollywood action films are notorious for casting as "terrorists" or "villains" individuals whose appearance is easily associated with whatever ethnicity or nationality happens to be currently receiving bad political press in the global news.

The conclusions we deduce from the assumptions films suggest to us may turn out to be false, but that just proves we were wrong to assume them. Part of the work of effective film narration is to lead audiences towards conclusions that will later be confirmed, challenged, or complicated, allowing audiences to be either surprised or satisfied. Take, for example, the opening scenes of Alfred Hitchcock's *Psycho* (1960). We start out with the natural assumption, confirmed by numerous film-going experiences, that the person whose point of view the film follows throughout the first act of the film is the protagonist. The film follows the point of view of Marion Crane (Vivien Leigh). So, she must be the protagonist. Of course, less than halfway through the film, she is murdered brutally while taking a shower. No protagonist would be killed less than halfway through the film, so she must not be the protagonist. Our initial assumption that films will follow the protagonist through the opening act must be false. Part of the shock audiences felt at the murder came from the fact that it contradicted what they had considered to that point.

Philosophy as commentary and scholarship

The method Aristotle employs throughout his work, and not merely in his logical treatises, is aimed at overcoming our tendency to form generalizations hastily, to rest on prejudice, or to accept authoritative opinions dogmatically. Nearly every time he introduces a new topic for consideration, he reviews first the familiar and common-sensical opinions on that subject, followed by the views of supposed experts, which he uses to illuminate the difficulties that arise in any serious attempt to understand the subject matter. His assumption throughout is that neither common sense opinions nor the views of presumed authorities can simply be wrong. What most people believe must have some basis in the phenomena under consideration, and those who have considered the subject seriously are likely to have reasons for the positions they arrive at. Yet they can't *all* be right, given that they disagree. So one of the criteria he adopts for an adequate account is that it must help us understand why most people think as they do and must incorporate what is reasonable from the opinions of experts. A similar approach, incidentally, is at the heart of good film criticism. A widely held consensus among audience members is a fact that can't be ignored, and what other critics have said about a film or film topic ought to be taken into account and taken seriously.

Much of the philosophical work produced during the medieval period consists of commentary, most notably on the works of Aristotle, but also on sacred texts, and on the writings of other philosophers, some of whom were themselves commenting on the writings of other philosophers. It might seem that such work would be derivative, prone to the blind acceptance of authority. In fact, there is a great deal of original thought to be found in such commentaries. Commenting on the work of other philosophers is in many ways analogous to film criticism. Some movie reviews seem to aim at no more than helping a reader decide whether to buy a ticket. Good film analysis, on the other hand, does far more. We have noted that a film, to be the film it is, needs an audience. This is not just because it exists to be watched, but because what it is cannot become apparent until it is watched, repeatedly, until what it is capable of showing an audience and what they are capable of seeing in it has become explicit. Good film criticism allows the film to be seen clearly, as if for the first time, to gauge whether it may stand the test of time, and draws out what could not have been appreciated upon its initial appearance. The point of reading and writing about old philosophical texts, likewise, is not to blindly accept and repeat what was said once before, but to reconsider its subject matter in light of its arguments, and to reassess the insights and perspective to which its words first gave readers access. Those who come later can also appreciate and articulate a text's capacity to illuminate a historical context in ways its author could not have foreseen.

Faith seeking understanding

An important theme of medieval philosophy – clearly articulated as early as Saint Augustine in the fourth century AD and repeated by Saint Anselm nearly 600 years later – is that the point of philosophy is not to teach what one ought to believe, but to explain and clarify what has already been accepted. Anselm's motto was "faith seeking understanding," and while the faith he presupposed concerned the teachings of Christianity, the approach can be generalized to other traditions and worldviews. Faith, as the medievals understood it, goes beyond mere belief. It entails commitment. It is what is presupposed by our practices. Everyone who comes to philosophy arrives with a specific background, formed by a determinate range of experiences and informed by their upbringing, education, and cultural inheritance. The existence of such commitments is not limited to those who belong to a religious tradition. Our commitments shape not only how we see the world, but what we value and how we live. It never seriously occurs to us to question such commitments, except on rare occasions, when something happens that doesn't make sense in light of them.

While "faith seeking understanding" begins with faith, it accepts that its significance and import may be poorly understood to begin with. In this respect, at least, the motto might be compared to Aristotle's insistence on beginning with common sense and authority, presuming that these can't be entirely wrong even as they may also be the source of some confusion. "Faith seeking understanding," does, though, appear to overlook the possibility that the presuppositional frameworks we inherit may be entirely wrongheaded or misleading. Or, at the very least, that they may contain biases that blind us to other, equally legitimate ways of making sense of the world.

Perhaps the most powerful and influential argument produced by Anselm, however, was aimed at encouraging the acknowledgment of truths independent of any particular perspective. It is a deceptively simple argument for the existence of God that has come to be known as the "Ontological argument." Anselm quotes a passage from the Bible, which states "The fool has said in his heart, 'there is no God'" (*Psalms* 14:1). He goes on to explain why the person described there is a fool. To say "there is no God" is to presume some idea of what God is or else the statement would be meaningless. God is not just some powerful being, but is supposed to be that being upon which all other beings depend. God, then, can only be thought of as the greatest conceivable being, or, as Anselm puts it, "something than which nothing greater can be thought" (*Proslogion* 99–100). To deny the existence of God is to suppose that the greatest conceivable being is a mere idea, something that doesn't exist except in thought, and has no power or influence in reality. Yet this is a manifest contradiction, because one can easily conceive of something greater than a mere thought. Whatever can be conceived as non-existent, or whose existence is wholly dependent upon another being, is clearly not the greatest conceivable being. So, since "something than which nothing greater can be thought" cannot even be conceived to not exist, it must be conceded to exist.

Plenty of ink has been spilled attempting to refute Anselm's argument, accusing him of playing tricks with words. A better challenge would be to clarify what it is supposed to prove. It should be clear at once that it can't prove the existence of a God conceived as some particularly powerful (and benevolent and wise) being among other beings. Such a being would remain subject to the limitations imposed upon it by the existence of other beings, even if they happened to be less powerful. That rules out the possibility of using the argument to defend one's own favored conception of divinity against that of another. There can only be one being that meets the definition: the absolute being, the being that contains within itself all reality, either directly or by being its cause. Anything that can be characterized as separate from other beings or limited in any way is not the greatest conceivable being, since one could always conceive of another being that contains it and more. The point of the proof is that not only the belief in particular things, but their very existence, presupposes the reality of the ultimate being. While individual things may or may not exist, or may exist for a time and then pass away, the ultimate being, the reality ultimately responsible for the world as we know it, cannot possibly not exist.

What Anselm's argument illustrates is the power of thought to gain insight into reality, independent of whatever we may be capable of learning from experience. It may not seem all that much, if all it reveals is that the ultimate reality must exist and transcends what we are capable of experiencing. Another important strand of medieval thought insisted that this is as far as thinking can take us. An enormously influential pseudonymous author from the late fifth century, later known as "Pseudo-Dionysius," held that none of the characteristics we associate with the things we experience and know about can apply to the ultimate reality, or God. At most, we can think about God negatively. If God is said to be good, or even to exist, it is not in the way things familiar to us are said to be good or to exist. While specific real things can be beautiful, whatever beauty we may suppose to belong to reality as such would be something that transcends our comprehension. While Anselm may have been right to insist, later, that we cannot deny the existence of an ultimate reality, the tradition of "negative theology" argues that we cannot understand what that means using reason alone. Such knowledge, according to numerous subsequent medieval thinkers, cannot arrive through either ordinary experience or reason, but only through either revelation or direct mystical encounters. The question how far experience and reason can take us, and how much we need to rely upon the authority of scripture in making sense of the world, was taken up repeatedly throughout the medieval period. In the late medieval period, during which philosophy moved out of monasteries and into schools, the various arguments about this question and many others were collected and organized for the purpose of educating prospective lawyers, doctors, and priests. Thinkers who became known as "scholastics" refined the vocabulary of philosophy, reawakened classical debates about the nature and existence of Platonic forms (or universals), and attempted to reconcile the insights of classical philosophy with the teachings of Christianity.

Thinking about thinking

The seventeenth-century French philosopher René Descartes, sometimes called the "father of modern philosophy," arguing that genuine progress could only be made by starting fresh, upon solid foundations, urged a clean break with prior philosophy. He compared the knowledge we inherit from the past to a massive edifice built up over generations, following a variety of distinct and incompatible architectural styles. To build upon this edifice would be folly; even if it had been built well, there would be no guarantee it had not weakened over time, and new additions could only be as stable as their foundations. He suggests that we should tear it all down and find solid ground in the form of unassailable truths that can serve as a foundation for a new philosophy. In spite of his insistence upon starting fresh, he was trained within the scholastic tradition and made use of its technical vocabulary throughout his work. He borrowed skeptical arguments in order to call into question claims to knowledge derived from the senses, and showed that the one thing we cannot doubt as long as we are thinking is our capacity for conscious thought. "Even though," he wrote,

> these things that I sense or imagine may perhaps be nothing at all outside me, nevertheless I am certain that these modes of thinking, which are cases of what I call sensing and imagining, insofar as they are merely modes of thinking, do exist within me.

> (Meditations on First Philosophy 70)

While we cannot be certain that there is anything that truly exists independently from our thoughts, our capacities to experience sensations, to form images, to make (or reject) assertions, are undeniable. Descartes made the capacity of thought to think about itself into the foundation of a new philosophical approach. He aimed to show, like Anselm, that reason has insight into realities that transcend human consciousness, but, unlike Anselm, faith had no role to play in it. He argued that math is not merely a mental construct, that physical realities conform to the truths discovered by geometry and algebra. His ultimate goal was to move beyond a model of philosophy built on conversation, and to establish unassailable truths about the world that would improve human lives.

While it would be difficult to find a cinematic equivalent to Cartesian science, films are quite well suited to the exploration of the doubts he raises in order to prepare the ground for certainty in science. Films are often compared to dreams, and one of the skeptical arguments that Descartes employs is to point out that when we are dreaming we accept what is happening to us as if it were real. Since there seems to be no way of conclusively establishing for any given experience that it is not the product of a dream, we should not accept anything to be true simply on the basis of our experience. Science fiction and fantasy films such as *The Matrix* (1999), *The Truman Show* (1998), *Inception* (2010), *Abre los Ojos* (1997), *and Vanilla Sky* (2001) can make vivid the power of such skeptical considerations, by leading the audience to accept, along with the protagonist, the reality of situations they will later discover to be dreamt or hallucinated.

Descartes is known for his emphasis on getting the method of philosophy right, and outlined his approach in the *Discourse on Method*. The first principle of method is that one should never accept anything as true but what is manifestly true and unable to be doubted. This is why he insisted upon doubting everything he had learned before grounding his philosophy in the power of thought to reflect upon itself. Next, he argued, we should break down complex subjects so that we can examine separately the ideas that make them up. Always seek, as much as possible, to build the understanding of complex ideas by beginning with simple ideas whose implications can be fully grasped. Finally, he insisted, we should regularly review the connection between the complex subject and its simple elements, so as to be sure not to leave anything out or to arrive at conclusions that are not fully understood.

The eighteenth-century Scottish philosopher David Hume employed a similar method as he attempted to systematically outline the powers and operations of the human mind. First, he broke down all of our thoughts into impressions and ideas. By the term impression, he wrote, "I mean all our more lively perceptions, when we hear, or see, or feel, or love, or hate, or desire, or will." He distinguished these from ideas, "which are the less lively perceptions, of which we are conscious, when we reflect on any of those sensations or movements above mentioned" (*An Enquiry Concerning Human Understanding* 10–1). Impressions are what we experience directly; ideas are reflections upon that experience. The difference between them is that impressions are more potent. They command our attention such that we cannot think them away. Consider the difference between watching a movie and reading a detailed summary afterwards. Movies deliver impressions, and the total experience of watching a movie occupies the attention of the viewer almost completely. The summary consists of ideas, which constrain the imagination much less since one can imagine what they describe in various ways. The description may call to mind the specifics, and may even call attention to details of the film one hadn't noticed, but will never be as vivid as the original experience.

Having drawn this distinction, Hume argues that all of our ideas are derived either directly or indirectly from impressions. This allows him to criticize claims based on ideas whose origin and import are suspect. "When we entertain any suspicion, that a philosophical term is employed without any meaning," he writes, "we need but enquire, *from what impression is that supposed idea derived?* And if it be impossible to assign any, this will serve to confirm our suspicion" (*An Enquiry Concerning Human Understanding* 13). He uses this criterion to argue against metaphysical speculation regarding the ultimate nature of reality. He considers popular and philosophical conceptions of the nature of the soul, the powers of nature, and the essence of things in order to show that our ideas regarding each of these are hopelessly vague and cannot be traced to specific experiences. Consequently, he urged restraint on the part of philosophers and scholars. They should define their terms carefully, Hume argued, and limit their claims about reality to those which can be assessed in light of experience.

A good deal of what takes place in film studies, and most of what you find in introductory film studies textbooks regarding film analysis and criticism, would fit quite comfortably within a Humean framework. There is a fairly sophisticated vocabulary for distinguishing between various elements of film and film techniques, and for comparing and grouping films according to historical period and genre. This vocabulary is applied to a wide variety of films, with careful descriptions and illustrations. What Hume would likely find far less appealing is much of film theory, in which the frameworks introduced for understanding film-related topics are often developed and justified independently from an empirical analysis of the films to which they are supposed to apply. To appreciate each theory often requires familiarity with a wide range of concepts that are defined in relation to each other, rather than in their relation to clearly specifiable aspects of cinema and of reality as they are experienced directly. Of course, the theorists he would likely criticize would, in turn, consider Hume to be hopelessly naïve in his assumption that anything is experienced directly.

Towards the end of the eighteenth century, the German philosopher Immanuel Kant began his own critical investigation of the power of human thought to gain insight into itself and the world. While inspired by Hume's project, Kant held that Hume's insistence that all concepts be tested experientially had led him to overlook the fact that our very capacity to have meaningful experiences presupposes our possession of a range of concepts that are independent of experience. Kant called such concepts "transcendental." He argued that we cannot learn such concepts from experience because we couldn't have experiences at all unless we possessed them. If I couldn't differentiate between one experience and another, for example, it wouldn't make sense to say that I'd had the experience of both. Yet in order to differentiate between one experience and another, I have to possess the capacity of mind to attend simultaneously to each and to characterize each as qualitatively distinct. My ability to grasp each as a certain kind of thing is just what it means, according to Kant, for me to have the concept of being a "certain kind of thing" and so this concept is not so much learned from experience but makes it possible in the first place.

Philosophy and history

Philosophers throughout the ancient and medieval periods made very little distinction between the fields that we would now call philosophy and science. Whether they put more emphasis on ethical and political questions, or on theological or metaphysical questions, or on the natural world, all were, equally, philosophers. That changed in the early modern period, beginning in the sixteenth century with thinkers such as Francis Bacon and Galileo Galilei. Descartes was a major influence on the formation of the new scientific method employed by thinkers such as Robert Boyle and Isaac Newton, who were known as "natural philosophers" to indicate their focus on mathematical and experimental reasonings aimed at predicting and controlling the operations of the natural world. Hume and Kant, writing in the eighteenth century, could take for granted the distinction between philosophy and natural science, and their philosophical work can be understood, at least in part, as an effort to clarify what questions remain for philosophy in the aftermath of the scientific revolution.

In the nineteenth century, the content of philosophy itself became historical. While Kant, for example, had written in the latter part of the eighteenth century about the importance of history, the majority of his work is aimed at the elucidation of unchanging rational truths regarding human cognition and action. Georg Friedrich Wilhelm Hegel, by contrast, argued that reason itself develops historically.

History, he considered, is rational, but not in the sense that we can employ timeless principles of logic to deduce the course of history. Rather, he held, it is by examining with care the development of human history that we come to understand what it means to be rational in the first place. As he puts it, "what is rational is actual; and what is actual is rational" (*Hegel's The Philosophy of Right* 8). Yet wisdom – the philosophical comprehension of history as a rational development – can only come after the fact. We cannot employ reason to predict its course in advance. In his famous statement "the owl of Minerva begins its flight only with the falling of dusk" (ibid. 10).

The historical unfolding of rationality is what Hegel called "dialectic." While the abstract character of dialectic can be described easily, actual dialectical development is always concrete and specific and does not, therefore, conform to any simple formula. Abstractly, dialectic is the process whereby a certain configuration of reality or of thought is shown to rely upon conditions that, once acknowledged, prove it isn't what it seemed to be. The acknowledgment of these conditions transforms the configuration, and the new configuration that emerges will turn out to be itself dependent on as yet unacknowledged conditions, whose character can only become fully clear in the course of the history through which they emerge. The word "dialectic" is also used to describe the Socratic method of investigating the character and implication of ideas in the course of conversation. History, to Hegel, is the unfolding of reality as a conversation with itself. Within this great conversation, certain specific individuals, social institutions, and political structures find themselves challenged, both by others and as a result of internal conflicts, and – as a result of their efforts to address these challenges – may subsequently find their nature clarified and their character changed.

Karl Marx, reacting against those who read Hegel's claim as a valorization of the political status quo, argued that the primary mechanism of dialectical historical change is economics, which forces political and social changes. Historical change becomes necessary, for example, when the social and political structures of a given society are inadequate to the task of producing the material goods required for that society to function. The culture and ideas that a society produces, including their religious and philosophical ideals, do not so much shape their activities as they are shaped by the demands of political economics. Film theorists such as Jean-Louis Baudry, writing in the twentieth century, employed Marxist ideas to argue that, irrespective of the particular details of a given film, the very structure of the cinematic apparatus ensures the passivity of its audience, and encourages their acceptance of the structures and ideals of the society that produces it. "It is," he writes, "an apparatus destined to obtain a precise ideological effect, necessary to the dominant ideology" ("Ideological Effects of the Basic Cinematographic Apparatus" 46).

The subtitle to Nietzsche's late book *Twilight of the Idols*, published near the end of the nineteenth century, is "how to philosophize with a hammer." His aim, in that book and throughout his work, is to shatter assumptions that had guided Western philosophy to that point. This might be seen as a simple renewal of ancient skepticism, or of the methodological skepticism through which Descartes attempted to tear down the edifice of existing knowledge in order to get a fresh start. Yet Nietzsche was not interested in withholding judgment, and didn't think, like Descartes, that we could establish certainties upon which to build new philosophical idols. He attempted to undermine what he considered to be problematic philosophical dogmas in order to enable his readers to grasp the viability of alternative hypotheses. He challenged, for example, the assumption that history is both rational and progressive. He proposed, as an alternative, the hypothesis that history amounts to a series of discontinuous trans-formations, whereby some powerful social configuration imposes its will on existing power structures, and in so doing alters how the past is interpreted. The appearance of progress is, then, the product of a retrospective assessment of the past in light of the transformations it made possible, and in light of the values whose enforcement it enabled.

One of Nietzsche's most influential innovations was the philosophical method he characterized as "genealogy." When we study the genealogy of a person we find they are the product of many distinct lineages, and that each of their ancestors is also a node in a network of branching and intersecting and entangled roots. Yet when we tell the story of history – whether it is the history of individuals, states, or ideas – we tend to treat it as if it were linear. Nietzsche's philosophical genealogy attempted to recover the non-linear complexity of the history of ideas and ideals. He attempted to trace the impact of past ways of thinking and doing things upon the present, and also to identify the alternative ways of thinking and acting that were once vital but have become lost to us, for reasons other than their lack of utility, or their irrationality. The core of his method is the careful reading of old texts, in search of patterns of reasoning that can-not easily make sense to us in light of current presuppositions. Presumably they did make sense once, and hypotheses regarding the way the people who produced those texts must have been thinking can help to highlight what is distinctive and problematic in "our" own ways of thinking.

In *On the Genealogy of Morals*, for example, Nietzsche argues that the assumption of a binary contrast between good and evil is utterly foreign to the language and texts of many ancient peoples. Their sense of "good" was an affirmation of the strengths they found in their culture. They had no conception of "evil," but at worst of peoples and ways of life they considered to be weak or inferior to their own. Contrasting different approaches to moral evaluation allows us to reconsider the significance of the moral values we may explicitly endorse, by showing them to be optional, rather than inevitable. The resistance we may experience in acknowledging alternatives may also indicate to us our allegiance to values we hadn't considered to be important. In particular, Nietzsche aims to undermine the apparent obviousness of the opposition between good and evil as this contrast appears within the Judeo-Christian tradition that had shaped European values. He argues that the designation of something as "good," within that tradition, is not the affirmative evaluation it appears to be. It is, rather, a reactionary and defensive self-assessment on the part of peoples who consid-ered themselves oppressed by more powerful groups, who, because of their strength and power, were designated by those whom they had overpowered as "evil."

Nietzsche's approach to philosophy might be described as experimental. He some-times speaks as if the great philosophical task – a task he sometimes reserves for the overman (*übermensch*) who would live "beyond good and evil" – is to experiment with new ways of life, looking to the past only so that it can help us move past the prejudices of the present that keep us from finding healthier and more authentic ways to be. American pragmatist philosophers writing at the turn of the century, such as William James, also conceived of life and philosophy in experimental terms. The term "pragmatism" refers to a method for solving philosophical problems and for clarify-ing concepts. It is to consider what difference it makes to how we act that we conceive things one way rather than another. Charles Sanders Peirce, credited as the founder of pragmatism, puts the pragmatic principle as follows: "Consider what effects, which might conceivably have practical bearings, we conceive the object of our conception to have. Then, our conception of those effects is the whole of our conception of the object" ("How to Make Our Ideas Clear" 31).

Take, for example, the concept of "truth." William James offered the following pragmatic account: "True ideas are those that we can assimilate, validate, corroborate, and verify. False ideas are those that we can not" (*Pragmatism and Other Writings* 88). This doesn't mean, as some have thought, that for the pragmatists what is true is what it would be beneficial to believe, as it might benefit a child (or her parents) for her to believe in Santa Claus, even if he doesn't exist, because it will make her happy or encourage her to behave well. What is beneficial to believe could only count as "truth" if we include far more than merely psychological and moral well-being in the catalog of benefits. It wouldn't benefit anyone to believe what is inconsistent with one's other beliefs, what doesn't cohere with reality as it is experienced, what no one else can confirm, and what doesn't stand up to scrutiny and rigorous testing. It would, on the other hand, be difficult to say what more there is to a statement being true than that it is consistent with other statements held to be true, and that it stands up to scrutiny and testing over time. The pragmatists tended to be fallibilists, which means that they are open to the possibility that a claim once considered to be true will later turn out to have not been true. That doesn't mean that it was once true and later false, but that the best we have to go on whenever we assert a claim to be true is our practical experience in the world to that point, and that if, later, we have experience that is contrary to that claim, we should be open-minded enough to admit that we'd been wrong. The truth or falsity of an idea, according to pragmatists, should make an enormous difference in practice. Indeed, for them, this is the only difference that matters.

Analytic versus continental

The twentieth century saw the birth of cinema. In the beginning just a novelty, its impact grew until it had become the most significant popular art form in the world by the 1950s. The century also saw the increasing professionalization of the philosophy discipline. While cinema caught the attention of some philosophers and other theoreticians early on, and while several important thinkers devoted significant attention to the new medium, the philosophy of film developed into a specialization within philosophy and in film studies only at the turn of the twenty-first century. With a few notable exceptions, mainstream philosophers at the beginning of the twentieth century tended to focus more on the relationship between philosophy and science than between philosophy and art. Some philosophers, impressed by the progress of the scientific disciplines, sought to emulate their methods in philosophy. Some saw the task of philosophy to be complementary to the work of the sciences, and sought to clarify what science is, how it ought to proceed, and how it is different from non-science (and nonsense). Others sought to clarify the differences between philosophical concerns and the subject matter of other areas of inquiry. Many twentieth-century philosophers consider the primary task of philosophy to be that of clarifying the meaning of concepts, both in our ordinary language and in technical fields. The question of whether and how we can interpret human behavior, culture, language, and cultural products (such as texts and artworks), has been a dominant preoccupation of philosophical work across the spectrum of specializations. While, along with most other major fields of inquiry, philosophy has become increasingly specialized, we can highlight briefly here a few of the most important methodological trends of twentieth-century philosophy.

The most dominant division within twentieth-century philosophy is between thinkers whose approach to solving philosophical problems has come to be characterized as "analytic," and the "continental" philosophers whose preoccupations and methodology are inherited primarily from European schools of thought. It is a somewhat strange division, since "analytic" refers primarily to a method of clarifying concepts, by way of analysis, and "continental" refers primarily to the continental region from which its primary influences herald. Yet the strangeness is somehow appropriate, since so-called "analytic" thinkers aim to analyze concepts and arguments in ways that can be abstracted from historical context, while so-called "continental" philosophers tend to consider the explicit engagement with the history of philosophy to be central to their project, regardless of its topical focus. Where analytic thinkers have engaged with the history of philosophy, there has been (at least until recently) a tendency to abstract arguments from texts and contexts, and to consider them as if they were contemporary. Early modern thinkers, such as Descartes and Hume, who share the spirit of analytic philosophy, and whose arguments can therefore be appreciated apart from their place in the broader trajectory of the history of philosophy, were influential on both schools; thinkers whose work emphasized the historical character of thought, such as Hegel and Nietzsche, by contrast, have long been taken seriously by continental philosophers, but until fairly recently have largely been ignored or severely criticized by analytics. By the end of the twentieth century, it should be noted, this point of contrast between analytic and continental schools of philosophy had become far less pronounced. This is due in part to the fact that in the last couple of decades in the twentieth century prominent thinkers from both camps, such as Jürgen Habermas in the continental tradition and Stanley Cavell and Richard Rorty from the analytic tradition, began to take the work of their counterparts quite seriously.

Wittgenstein and analytic philosophy

Two important schools of early analytic philosophy are logical positivism and ordinary language philosophy. While the influence of both schools had waned by the early 1970s, they nevertheless illustrate a style and some of the range of concerns that have continued to characterize analytic approaches to philosophy. Both were strongly impacted by the work of the Austrian philosopher Ludwig Wittgenstein. His early text, the *Tractatus Logico-Philosophicus*, first published in 1921, inspired the logical positivists. His later work, especially his 1945 *Philosophical Investigations*, offered a distinctive model for doing philosophy that was emulated by ordinary language philosophers. Both works are concerned with questions of meaning. They examine how, for example, words and thoughts acquire their significance, and explore the difference between meaningful and meaningless claims.

In the *Tractatus*, Wittgenstein argued that to be meaningful, propositions must depict precise facts about the world, such as "the pen on the table is red." We can, of course, create sentences that don't depict precise facts in the world, such as "the pen on the table is furious." Such sentences may be grammatical, yet are meaningless. It is impossible to say what observations would encourage us to accept or deny them. Statements about values, likewise, are meaningless, and many of the claims that philosophers make about subjects like God, beauty, and morality lack meaning as well.

In fact, Wittgenstein appears to have thought that these subjects remained important, even vital, but that we could not sensibly argue about them, and that we'd do better not to speak of them at all. In this respect, his thinking might be compared to that of Kant, who held that we live under the guidance of ideals that we could never prove and about which we can have no knowledge. The logical positivists, however, read Wittgenstein's argument as a repudiation of much of the history of philosophy. We can only make meaningful statements regarding what can be observed and described in factual terms. The positivists held that philosophy ought to proceed on the model they attributed to science. We define our terms carefully, make observations, form generalizations based on those observations – making sure that these generalizations can be tested by further observations – and form theories to make predictions regarding future observations. Philosophical claims that cannot be tested based on observations should either be reformulated or repudiated as nonsense. A.J. Ayer's *Language, Truth, and Logic* is an admirably clear and concise expression of the general approach.

By the time he came to write *Philosophical Investigations*, Wittgenstein seems to have concluded that there is no straightforward way of determining which statements are meaningful. To make sense of any statement, whether it is a factual description or a characterization of values, requires us to participate in what he calls the "complicated form of life" within which language takes shape (174). He considers a range of examples to show that perfectly sensible statements become nonsense when they are employed outside of the contexts in which they are ordinarily used. He argues moreover that the meaning of concepts is not univocal, so that the successful employment of a concept in one context doesn't guarantee it will be understood in another. At most, there is a "family resemblance" between the range of conceptual meanings. Philosophy, according to Wittgenstein, can function as a kind of therapy, assisting us to overcome the confusions that arise when we misuse language and apply sensible concepts where they don't make sense. He holds that many of the most enduring philosophical problems arise as a result of such misuse of language. The task, as Wittgenstein sees it, is not so much to solve such problems as to dissolve them.

So-called "ordinary language philosophers" took up the challenge of solving philosophical problems by clarifying the contexts within which philosophical concepts can be appropriately employed. Gilbert Ryle, for example, argued that the so-called mind-body problem arises as a result of a kind of conceptual confusion he characterized as "category mistakes." The examples he uses to illustrate such mistakes are all cases of confusing conditioned realities with the conditions that make them possible, treating conditioned realities as if they were just one other thing, just like the things that serve as their components or their causes. It would be, for example, a category mistake to suppose that the movie *Jurassic Park* was the same kind of thing as the recording media on which copies of the movie can be found. It wouldn't make sense to ask, upon viewing various copies of the movie, and various playback devices, and projectors, and theaters: which one of these is the movie? It is not any one of them, but that doesn't, as we've seen, make the movie a mysterious reality, existing somewhere outside of or beyond the physical realm in which its recordings and the equipment exist. The movie is, rather, the specific and repeatable event that unfolds for an audience whenever such a copy is played and its image is displayed, an event that would only be possible given the existence of copies and playback equipment. Similarly, Ryle argues, the fact that we talk about mental entities such as beliefs and emotions should not mislead us into thinking that they are ghostly things inside of the body which somehow cause the body to act. Ascribing beliefs and emotions to a person is, rather, a convenient manner of talking about the ways in which that person is likely to interact with other people and the world as a result, in part, of the interaction between physical events taking place inside and outside of their bodies.

Analytic philosophy gets its name from the overriding interest of its proponents in defining key terms through analysis, by breaking concepts down into their constituent elements. Philosophers seek to go beyond the dictionary definition of philosophical terms, and to identify necessary and sufficient conditions for their correct employment. We might illustrate the difference between these by considering what must occur for a film screening to take place. There would need to be some kind of screen, something that would allow an audience to view the film. That is a necessary condition. But the existence of a screen alone is not sufficient, since something needs to be projected or displayed on the screen. If what was displayed was a still image, it wouldn't be the screening of a film. Of course, there are films in which no motion takes place, such as Derek Jarman's *Blue* (1993), in which the screen displays the same blue shade throughout – but that film does include sound, and it wouldn't count as a screening of that film simply to project a blue slide. A sufficient set of conditions for a film screening would be, say, that a specific film is projected for the duration of the film onto a standard sized screen in a commercial movie theater. Yet that's not the only way to screen a film, so these aren't necessary conditions.

Many philosophers hold that to define a concept adequately requires the specification of both necessary and sufficient conditions for its application. One way that philosophers attempt to identify such conditions is through the use of thought experiments. A historically popular way of defining knowledge, first clearly formulated in Plato's dialogue the *Theaetetus*, is that to have knowledge is to have justified true belief. It seems that this definition states both necessary and sufficient conditions for knowledge. To have knowledge one must believe what one knows. That is necessary, but not sufficient. What one claims to know must also be true, since we wouldn't say it is known if it was false. Finally, it wouldn't be enough if one just so happened to believe a true fact. That would be a lucky guess, not knowledge. One should believe it for good reasons. Believing something true for the right reasons seems to be enough, a necessary and sufficient condition for knowledge. Yet a series of thought experiments, modeled on one first formulated in a famous article by Edmund Gettier, suggests that even these conditions are insufficient. The experiments involve cases where someone believes something that is true and for very good reasons – reasons that would ordinarily count as a justification – except that in this case there are facts, unknown to the supposed knower, that undermine the relevance of the evidence. We might imagine such a case involving film.

Suppose, on a whim, someone walked into a movie theater that was advertising an Alfred Hitchcock festival. He hadn't seen many Hitchcock films, only heard he was a famous filmmaker, so he didn't know what to expect. He decides to see the film *The Man Who Knew Too Much* (1956), and the cashier hands him a ticket. As it turns out the ticket is printed with the wrong theater number, and the line for popcorn is long so he takes his seat in the wrong theater, the one that is supposed to be playing Hitchcock's *The Wrong Man* (1956). He arrives a few moments after the movie starts, just after the title of the film appears on the screen. Yet the distributors have also made a mistake, sending two copies of *The Man Who Knew Too Much*, one of which is labeled incorrectly. So he believes he saw *The Man Who Knew Too Much*, he has as good reasons for thinking this as anybody who claims to have seen a movie for the first time, and he actually did see it, but only on accident. If he'd seen *The Wrong Man* instead he would have had the same belief. Later on when he is asked whether he had ever seen any Hitchcock films he might say "I saw *The Man Who Knew Too Much* once." Does he *know* that he's seen it? Gettier examples are generally taken to imply that more is required for knowledge than adopting beliefs for reasons that in most cases would ensure that they are true. There is a lot of disagreement, though, about what else is required.

The point of such thought experiments is to clarify our intuitions regarding the concept in question, so that we can assess more precisely the conditions for its use. Here, even though what he happens to believe is true, his evidence for believing it would be equally sound evidence for believing something else. This suggests that having good reasons for believing something true is not enough for knowledge. One of the reasons that analytic philosophers in the past couple of decades have become interested in films is for their capacity to function as particularly vivid thought experiments. Thomas Wartenberg has argued in his book *Thinking on Screen: Film as Philosophy* that it is primarily for their ability to illustrate philosophical concerns and to sharpen our intuitions regarding philosophical concepts that films can be considered to be philosophical.

Phenomenology and continental philosophy

Perhaps the most significant and influential movement within continental philosophy is phenomenology. There are important precursors to phenomenology in the post-Kantian tradition. Hegel's most enduringly influential work, published in 1807, is in fact titled the *Phenomenology of Spirit*. Edmund Husserl, however, writing at the end of the nineteenth century and through the first few decades of the twentieth is considered the movement's principal founder. The method and aim of phenomenology can perhaps best be described as the rigorous description of the structure of experience. Normally when we describe our experiences, we focus our description on the object of that experience. We say *what* it is that we experience. "My *Alien* DVD is on my desk," for example. Phenomenology encourages us to attend also to *how* it is experienced, and especially to the conditions within the experience that make it possible for us to experience the object as we do.

The most obvious thing to notice is that my experience of the DVD is by way of vision. I might have said, instead, that "I *see* my *Alien* DVD on the desk," which already calls attention to an important structure of the experience. It is not just that the DVD shows up as there, on my desk. It shows up *to me*, and appears to me visually. So its appearance implies my relationship to it. What shows up is not just the DVD, but my own way of being towards it. To see it, for example, I have to be looking in its direction. I have to be close enough to discern it, but not so close that there isn't a spatial distance between me and it. It isn't enough to have my eyes pointed in the right direction. I have to direct my attention towards it, so as to notice it and pick it out as something distinct from the many other books and things that surround it on my messy desk. I don't see it in its entirety but at most from a particular side; yet to see it as a DVD disk is to see it as something that has another side. If I were to try and pick it up and turn it over but couldn't grasp it, or if it disappeared when I attempted to move it, I would have to say I'd been mistaken when I thought I saw a DVD. It must really have been some kind of illusion. Even if I don't try to pick it up, to experience it as a DVD disk is to experience it as something I *could* pick up and turn over. If I did I would expect to see its shiny backside, rather than the front with the title printed on it. So when I see the disk, I don't just experience an object. I experience it in relation to me, and I experience with it the expectations I have built up through dealing with similar objects in the past, and experience through it my own capacities for interaction with such objects.

While I am there with the object in the experience of it, I do not appear to myself directly, as if I were just another object there in the vicinity of the disk. It appears to me as a thing. I don't appear to myself as a thing. I appear, rather, as that to which and for-which the thing appears. We might compare my indirect appearance with the object to the way that the movie camera is implied by the appearance of a moving image. We don't see the camera itself, but the image that does appear could only appear as a result of a camera pointing in its direction. Specific qualities of the image might even allow us to infer what kind of camera it was. The image would, then, appear as the image of, say, an Arriflex 35. Similarly, my appearance with the disk is not the appearance of an object, but is the reason why the object appears in the way that it does. I am there with the disk, in other words, as the interested perspective from which it appears. My orientation, my specific perceptual capacities, my powers of attention, all have an impact on how the object appears. I am also there in the experience through the fact that this moment of the object's appearance has a history and a future. The DVD doesn't just show up suddenly. It appears to me from the moment I notice it as already having been there for a while, and as something that will remain in place unless I or someone else picks it up. It appears to me, moreover, not just as an inert object that can only sit there. It appears to me as something I can pick up and put into the player in my computer, so that I can watch the film again. All of this is part of the experience of this simple object. It is how it appears to me. None of these aspects of the object's experience can be explained by or reduced to its mere physical presence. They are the result of its presence to me – a being capable of having experience – and of my presence to it.

Every experience of an object is going to be oriented in some way. We can never adopt what Thomas Nagel has described as "the view from nowhere." We only ever have views from particular, finite, perspectives. How any object appears to me is shaped not only by my spatial orientation towards it, but by the way in which my encounter with it now is shaped by my other experiences, and my expectations regarding the future – all of this is part of what Husserl describes as "intentionality," the specific way in which consciousness orients itself towards and takes up – "intends" – the object of which it is conscious. The first and most basic lesson of phenomenology is that there can never be an object of experience without some such contextualizing orientation towards that object. There can be no consciousness without intentionality. Phenomenology, as Husserl introduced it, aims to draw out from this richness of intentional experience what is universal in it. It aims to discover the "what it must be like" for anyone to have an experience of specific types of objects, whether they are simple material objects like my *Alien* disk, objects that unfold over time like musical performances or movies, or conscious beings like myself, who also have a determinate but distinct perspective on the world. In order to make this possible, the first step of the phenomenological method is to let go of any assumptions we might have about what the world is like that have been drawn from common sense, science, or culture. Phenomenology is the attempt to rigorously describe how the world appears within experience, so the phenomenologist attempts first to "bracket" or set aside any preconceived notions regarding what it might be like independently of how it is experienced.

Subsequent philosophers have drawn upon the methods of phenomenology in order to address specific philosophical problems. Martin Heidegger, for example, adapted the phenomenological approach to illuminate a question he considered to be both central to and obscured by the history of philosophy: the question of being, the question of what it means to be, or, to put it paradoxically, the question of what "is" is. It is a question that, as he argues in *Being and Time* (1927), cannot be approached directly. It doesn't seem at first like the question makes sense, given that we have to presuppose an answer even to pose the question. You can't just ask "what *is* is?" and expect an illuminating response – you have to orient the question somehow towards something familiar. He decides to approach the question of being by pursuing a phenomenological investigation of a special kind of being, which is itself defined by the question of its own being: the question of what it is and ought to be. This kind of being is, of course, the human being, whose existence he designates as "*Dasein*" (in German) or as "being there" (in English). To be human, he notes, is not merely to be a thing among things, but to be that for which there are things. We don't experience ourselves as things, but as that for which and to which things appear. To be human is to be a situated orientation, a clearing or a space among beings, a "there" where other beings appear.

Jean-Paul Sartre, though influenced by Heidegger, was more interested in the problems of human existence than in the question of being per se. The core principle of existentialism, a philosophical movement to which he contributed while rejecting the label of an existentialist, is that for human beings, at least, existence precedes essence. What it is to be a human being (their essence) is not something that can be defined in advance; it is a product of their activity, the product of their manner of existing. Human beings are, in other words, what they make of themselves. This is, really, just another way of putting Heidegger's claim that human being is that kind of being whose being is in question. Sartre, though, focuses on the ways that our way of being shapes our experience and activity. First of all, it means that we are aware, at least dimly, of our freedom and responsibility. We are not given the meaning of our lives, we have to choose it, and we are, therefore, responsible for what we make of ourselves. We can't choose the home into which we are born, we can't choose our ethnicity, our genetic predispositions, our society, our historical moment – but we can't help but choose how we take these up, what we make of ourselves in light of the possibilities into which we are "thrown." To the extent that we are aware of this, it is a source of great anxiety. Every moment we have to decide what we are going to make of our circumstances, and what we are going to become, and there is no one, not even a God, whom we can blame for the impact of our choices. Most of us try to evade this responsibility. We fall into the patterns of activity we observe others adopting. We adopt a role, we live by habit. This is what Sartre calls "bad faith," or "inauthenticity."

Sartre, along with other existentialist thinkers such as Simone de Beauvoir and Albert Camus – and Søren Kierkegaard before them – did not merely write philosophical treatises. They wrote fictional and semi-fictional explorations of philosophical themes, in novels, plays, and autobiographical accounts. Sartre even wrote screenplays. Given that life as it is lived is the subject matter of their philosophy, it was equally susceptible to exploration through art, literature, and cinema. Jean-Luc Godard, whose film *Breathless* (1960) will be the subject of the final part of this book, drew inspiration from existentialist literature as he developed his own cinematic style and preoccupations. He may have learned from his reading that to observe interesting characters having conversations about ideas and about life can be as compelling as to see them in action. By the 1960s, existentialism's importance within continental philosophy – especially in France – was eclipsed by the influence of other philosophical and literary movements such as structuralism, which were less influenced by phenomenology.

The core method of structuralism is to explain social and cultural phenomena as if they formed part of a language. The key to language, for the structuralists, is that linguistic terms don't have meaning in themselves. Yet there is no meaning outside of language. There is no realm of pure meaning – such as a Platonic realm of the forms – that first gives meaning to language. The terms and sentences of language get their meanings as a result of their structured and relatively stable relationships to other elements of the language. The structuralists held that the same was true of social and cultural phenomena. Structuralist film theorists such as Christian Metz applied this theory to the study of cinema, insisting that the significance of any given shot or technique could only be determined in relation to the other shots of a film, and in relation to cinema as a whole. Cinema is not quite a language, since the same shot or sequence of shots can mean something very different in one film than they do in another, depending on the other shots that surround it. Yet there are certain codes or patterns that recur both within cinema and in the larger culture, which are readily understood by those who participate within that culture, and which shape the ways in which a given film that employs them is understood.

The so-called "postmodern" movement, which became popular within continental philosophy in the last few decades of the twentieth century and had a significant influence on developments in several disciplines outside of philosophy, including Film Studies, represented the attempt on the part of a number of thinkers to challenge any philosophical approach that claimed to offer a "theory of everything," a "Grand narrative," or a story that explains it all. No one ever seriously suggested that traditional philosophical approaches are just wrong, or have no value at all, or that in the absence of a single best interpretation of matters there is no meaning at all, and that any way of making sense of things is as good as any other. Rather, they argued – and it is hard to disagree with them – that no theoretical approach (such as phenomenology or structuralism) and no story of history (like those offered by Hegel or by Marx) can ever claim to have the last word such that philosophy is finished. Each new answer only raises new questions. By taking the history of philosophy seriously, we can build upon its great conversation. We can learn from Nietzsche, for example, that history needn't always build in a linear fashion. Sometimes, as in a good conversation, someone will introduce an entirely novel idea that redirects the flow of the discourse. This may even mean that some questions that once seemed important go unanswered, with a slim chance they'll be picked up later. We can also learn from thinkers like Plato, from the beginning, and Sartre, our near contemporary, and from the many artists and writers and filmmakers who inspired the thinking of others, as we attempt to find new ways of contributing to the great philosophical conversation, through dialogues, literature, theater, and, now, film.

Film's philosophical affinities

Films, like philosophy, can be about almost anything, and can adopt a wide range of styles. Given that films are able to address nearly any conceivable subject, they can certainly address many of the subjects philosophers have talked about. Perhaps they can't effectively explore abstract topics like modal logic – which deals with inferences

from statements about what is possible, actual, or necessary – except by having someone on screen talking about it. Yet they can vividly depict the kinds of alternate realities and possible worlds that philosophers sometimes invoke to help make sense of it.
They may not easily go into the depth one might achieve in a treatise or a novel, yet
in a short amount of time they can deliver a compelling message and convince audiences to care about subjects they'd never considered before. Arguably, the films that
fascinate most, and certainly the most popular films, tell stories about people, whether
documentary or fictional. They can, naturally, depict people who care about, and
think about, philosophical subjects. Or, films might show that whether or not the people they depict actually think about such things, their situations and actions can best
be understood in relation to philosophical themes. There are films about faith, and
religion, featuring characters who believe in a higher meaning or purpose to their lives
than the values they perceive all around them. Films can feature those who doubt what
they'd long believed, and those who question the things they considered to be real.
They can lead us to consider whether their beliefs and doubts should be taken seriously. Films can depict some of the ways that sense perception and memory are biased
and unreliable. They tell stories about people behaving in ways we either endorse or
disapprove of, sometimes presenting evidence that what they do is right or wrong, and
sometimes suggesting that the attitudes that condemn them are themselves unfounded.
Films can, like other great works of art, push us to see and think differently.

So, films can both entertain their audiences and engage their reflection on some
of the traditional subject matters of philosophy: questions regarding knowledge and
the justification of beliefs, questions about how we ought to act, about the nature of
art, and what is ultimately real. Not every film does any of these things directly, and
some films seem to do none of them. Every film is, though, obviously, relevant to
philosophical questions about the nature of film. Edward Small argued specifically for
the importance of the genre of experimental films by suggesting that its output is best
understood as a kind of "direct theory" – that its major function is "to theorize upon
its own substance by reflecting back upon its own intrinsic semiotic system(s)" (*Direct
Theory* 5). One might argue, more broadly, that narrative fiction and documentary
films also have the potential to generate reflection on the nature of film as an expressive medium and art form. Each film has the potential to teach us what films are capable of, and to challenge any widely held assumptions about what it takes for films to be
successful. There are, though, in addition, certain broader philosophical themes that
successful narrative and documentary films evoke, as a result of characteristic features
of the medium. Other philosophical subjects and questions may not be intrinsic to the
nature of cinema, but nevertheless come naturally to it. Let's call these film's philosophical affinities. In what follows I'll outline briefly a few of the most obvious ones.

Perhaps the most significant affinity is metaphysical, and Parts Two and Three of
this book will examine this in detail. Films present us with what seems to be real, but
that we recognize to be merely an appearance. That means that to think about film as
a medium requires that we consider the basic question of metaphysics, a question that
has been at the heart of philosophy since its beginnings. It is the question whether and
how we can differentiate between appearances and reality, how we should characterize
reality when we only ever have access to its appearances, and whether we can have any
insight at all into what is ultimately real, independently of how it appears to us. In fact,
it is this metaphysical affinity that might be said to be the root of all the others. It is
because films have the capacity to evoke reality so powerfully that our reflections upon

what they present us are relevant to our understanding of the realities we experience outside of the cinema. It is because successful films encourage us to suspend disbelief that they offer us an occasion to reflect upon what we are willing to accept as possible. The fact that, at the same time as we suspend disbelief we don't actually believe it, and are always at least dimly aware that what we are watching is not real, can also enable us to achieve the critical distance that helps to sharpen our intuitions. When observing, say, the actions of a fictional character on screen, we may assess their morality in the same way that we would a person from our social circle. Yet, since their actions don't affect us, and in the end we have to admit they don't affect anyone directly, we are in a better position after the fact to reflect on the justice of our judgments.

Of course, while the actions of fictional characters on screen don't affect anyone directly they may affect their audiences indirectly by influencing their behavior. The question of film's impact, and of the power of its representations to effect how people interpret the world and act, is a question with clear philosophical relevance. While films may only be an appearance, they do nevertheless appear within the real world and have real-world consequences. This was, in part, why Plato raised concerns about Greek theater and poetry in his *Republic*. He worried that children, especially, learn how to act and what they should aspire to through the stories they absorb from a very young age. Plato's characterization of this concern, and of the possible relevance it might have to movies, was central to *Shadow Philosophy: Plato's Cave and Cinema* (2014), which can be read as a companion to the present book. A range of related questions regarding how cinema draws upon and reinforces or modifies our moral intuitions and attitudes are discussed in some detail in Robert Sinnerbrink's *Cinematic Ethics: Exploring Ethical Experience through Film* (2015).

When we watch a film about people, we seem to see them while remaining unseen. If they were real it would be voyeurism. Questions regarding the ethics of observation and the ethics of representation thus also arise naturally in considerations of film. Such themes are made explicit in films like Alfred Hitchcock's *Rear Window* (1954), in which a recuperating photographer alleviates the boredom of being stuck in a wheelchair in his apartment by peering through the windows of his neighbors. Viewers of the film can't help but notice that they, too, are peering through a window into the lives of this photographer and his socialite girlfriend. Laura Mulvey, in a famous article entitled "Visual Pleasure and Narrative Cinema," (1975) argues that much of mainstream cinema is designed to appeal to such voyeuristic curiosity, which she calls "scopophilia." She argues, however, that the gaze catered to in classical Hollywood films is distinctively male. Leading women in such films tend to be represented as objects to be looked at, framed and lit in ways that make them attractive to the viewer. They function as both erotic objects for the active male protagonist and as a source of visual pleasure for the audience. Audiences are encouraged to identify with the active male protagonist, but the interest that he takes in the "love interest" allows the audience to pretend that the pleasure they take in looking at her is not guilty. The film is designed to allow them to attribute the gaze that takes in her appeal to the male protagonist. They can pretend, in other words, that they are not looking at her, but are only being shown what he looks at.

Something similar can be said about cinematic representations generally, where audiences are encouraged and enabled to overlook their own complicity in the problematic character of the representations in films they enjoy. People of a marginalized or minority status are often portrayed on film in ways that conform to widely held stereotypes on the part of the audience. Yet audience members who might not admit to such a stereotype or who might question it if it were articulated clearly by their peers, can nevertheless suspend such doubts as they suspend their disbelief in order to enjoy the entertaining spectacle. The impact, however, is that they are less likely later to find plausible any cinematic depictions that break with the stereotypes to which they've grown accustomed.

In one of his rare comments on cinema, the French philosopher Maurice Merleau-Ponty suggested that filmmakers share a "certain way of being" with phenomenological and existential philosophers. Film, he argued, is particularly well suited to exploring and revealing the way that our inner lives and thoughts are expressed by our manner of being in the world. Films do not need to tell us what characters are thinking. They can show it. The capacity of film to draw in close to reveal facial expression and gesture, and to pull back to show the nuances of human activity and interaction, allows film to participate with phenomenology in its demonstration that we need not posit a metaphysical divide between the mind and the body, or between intentions and actions. "That is why," he writes,

> the movies can be so gripping in their presentation of man: they do not give us his *thoughts*, as novels have done for so long, but his conduct or behavior. They directly present to us that special way of being in the world, of dealing with things and other people, which we can see in the sign language of gesture and gaze and which clearly defines each person we know.
>
> ("The Film and the New Psychology" 150)

Good films have the capacity to show us who we are and how we think, precisely by showing us (with precision) how we act.

Stanley Cavell, one of the most prominent analytic philosophers to have engaged seriously with film in the twentieth century, went further than Merleau-Ponty when he wrote that

> to my way of thinking the creation of film was as if meant for philosophy – meant to reorient everything philosophy has said about reality and its representation, about art and imitation, about greatness and conventionality, about judgment and pleasure, about skepticism and transcendence, about language and expression.
>
> (Contesting Tears xii)

Of these the philosophical concern he focused on most powerfully in his analysis of film was skepticism. Film, he argued, has the capacity to remind us of our natural condition, of standing outside or apart from the world in which we take an interest. It helps us to reconcile ourselves to this condition, which entails that we can never know things as they are but only as they appear to us. "It is as though the world's projection explains our forms of unknownness and our inability to know" (*The World Viewed* 42).

Cavell was, however, less interested in the abstract philosophical question whether we can know anything for sure, than in the ways film can highlight how skeptical concerns are always a going issue for all of us, and shape how we live. He was interested in the way that a kind of skepticism is lived out in our relationships with other people, in the doubts we might harbor about whether we can trust another or trust ourselves to stick with another. He was interested, for example, in the doubts that might lead a couple to discover that they no longer speak the same language and can no longer understand how to remain together. He found the most rewarding film material for such investigations in the genre of golden age Hollywood films that he characterized as "comedies of remarriage," which he defined and examined in detail in a book called *Pursuits of Happiness* (1984). Each of the films he considers involves a couple, usually married, who have broken up or are on the brink of a break-up. The circumstances of the film bring them back together. The question the film poses is whether they can really be together, what it would take and what it would mean for the two to discover that they belong together, that they can have more than a merely legal marriage but a marriage of the minds, a genuine and ongoing conversation. The details of his accounts defy easy summary, but the richness of his descriptions show that much can be said about such subjects as knowledge, self-knowledge, communication, recognition, mutual understanding, gender, identity, relationships, and marriage that had not adequately been explored by philosophers but whose importance was clearly demonstrated by the appeal of these films.

In his massive and detailed series of lectures on the character and history of art delivered between 1818 and 1829, G.W.F. Hegel argues that from its beginnings art has aimed to reconcile the peoples who produce and appreciate it with what they considered to be the absolute, by providing them with a sensuous experience of what they took to be ultimately real. Each developing stage in the history of art can be seen as building upon and challenging the limitations of prior ways of representing what is ultimately real and important. What has traditionally been conceived to be ultimately real was god, and art has depicted the divine and the sacred in various ways throughout history. The final stage of this development, according to Hegel, was in the art of the Renaissance and beyond, when artists recognized human life and the world of human interests to be the only reality with which we can or need to be reconciled. "Herewith," he writes,

> the artist acquires his subject-matter in himself ... nothing that can be living in the human breast is alien to that spirit any more ... no interest is excluded—for art does not need any longer to represent only what is absolutely at home at one of its specific stages, but everything in which man as such is capable of being at home.
>
> (Aesthetics 607)

He finds the representation of this subject matter exemplified in Romantic poetry, in theater and music, and in some of the painting styles that had developed in the nineteenth century. Yet it is hard to conceive of an art form more suited to exploring human life and interests in all of its richness and variety than cinema, which only developed its full expressive powers roughly a century after Hegel had completed his lectures.

Given this, we might say that film has a natural affinity with the philosophical exploration of human life, society, and culture. Film operates within the context of intersubjective human life, which, according to Hegel, needs to be understood according to what he called the "logic of recognition." To be a self-conscious human being it is not enough to have a human form – to have, for example, a large brain that allows one to adapt, to walk upright, and be able to use hands for grasping things and potentially making tools. To be self-conscious as a human being, according to Hegel, requires that I be capable of recognizing others as human beings, and that they be capable of recognizing me, and that we each recognize each other as capable of recognizing one another. Communities, as Hegel puts it, are not merely made up of a bunch of different people existing in isolation, but exist as "the unity of the different independent self-consciousnesses which, in their opposition, enjoy perfect freedom and independence: 'I' that is 'We' and 'We' that is 'I'" (*Phenomenology of Spirit* 110). One cannot be human by oneself, in other words, and it is only as all of these requirements are met that the capacities we ordinarily think of as human, such as language and culture, become possible. Film would not be possible without it; a being who wasn't operating according to the logic of recognition would not be able to appreciate a film.

It is commonly said that to appreciate and enjoy films one must "suspend disbelief." Yet unbelievable things happen all of the time in films that can nevertheless be appreciated and enjoyed. What we need to believe, or at least to accept for the duration of the film, is that the characters we observe on screen are behaving as people would. We need to recognize them as human characters, and we cannot appreciate their actions and adventures unless this condition is met. We can accept superheroes, science fiction, and magic. We can come to care about the love life of an imprisoned aquatic humanoid who falls in love with the janitor who is kind to him and treats him as a person in Guillermo del Toro's *The Shape of Water* (2017). What we can't accept is bad acting, or characters written to behave in ways that don't make sense, given our understanding of who they are and what they want. Characters who look like people but behave unlike humans jar us out of our immersion in films far more than the appearance of aliens or improbable coincidences.

This means that films can make it possible for us to reflect directly upon what we are willing to accept as human. It also means that films have the potential to broaden our capacity to recognize human activity, in the lives of peoples to whom we might otherwise have very little exposure. This is one of the reasons why questions of representation have become so important in discussions of film and television lately. Film and television – and the advertisements that support them – are the most widely disseminated media for communicating with people about what it means to be a person. The stories we tell, who we tell them about, and who gets to tell them, have a profound influence in how we collectively (the "I" that is "We" and the "We" that is "I") determine who it is we are and how it is possible and desirable to be. This is perhaps films most powerful and important philosophical affinity. Yet it rests on the fact that we make sense of films in roughly the same way that we make sense of our lives. This is possible because film gives us an appearance of reality. What this means and how it works will be the focus of the next part of this book.

Before turning our focus to the relation between cinema, on the one hand, and the philosophical tension between appearance and reality, on the other, it will help to introduce some basic background information regarding cinema, and to develop an introductory framework of concepts and methods that apply to the analysis of every film.

2 What is film?

Film has a long history. It extends back at least to the experiments of Edward Muybridge at the end of the nineteenth century, and arguably even further to shadow puppetry and "magic lantern" shows and to a variety of toys and devices that created the appearance of movement. Muybridge's advance was to draw his sequential imagery directly from nature, by way of photography. He developed techniques for taking photographs in rapid succession, and his first and most famous experiment proved that galloping horses did, in fact, raise all four legs at once. Not long afterwards, Thomas Edison patented a motion picture camera developed by his employee William Dickson. It shot sequential photographs onto rolls of film, and these photographs could be viewed through a peephole in a box known as the "kinetoscope." It was Edison's company that established the standard 35mm width of the filmstrip, but it was the French Lumière Brothers who, inspired by Edison, first managed to develop a motion picture camera that was also able to project its images onto a screen. While it had long been possible to create the illusion of motion by means of devices that displayed subtly varied images in rapid succession, film as we know it was born when these successive images could be captured from the real world and then projected sequentially to deliver a shared experience to an audience.

Film has evolved quite a bit since then. At first, it was enough just to capture a situation with a motion picture camera and project it on a screen. Audiences were fascinated by the depiction of small, everyday events such as an intimate kiss or a group of workers leaving a factory. Filmmakers such as the stage magician Georges Méliès went further, employing special photographic techniques to create magical spectacles, in which objects on screen would disappear and then reappear elsewhere, or where images of varying scales, such as people and a goldfish, could be superimposed alongside one another. Early filmmakers, including Méliès, tended to treat the screen as a stage, employing a fixed camera to capture continuous events taking place within the boundaries of a single framing of the camera. It wasn't long before the capacity to edit clips together was used to depict more complicated stories involving many locations and depicting actions from distinct points of view. Subsequent developments in cinema included the advent of color photography and the inclusion of sound. Such developments were, at first, resisted by some who considered them to detract from the purity of the art of motion pictures. Changes in the size and aspect ratio of the screen, and in the sophistication of the sound delivery system, have made it possible for filmmakers to tell different kinds of stories on screen. Yet the fundamental nature of the cinematic experience, of an audience in a darkened room confronted by projected moving images, remained fundamentally unchanged throughout the twentieth century. It is an open question whether modern innovations – the advent of digital filmmaking and distribution, the latest 3D and ultra-high resolution, increased frame rate projection technologies, or the availability of smaller and more private screens to view them – have introduced fundamental changes into the nature of the cinema.

There are several sides to cinema, each of which contributes to the overall experience of watching and making sense of films. Popular (and even scholarly) discussions don't always distinguish carefully between these, but understanding movies and their meanings requires that we do. There is, first, the industrial side of cinema, the business of filmmaking and marketing. Next, the technique and artistry involved in making films. Then the audience, who come to the film with expectations drawn both from their experiences watching other films and their experiences in the world outside of the theater, and who respond to the film in a variety of ways. The film itself – the finished product – has several differentiable elements and features. Finally, we need to consider the impact and significance of the film, the way in which the details of the film combine to deliver a meaningful experience to its audience.

Films are products, funded by an industry and created by artists and professionals making use of a lot of expensive equipment. Their production takes place in a series of overlapping stages, and making them usually takes a long time. Getting them out into the world to be seen takes even longer. The finished product, whether it appears on screen in the cinema, or on a DVD or Blu-ray or online, can then be enjoyed by the public and assessed and analysed by critics. A film's success, whether this is defined commercially or critically, depends upon the impact it has on its audiences; its meaning and import has to do less with how it is conceived, by its director or producers, and more with how it is received, whether in its initial critical and commercial reception, or in subsequent encounters by those who give it a chance to outgrow its initial reputation and hype and to be assessed on its own merits. Let us now consider each of these features for their relevance to film's philosophical import: the film industry; film production; the audience; the finished product; and the film experience.

Film industry

Films are, first of all, made to make money. The artistry and industry of film are interconnected, insofar as it usually costs a lot of money to make a film and, whether or not a film's concept is considered to have artistic or social merit, investors generally only provide that money when they can reasonably anticipate a return on their investment. Of course, the fact that films are products, expected to generate a profit, doesn't tell us all that much about them, and doesn't explain why some films have an enduring appeal. People (sometimes) pay to see movies, just as people spend money on food, transportation, clothing, housing, medicine, books, memberships, charity, and so much more. What matters more is why they spend their time and money on movies – especially given that as a result of television and the internet, people don't always pay directly for the movies they watch – and what they expect to get for their investment. If what they want is just to pass the time, avoiding boredom, the movie counts as "good" if audiences consider it promising enough to go see it and exciting enough to spread the word afterwards. Nowadays, what really matters for success – from an industry standpoint – is whether enough were willing to buy a ticket and see it on the opening weekend – or buy a DVD or watch it pay-per-view later – which usually means it was marketed well or got good word of mouth. That isn't enough, however, to account for the artistic and critical success or failure of a film.

Most films manage to outlive the initial box office-based assessment of their over-all worth, and the critical and popular response that lingers usually provides a more reliable measure of what the film meant and of its overall importance. The films considered in this book can be considered successful for reasons that go beyond economics. They tell stories and communicate in ways that continue to resonate with critics and audiences long after their initial theatrical run. A full assessment of their worth and meaning, therefore, requires that we look to factors other than merely economic measures of success.

Film production

Generally speaking, there are three major stages of film production. It all begins with the pre-production stage, during which an idea for a film is formulated, a screenplay or at least a summary (known as a "treatment") is written, and the film is vetted by producers, who begin raising funds, planning, and hiring, so it can then get made. The most important hire is the director, who takes part in the planning and decides on the cast, and is the key player during the production stage. While he or she usually remains supervised by producers (and studio executives), the director works directly with the actors, and collaborates with a cinematographer and a whole host of other technicians in order to carry out the plan developed during pre-production and shoot the film. Finally, there is the post-production stage, during which the film is processed and edited, and effects and a soundtrack are added. If the film has already been slot-ted for a theatrical release, it is during this final stage that the marketing team begins preparing trailers, posters, and other advertisement materials. Some films, and espe-cially films considered "independent," arrive at the post-production stage without an established distribution plan, which means that they were made in the hopes of being sold later on to a company that would arrange for their marketing and release. Such films are often submitted for inclusion in film festivals, where their producers hope they will get good press and catch the attention of a distribution company, who will either buy them outright, or will at least buy the rights to distribute them within some territory of the world.

Except where films are largely improvised – and where they are said to be, it's often exaggerated – they start out with a screenplay. Screenplays can be more or less detailed, but they tend to fit into a general storytelling pattern. Characters are intro-duced, and they do something or something happens to them that creates a crisis – or at least a difficulty they must face by taking action. What they do changes their situ-ation and, usually, escalates or transforms the crisis they face. What they do to deal with the elevated crisis creates a new situation which could be either a resolution to the crisis or a starting point for a very different situation than the one they'd started out in. There's often, especially in mainstream Hollywood films, also what's called a "B-story," where the hero or heroine not only has to face up to some kind of crisis, but also has a love interest or wants to reconnect with an estranged family member, so that in the end he or she not only solves the problem but also "gets the girl" (or the guy), re-wins the respect of a child, or manages to reconcile with an estranged spouse. It is sometimes useful to consider this rough storytelling pattern as akin to the standard three-act structure usually seen in traditional theater, where the first act introduces the character and the crisis, the second act depicts the immediate and varied consequences of their response, and the third act shows the resolution or transformation in their circumstance that results from facing up to those consequences, while the B-story serves as a through line throughout.

Screenplays can be commissioned by a studio or producer, or they can be written independently (on "spec") by a writer who hopes to sell the story later. Sometimes the writer is also the director, in which case an expectation of how the film will end up being shot and arranged will likely play a role in the writing. Where the writer is not expected to direct, it is customary that the screenplay includes very little in the way of explicit directions regarding how it will be filmed. Those decisions – as well as decisions on what to cut and how to rearrange things in order to streamline the story – would then be left up to the director and her team, so that the same screenplay in two director's hands could produce two very different films.

These facts have some bearing on the ultimate significance of the finished product, given that a question we often ask when we are thinking about films is who made them. One correct answer to this question is that a whole team of professionals collaborated to make the film. When it comes to making sense of the film, however, it is sometimes more helpful to note that there is a single person or team of people primarily responsible for the story, look, or thematic content of the film. One reason for this is that we can often best see what is distinctive about a film when we compare and contrast it with other films. We can, of course, always compare a film with others of the same genre or type, such as other Westerns or other suspense thrillers, or to other films made within the same year, country, or era. According to the so-called "auteur theory," however, what is truly distinctive to a particular film can best be understood when it is considered together with other films by the same "author" or "auteur." This does beg the question who should be considered a film's "author" when a whole host of professionals are involved in its production. The right answer might be the writer, or the producer, or even the studio head. It would depend upon how much creative input that person had. Most commonly, however, the director is considered the auteur, which is why some films prominently note in their credits that it was, say, "A Martin Scorsese Film" or "A Spike Lee Joint," or "A film by..." whoever else directed it. While that kind of designation is arguably overused – it does probably fit in the cases of both Lee and Scorsese – it sometimes makes sense to say that the director was primarily responsible for the content of the film, especially when the director is also the writer, was heavily involved in pre-production, and oversaw not only the production but also the editing and post-production process. While this may be common in the realm of low-budget independent filmmaking, it is somewhat rare when it comes to major Hollywood studio productions. Still, even in the studios, some directors, trusted by their investors, have a "final cut" clause in their contract. This means they get to decide on the overall shape of the film, and that, within certain limits, and as long as the directors meet contractual obligations, the studio cannot release the film until it meets the director's approval.

Invoking an "auteur" in an interpretation of a film – which just means considering that work in connection with a body of work by the same person – makes sense when that comparison does in fact offer insight into the film's theme and approach. It is, essentially, a hypothesis: that other works by the same filmmaker will provide a useful reference point for understanding a particular film. It has to be tested carefully, by considering a body of films by the same "auteur" together and seeing whether there are illuminating continuities or contrasts. As with any interpretive claims, such hypotheses may or may not turn out to be viable. That a filmmaker can be considered an "auteur," however, doesn't mean that what that director, producer, or writer happens to say about the film is the final word on its significance. Notably, some auteur directors, such as David Lynch, refuse to try and explain their films, insisting that is a task for the audience. Where filmmakers do talk about the meaning of their work, what they say should probably be taken seriously, but they aren't the ultimate arbiters of its meaning. Hitchcock's assessment of his own work and of its import and significance, for example, is just one opinion among thousands, probably more illuminating than many of them, but not automatically superior to all of them. However much its director or maker contributed to the overall look and feel and thematics of a film, once it is out in the public sphere, it has to be interpreted on its own merits.

Once the film is conceived and planned out, a filmmaking team and actors are hired, and prep work such as location scouting, set building, storyboarding, script readings, rehearsals, training, budgeting, and project planning has been carried out, the actual production stage of the film can begin. For the most part, this involves the cast and crew going to the locations where the film will be shot – whether that is a real-world place that fits the story or a fabricated set in a studio – and working out the shots and scenes with the necessary technicians and camera crew and actors, and then shooting those scenes. Some filmmaking teams have the final result they aim for mapped out precisely in advance and it is then a matter of working with the crew and the actors to realize that vision. In some cases that is not possible, and sometimes not even desirable, and there is some improvisation on set or on location to work out the details for each scene. Last-minute adjustments may be made to the lighting, camera movement and framing, the dialogue and tone, and perhaps even makeup, set design, costuming, and special effects dialogue and tone of the acting. All of this is (usually) done quite deliberately and with care, in the hopes of telling a story with a specific style, where each shot must contribute to the telling of that story and towards generating a feeling and attitudes in the audience regarding the significance of that story.

A lot goes on "behind the scenes" of every scene that ends up on screen. For the most part, though, we can understand films without knowing much regarding the technical details of, say, cinematography and lighting, or about camera types and lens specifications, or about the many jobs on set, such as gaffers and script supervisors and PAs and grips. What is most important is what contributes to the look and feel of the final product. There is a difference between the technical knowledge and vocabulary employed by the professionals who make films, and the critical knowledge and vocabulary employed by those who pay close attention to their details and structure. There can also be a substantial gap between how and why a particular cinematic element was designed and included, and its ultimate impact on the experience of its audience. Having the technical expertise, and sharing the vocabulary, of the cinematographer is not essential. You don't really need to know the difference between a dolly and a Steadicam, but can learn to notice the difference between a shot that tracks an action smoothly and steadily in a straight line or along a gentle arc, and a shot that seems almost to float along with actors, in and out of buildings, through a crowd and around corners and over obstacles. Having noticed the difference, and having described it precisely, what is most important is to consider just what difference it makes to the overall feeling and significance of the scene and of the story.

Of all the filmed material shot on set or on location, what does end up on screen results from decisions that are ultimately made during the editing process, which takes place during the post-production stage of filmmaking. It is also during this stage that the film gets its final soundtrack, and when the visual effects – ranging from lighting adjustments and sound mixing and color correction to the addition of computer-generated imagery – are finalized. It is often said that the film is created in the editing room. It is there that filmed material is selected and organized into a more or less coherent whole. Traditionally, editing involved the actual cutting and splicing together of developed strips of celluloid. Editing, these days, takes place mostly on computer, where selections from clips either shot originally on a video camera or drawn from digital copies of sequences shot with a film camera, are arranged and rearranged in ways that don't involve actually cutting film. Over the past couple of decades, in fact, film has changed dramatically insofar as settings and even characters and their performances can be significantly altered or even – on very big budget films – created entirely from scratch and added to the final project during post-production. The use of computer imagery to pre-visualize scenes and the ability to "fix" problems with cinematography or even to modify performances have blurred the line between the stages of pre-production, production, and post-production. It has even become an open question whether film in the digital age has changed so radically as to become a new art form. So far, even where films incorporate large amounts of CGI, they tend to follow – loosely, and with a faster, sometimes more chaotic pace – the patterns of framing and editing developed during a previous era, and tend to do so in the service of stories that follow roughly the same pattern that films have followed for a long time. At this point, then, the use of CGI to escape from the photographic limitations of the film camera does expand upon the range of what is possible to depict on screen, but for the most part hasn't radically changed the nature of cinema.

The audience

The final stage of film production is getting it out there in front of an audience. People need to hear about a film, and then it needs to show up in theaters (or, more recently, online or on cable) where they can see it. Even word of mouth campaigns are directed, and lots of people have to manage to see a film before they'll spread the word. Marketing takes time, expertise, and money, and isn't something that just happens when a film is finished. It can even have a major impact on how movies get made. It is common practice, for example, to test unfinished films in front of an audience, and make final editing decisions (and even, sometimes, re-shoots of entire scenes) at that point. Except, perhaps, in the case of ultra-low-budget independents, films don't even get started unless someone has a reasonable expectation that enough people will pay to see it to generate a profit. Still, as noted above, no matter how much time, money, and effort is spent on spreading the word and trying to get audiences excited to see it on opening night, some films still fall flat, and others take their time to find an appreciative audience.

It has become a cliché to say, when it comes to predicting which films will fail and which will flop, that "nobody knows anything!" William Goldman, who made that phrase famous in his 1983 bestseller *Adventures in the Screen Trade*, just might have been right – even if studio executives keep trying to prove him wrong by churning out superfluous, but almost inevitably profitable, sequels of successful flicks – but the

German philosopher Georg Wilhelm Friedrich Hegel may have said it better when he wrote, regarding historical phenomena generally, that "the Owl of Minerva only takes flight with the coming of dusk" (*Hegel's The Philosophy of Right* 10). We can't say in advance with any degree of certainty what films will work with an audience and find critical and commercial success, but wisdom (symbolized here by the owl associated with the goddess Minerva, aka Athena) *can* emerge after the fact. In the wake of the success or failure of a specific film or of a range of films of a certain type, we can reflect helpfully upon the social, cultural, historical, and economic reasons it either resonated or failed to connect.

Audiences vary quite a bit in their response to films. Even films widely considered to be successful have their detractors, and may in fact owe their success to their appeal among a narrowly specific constituency, such as the white male American teenager. While it is the job of marketers to determine who is most likely to enjoy a particular film, and to target them in advertisements, an important aspect of understanding movies is understanding their audiences.

There is a wide variety of academic approaches to thinking about cinematic audiences. One approach to thinking about the film audience is largely historical or quantitative, focused on who films appeal to and how they are received by specific groups, and how they impact those groups. Reception studies adopts the view that films don't have a fixed meaning in themselves, but that what they mean is what they have meant for specific viewers, and this is a question that can only be answered historically and empirically. Some theorists, by contrast, argued that the position of the spectator in relation to the image is, as it were, built into the very apparatus of cinema. By virtue of sitting in a dark room, confronted by the moving image of exciting events outside of his control, the audience member has his passive position with respect to the real world outside of him reinforced, at the same time as, paradoxically, his desires to be active are vicariously satisfied through the filmed fantasy. Other film theorists, such as Laura Mulvey, argued that the spectator implied by the apparatus of cinema was characteristically masculine, and that cinema catered to male desires, encouraging the viewer to identify with a male protagonist and to be aroused by the female "love interest" ("Visual Pleasure in Narrative Cinema"). She also, along with other critical film theorists, called for a different kind of filmmaking practice that would upset the ideological frameworks built into the workings of mainstream cinema and would disrupt the passivity of the spectator, making him or her aware of cinema's manipulations. Others have responded that the spectator always does play an active role in making sense of movies, and that even in mainstream cinema there is usually room for the viewer to adopt a range of attitudes about the film. A viewer might, for example, identify with characters other than the presumed protagonist.

Theory aside, it is a fact that audiences come to the movies with attitudes and expectations they've cultivated elsewhere, both in the real world outside of the theater and as a result of their having grown up in a media-saturated culture. The feelings a film evokes and the meanings viewers draw from it are affected by their past experiences and current dispositions, with the result that different people can watch the same film at the same time and have it impact them very differently. Film is neither simply what is on the screen, nor is it what the film industry or the filmmaker say or hope it will be. Films are what people make of them – how they are seen and interpreted by audiences – but they are also more than what can be grasped of them on an initial viewing by an uncritical audience. Different viewers will interpret films variously, just as people make sense of situations drawn from everyday life in a variety of ways, depending upon their background and assumptions.

What makes films different from everyday situations, however, is that they can be repeated, that the same film can be viewed more than once. After seeing a film a second time, our initial impressions of it may be corrected. We may notice things we hadn't seen initially. Descriptive and interpretive claims regarding the film can be checked against the evidence gathered during a third or a fourth viewing. While films are what people make of them, what can be made of them isn't fully clear until the work of critical assessment has been done, and even that is never enough to establish a consensus. New interpretive accounts can always come along and encourage those who love a film to look at it differently. The best films sustain multiple interpretations, but unlike the diversity of initial reactions, interpretive assessments of a film are supported by evidence and arguments and can, therefore, themselves be criticized and assessed. The point of all this is not to shut down discussion by coming up with the one true or best interpretation, but to take advantage of the complexity of the film experience in order to arrive at new and enriched thoughts about reality, art, and the range of human experience.

Formal analysis

Decisions made during the production stage of filmmaking, such as what and where to shoot, how to frame it, what aspect ratio to employ, what camera and lenses to use, how to move the camera while shooting, how to dress the set, costume the actors and direct their performances, all have an impact on the look and feel of the completed film. Decisions made during the post-production process, about which clips to include in what order, and what music and sound effects to add, and how the film will be processed, and what effects will be added, are also, ultimately, important for how they give shape to a finished product. Still, even without an intimate understanding of the specific technical details of the production and post-production process, one can watch the finished film and describe how it works with a fairly high degree of precision. A helpful starting point for such descriptions of the finished product, focused upon how it is experienced by audiences, is to distinguish between, on the one hand, the framing and, on the other, the ordering (what results from editing) of the screened moving image – a simple, common sense contrast that is closely related to the more technical distinction, often taught in introductory film appreciation courses, between *mise-en-scène* and *montage*. Examining the significance of the ways in which images are framed and arranged within a film is called "formal analysis" because it focuses on the form of the finished product. It focuses on the way in which the content of a film is presented.

Mise-en-scène is French, drawn from the context of the theater; it means, roughly, "placing on the stage." Its meaning in cinema studies is ambivalent, as it is sometimes used narrowly to refer to the composition or arrangement of elements in front of the camera, elements such as actors, settings, costume, set, and lighting. In that sense, it would be contrasted with cinematography, which is about the work of the camera, how it focuses upon and frames those elements and moves among them. Instead of just referring to what is in front of the camera at the time of shooting, *Mise-en-scène* is also often used to signify the outcome, the finished product, the arrangement of elements upon the screen that results when just those moving elements in front of the camera are shot by a moving camera in a specific way. The preferred term employed here is "framing," which eliminates some of that ambiguity by focusing just on this finished result. It also emphasizes that the finished result is a framed moving image, a mobile arrangement of moving elements that the viewer (usually) experiences as a selection from a larger horizon of possible elements, a window onto a world.

Montage, another French term, refers to the sequential arrangement of moving image clips during the editing process. Of course, there is an overlap between *mise-en-scène* and *montage*, because decisions about what to film and how to film it have a bearing on how it will cut together later. If a conversation in a coffee shop is only shot wide from the side of the table where a man and woman face each other, there will be no chance later to edit back and forth between close-ups of their faces as they listen or respond to what the other says. A camera moving through a crowded room, focusing here on someone's face, there on a gesture or embrace and then moving back to take it all in, will leave little room for actual cutting between a wide frame of the room and a close look at details, but effectively already accomplishes an ordered arrangement of framed imagery by way of its deliberate movements. Cinematography, we might say, is already editing, insofar as it both constrains the possibility of editing choices later and insofar as in its mobile framing of the image it is already performing both a selection and a sequencing. Still, there is a difference, and where framing establishes the spatiality of the image, ordering provides it with its distinctive mode and style of temporal continuity. The term "ordering" calls for paying attention both to the sequence of events depicted on screen and to the deliberateness and impact of the way they are temporally organized in the film, whether, for example, the whole arrangement is the result of long takes in which the movement of the camera tells the story or of short clips edited together, or whether the breaks between clips are jarring or barely noticeable.

Framing

To speak of the framing of the cinematic image is to call attention to a number of its important features, but an immediate caution is in order, since it also suggests a comparison with painting. With paintings, the frame is a supplement that surrounds and presents an image essentially complete without it. The painting's frame, we might say, calls attention just to the completeness of the painted image, to the fact it was composed and created to fit within the limits of a given canvas or space, and to stand on its own, self-sufficient and self-explanatory. In film, by contrast, the imagery flows. The frame is both selective and open-ended, revealing to us a range of unfolding situations from a variety of perspectives, and only when the light fades and it is finished does it hang together as a whole. The frame, moreover, doesn't extend beyond the image, and isn't part of the image either. What we call its "framing" is, rather, the mode of its appearance to us: that it is only "so far" visible, that it appears to us within the limits of a projected rectangle of light. The borders of this illuminated pane are not, however, limits of the image. They do not so much limit the image as they limit us. They limit what we can see of it, now, and yet each moment we anticipate that the frame will show us more. The image, as it appears, belongs to a visible horizon that we can see extends beyond the frame, but is only visible to us within that frame.

We can, of course, see beyond the frame, but to look outside of or away from the frame is to stop watching the movie, to let it lose its grip on our attention. To watch the movie is to succumb to the frame, to let what appears within the specific limits of a lit-up rectangular space become the object of our focus, at least for the film's duration, and to let the "real world" of everyday life outside of those limits fade into the background of our attention. The frame is also immobile, relative to us. It appears in front of us in the same space, and we can't change what it reveals by changing our place relative to it. It isn't like a window, where we might see more by moving to one side or another. To watch it is to accept our limits. It is to acknowledge that we can't change what is unfolding before us. While it appears to us in the now, the future it unfolds into is already finished. While its dynamic movements and unpredicted outcomes are unknown to us they are (at least tacitly) known by us to be something we can't do anything about. Otherwise, we might want to try and do something about what we see happening on screen, and one of the pleasures (and, sometimes, frustrations) of cinema is that while we may think and feel and experience a great deal, we can remain detached, as we are not responsible for what is taking place before us and are unable to affect it, as much as we sometimes wish that we could.

The frame does appear to move, but only relative to the visible horizon it reveals. Its relation to that horizon is, at least potentially, in a constant state of flux. Its location relative to the audience, by contrast, tends to be fixed. While the ratio between the width of the screen to the height of the screen – known as the "aspect ratio" – can vary from film to film, it also tends to remain the same throughout a given film. The aspect ratio is defined as the relation between the width of the image and its height. The early standard for silent cinema was a ratio of 4 to 3 (expressed as "4:3" or "1.33:1"). The most common ("widescreen") aspect ratio for cinematic projection is currently 1.85:1, which means that the width of the screen is nearly twice that of the height. The choice of aspect ratio does impact what can be revealed within the frame. A wide framing, for example, tends to be better for films in which landscape is prominent or where there is a need to show characters moving about on screen; an aspect ratio that is closer to a square tends to be appropriate for films where the emphasis is on characters and the subtleties of their interactions.

While the size of the frame relative to the audience remains unchanged, its size and location and even orientation relative to the world it depicts can vary greatly. It can move about within the space of the people and things it shows us, it can narrow in upon a clock or a hand or a face, and can expand to reveal much more. It can even shift discontinuously, from one perspective to another. Given that the frame, which doesn't change in size relative to its audience, can nevertheless expand or contract relative to the world of objects it displays, some of the most helpful basic descriptive vocabulary employed in film analysis is designed to clarify the framing of a particular shot by calling attention to its scale, by specifying just how much of that world it includes. It is notable, though, that the primary object, or measure, in terms of which the scale of the image is defined is the human body, which appears to indicate that, for the most part, what is primarily of interest in cinema is its capacity to reveal to us a human world.

"Close-up" names a framing just wide enough to encompass a human face, and perhaps also the shoulders. An "extreme close-up" goes even further, narrowing in on just a portion of the face, such as the eyes or the mouth. We also speak of close-ups focused on objects, and when they appear it is precisely to make those objects or their aspects fully visible, to set them apart from a background, so their details stand out clearly. The "medium shot" is defined as that kind of framing that encompasses the upper

Figure 2.1 Shot types in *The Last Jedi* (2017).

part of the human body, usually from the waist to the top of the head, leaving room to show hand or arm gestures or other dispositions of the upper body. What used to be called the "cowboy shot" or, in Europe, the "American shot," was a medium shot that encompassed the hips as well, so that gun belts were included. A medium "two-shot" does the same thing as a medium shot, but is wide enough to include two bodies from the waist upwards, often to show them facing one another, engaged in conversation. An "over the shoulder" is usually a medium or close-up, focused on someone's face but from behind another she is facing; editing back and forth between a shot like this and its reverse, from over the other's shoulder, is a common way to capture a conversation, because it allows the frame to reveal the expressions of both as they speak and the reactions of each to the other. A "long shot" is usually defined as a framing that includes the entire person or group of persons, and shows them within and interacting with a specific surrounding. The "extreme long shot" emphasizes the setting, which may or may not include a person, but if it does they are usually small in comparison to the depicted location. When the function of a long or extreme long shot is to situate the action that will follow or that preceded it on screen in relation to where it is supposed to take place, it is called an "establishing shot."

Some ways of framing a situation appear to put the people on screen in close proximity to each other, filling up the screen. This may feel either cramped or intimate, depending on other cues we get from the context and the performances; this is described as "tight framing." Characters can also be more loosely framed, with room between them and room around them, suggesting, perhaps, an emotional distance, or, in other contexts, an easy-going familiarity. Characters might also be framed within the frame, by a window or a doorway, and this double framing might suggest that they are trapped, or, in some cases, might serve to remind the viewers they are watching a movie.

A framing of situations from above might suggest an omniscient point of view, or might suggest the helplessness of the people it depicts underneath. The framing of a face from below, or of one person elevated over another, can suggest that the person above is ominous or has the upper hand. A frame that is tilted relative to the horizon, what used to be called a "Dutch angle shot," can be unsettling, and give the feeling something's wrong or that it is a dream or that it captures a drunken perspective.

Of course, framing is not static. A camera moving from side to side from a fixed point, a move known as "panning," can deliver a changing perspective on screen similar to that of turning the head to look along the horizon. "Tilting" results from changing the orientation of the camera along a horizontal axis, either upwards or downwards, which can suggest an elevating or lowering of the gaze. A moving camera can "track" a movement, following along as a person walks the streets or as a car barrels down the highway. The camera can move closer or further away from a person or object, either in a steady movement on a dolly that rolls along a track or in a handheld shot, and the impact on screen is different than if the camera doesn't move and the narrowing in or widening on a particular object is accomplished by means of a telephoto or zoom lens. With a zoom lens, it doesn't feel that we get closer to the object, so much as make it larger on the screen. Another impact of zooming is that it changes the focal length of the lens, and this affects the range of what is in focus. A long lens has a narrow depth of field, so that what is behind the subject goes out of focus. A wide lens, by contrast, allows all that's on screen to remain sharply in focus.

Other elements of the framed image that convey information and affect how it affects us include the lighting and the color, the set design, and the acting. Brightly lit images, known as "high key," are fairly common in comedies; horror films and films focused on crime tend to be "low key," often taking place largely in darkened rooms, or alleyways, or in shadows. Images can be "high contrast," where the brights and the darks are sharply distinguishable, or they can be "low contrast" which tends to give the image a flatter appearance. Some films are black and white, and even when color film is available some filmmakers still choose to shoot this way, which cuts down on some of the potentially distracting details of the real world being filmed and puts the emphasis on the composition of the image and the acting. Some films are colored "naturally," in ways that don't call attention to themselves, while others emphasize specific colors, that evoke a mood, such as reds or blues, or focus on warm toned colors or cold ones. Settings, also, can appear natural, and can be shot in real locations, or they can be shot in a studio and may appear highly stylized. Acting styles can range from cartoonish and exaggerated to highly nuanced and subtle. Some actors ("stars") are chosen because their familiar off-screen persona and mannerisms in front of the camera already, naturally, fit the role; others are practically unrecognizable from one film to the next, because they manage to inhabit fully each new role. In some cases, directors choose to hire non-actors, who won't be recognizable to the audience, but whose real-life persona fits closely to what is required on screen. All of these choices make a difference to the overall impact of a film, and noticing such details is critical for those who hope to provide a nuanced account of its significance.

Above all, framing is about composition. It is about the deliberate organization of the overall image. To discuss framing is to note there is significance to the arrangement of the elements on screen and to their relative movements. That doesn't mean it always "means" something profound or conveys a message that could just as well be specified verbally. Some details merely hint at significance. They make a minor difference that contributes to the overall mood of a work, and disposes the audience to respond to the rest differently than if the details had been omitted. Sometimes, though, they might mean something more specific, as we might notice that the preponderance of red in a particular scene suggests or accentuates the jealousy or rage or passion felt but unexpressed by a character; but note that still this significance is more felt by the audience than brought to explicit awareness, and that can be an advantage. Were the character to say that she was jealous, we might not feel it as powerfully or might find it unconvincing. We might then be unprepared for, and unwilling to accept, the suddenness of the shocking act through which she subsequently expresses that jealous rage. The color, the lighting, the costuming, the scale of the frame relative to the objects it depicts, the arrangement of actors and other objects relative to each other and to a setting and to the frame, their movements and the movement of the frame relative to all of them – all together these form the composition, which can carry with it a significance that is grasped intuitively rather than inferred or considered. It might, also, sink in slowly but leave us with a potent impression that can't be simply shrugged off, and that orients thoughts rather than provoking them directly. After the fact, however, we can consider how all of these elements worked together to create their compelling impression, and contribute to the felt significance of the film as a whole.

Ordering (the edit)

Apart from framing, the other core dimension of film form is its ordering. Films display a series of moving image sequences, each of which can be analyzed on its own, but whose ultimate impact and import result from their order and combination. The influential early Russian filmmaker and theorist Lev Kuleshov illustrated the power of combining moving image sequences through editing (or *montage*) when he juxtaposed a shot of an actor's apparently expressionless face with three different images: a bowl of soup, a beautiful woman, and, finally, a child in a coffin. Those who saw the first combination considered the face to express hunger; those who saw the second could swear they saw lust, and those who saw the last interpreted his expression as one of grief. This result displays what has come to be known as the "Kuleshov Effect," which was hugely influential for Soviet filmmakers and continues to serve as one of the basic principles of editing: that when audiences see a series of images, they will look for a connection, and if the connection isn't obvious they will themselves contribute the idea or the framework or the feeling that links them together.

In most films, the most obvious connection is spatio-temporal. The frame displays a moving shot or sequence, and then cuts to another: this usually implies that the first sequence of events happened first, followed by the other. It sometimes suggests both shots depict things taking place in proximity, as when one shot displays a man on a mountain looking in the distance and the next displays an extreme wide shot of a valley. We assume, then, he is looking down upon the valley. Even where this inference appears obvious, it's never certain. In Kuleshov's experiment, for example, the image of the actor followed by an image of soup might suggest he is hungry because from seeing an image of him looking somewhere and then an image of soup, audiences infer that the soup is nearby and it's what he is looking at. It needn't be, and he isn't. The original shot of his face was (allegedly) taken from the context of another (abandoned) film entirely, and the connection with soup (and with a woman and a child) was arranged purely for the purpose of the experiment.

The eighteenth-century British philosopher David Hume argued that whenever we are presented with a series of impressions, whether drawn from everyday life or from art, we tend to associate in our minds those that seem similar or that appear to us alongside one another or in sequence. While he held that these associations could easily be arbitrary and that many were completely spurious, since they always could have been combined differently, the German philosopher Immanuel Kant responded that it was in any case necessary to impose some order upon our impressions. Otherwise, they would be a mere jumble, that would not make sense to us at all, and the fact is that our experiences do, more or less, make sense. It is, Kant argued, a necessary condition for having experience that we differentiate between the elements of our sensory encounters and impose upon them a structure, fitting impressions into the assumed framework of a coherent spatio-temporal and causal order. Otherwise, we couldn't even see or say what it was we had experienced. He held that much of this structuring activity occurs, as it were, below the level of consciousness, precisely because to become conscious of what we experience presupposes that this structuring takes place.

If it is true that we impose order upon our impressions, so that they conform to our need to perceive the world as an enduring and continuous spatio-temporal whole that is never fully given, then our experience of film, too, will conform to that order. The film will begin and end at a definite time, and display within the framework of a determinate shape, and in a specific location. One impression from the screen will follow the next, something will happen and then something else, and what we see there will be determinate and specifiable, even if it isn't clear all at once what it all means or amounts to. Yet while the images we see on screen do follow a definite order, occurring at a specific time and in a specific place that is part of our everyday world, the events they depict occur along their own timeline and in their own space. They needn't (and often don't) display themselves to us in order, and the screen can easily shift from depicting events happening in one place and events taking place elsewhere. In fact, it's not even strictly accurate to say they occur along a timeline or within a continuous space.

What we see on screen needn't be and often isn't continuous; not only are there gaps, there are sometimes inconsistencies, and those aren't always mistakes. Filmmakers talk about "continuity errors" when, say, a character lights a cigarette in one shot and then, in a cut to what appears to be mere moments later, as another character finishes the sentence she'd begun while it was lit, the cigarette appears burned down halfway. Such errors are only a problem if they're likely to be noticed, causing audiences to lose their absorption in the scene – and even then they're not a problem if they were included deliberately and precisely to have a jarring effect upon the audience. Inconsistencies can also signal something else. They can imply the subjective nature of a character's perceptions or memories. A sequence may show an event that is later revealed to have been merely imagined or misremembered. Films can, however, also simply show events that are inconsistent, without ever revealing which, if any, version was mistaken. Then it is up to the audience to decide what it means, and there are various possibilities. An inconsistency in time or in space could most easily be interpreted as a mistake or a hallucination or fantasy, or as the product of unreliable narration, but it might also suggest that reality is more complex than can be captured in a single linear construction, or might depict, without explanation of a narrative preference, a range of alternative possible outcomes to a situation.

Most often, however, editing aims to avoid inconsistency, to arrange images in ways that both communicate clearly what is taking place and where in the world depicted on screen it is supposed to be taking place, and which allow the audience time to apprehend essential information. Stories can, of course, be told out of order, as in a film like *Citizen Kane* (1941), that begins with the death of its main character, and proceeds both forward in time, following a reporter's attempt to make sense of his final words, and backwards, through a series of flashbacks depicting his life. Still, even where films are told out of order, there is usually some indication that's what's happening. There are often clear cues, for example, regarding when a scene is a flashback and when a scene is imagined or dreamed.

There are a variety of editing styles and a variety of ends that can be accomplished through editing. Some filmmakers prefer to capture the setting and the action with as few cuts as possible. They might employ long takes and deep focus camera work to put the emphasis on what is taking place in front of the camera. Some consider this approach to be a hallmark of "realism," in part because deep focus camera work is unforgiving, showing every detail, and long takes don't allow for a lot of manipulation through the selection of various bits and pieces of different performances after the fact. They give more room for the unexpected event or the accident to play a role in the final display. To experience long takes as an audience, also, requires more patience, and allows for the audience to select which elements to attend to, and because they have time to think about what they are seeing, permits a greater range of interpretive flexibility.

Another much more common approach to editing focuses on story, and aims to show only those elements required to tell the story clearly, holding on to each shot just long enough to make clear what is happening, and selecting from among various possible framings those that most effectively elicit the appropriate feelings and convey just the information necessary to follow the plot. The main criteria of this approach, often described as "continuity" editing, is that the images should be selected for maximum clarity regarding where, and when, and what takes place in the film. While the action tends to be chopped up into little bits, they are arranged in such a way that this division is barely noticeable, and each shot flows naturally into the next in order to communicate a continuous series of actions and events.

In Hitchcock's film *Vertigo* (1958), Scottie (played by Jimmy Stewart) is talking with his best friend Midge (Barbara Bel Geddes). He was recovering from an unfortunate accident, during which he'd discovered his unnatural fear of heights and

Figure 2.2 Midge and Scotty in *Vertigo* (1958).

inadvertently caused a fellow policeman to fall to his death. He asks her about a fancy new bra, and then, as he moves to recline on her couch, asks about her love life. The frame cuts to a medium shot of her curious reaction. "That's following a train of thought," she replies. Then the frame cuts back to him as he sits, "well….," he replies. Then we see her, seated and drawing, looking down at her draft board. "Normal," she says, not looking up, and the frame lingers with her as he asks "Aren't you ever going to get married?" She replies, with barely a glance in his direction, "you know there's only one man in the world for me." Cut to a shot of him, now reclining, with an amused grin on his face, because of course he knows the answer to his question. "You mean me?" he asks, and then adds, while shaking his cane in her direction, "we were engaged, though, once, weren't we?" The way he says it makes it sound like an afterthought, suggesting that for him the memory is vague and almost trivial.

The frame now cuts to a close up, with only Midge's face in focus. The background is blurred so that the reactions on her face are the only noticeable details. She is still looking down and smiles tightly for a moment. "Three whole weeks." The frame then cuts back to the medium shot of him reclining on the couch as he smiles broadly, recalling fondly, "Good old college days…." Then he raises his cane and shakes it at her to proclaim, "but you were the one to call off the engagement, you remember?" We return to the close-up of Midge, still facing the draft board but her eyes glance up sharply through the frames of her glasses, her lips pursed, as he continues, "I'm still available." The close up shows us the reaction she deliberately hides from him. She remembers things quite differently, and he's not nearly as available as he suggests. The frame returns to him as he glances down at his feet and mutters, "available Ferguson…" He may still be single, but we saw from her reaction that he's not available to her.

This scene could have been cut quite differently, with the dialogue unchanged, but then we likely wouldn't learn nearly as much about Scottie's relationship with Midge. We'd know they'd been engaged, but not that they have very different memories of

Figure 2.3 Close-up of Midge in *Vertigo* (1958).

how things ended. We'd know that she's still fond of him, but not that the memories are painful, or that he is so willfully oblivious of his best friend's true feelings, and so easily capable of overlooking his own culpabilities. All these facts about Scottie and his manner of relating to women, so critical to understanding what follows in the film, are communicated quite precisely through the power of editing. What is notable, too, is that the scene seems seamless. Even though the frame cuts from him and then to her and back, from a shot of him reclining to a close-up of her face, the breaks don't feel jarring at all – we barely notice – because they are linked both by their proximity in time and space, all occurring in the same room, and by the continuous character of an event, which in this case is a conversation. The cuts, in fact, follow, more or less, our interests in that conversation, as when Scottie says something we expect that Midge will react, and immediately the frame shows us that reaction. It doesn't only follow our interest, but leads it as well. That the frame lingers with Midge as Scottie asks if she'll ever get married, and lets us see how deliberately she avoids letting him see her reactions, helps us begin to care about her as we grasp that this is a painful subject and that her affections for Scottie are something he both takes for granted and takes advantage of.

Editing not only manages to keep the focus on essentials, and to orient audience attention to the details that communicate character and feeling and that best tell the story, but it can also put on display realities that would be difficult or even impossible to capture in a single shot of whatever duration. A crowd, for example, could be shown from overhead in an extreme long shot, but the fact the actions of the crowd are actions of individuals, each responding to their immediate surroundings, is not something that would show up or be clear from the impersonal distance of the long shot. Cutting back and forth between extreme long shots focused on the many, to long shots displaying individuals interacting with situations in their proximity, and to medium and close-up framings that display their individualized expressions and reactions – as occurs so potently in the rightly famous Odessa Steps sequence of Sergei Eisenstein's *Battleship Potemkin* (1925) – does manage both to show what takes place among the crowd as a collective activity and as having deeply personal impacts. A car chase, likewise, could be shown from the vantage of a single camera mounted on a third car or in a helicopter overhead. But add cameras placed on, and inside of, both cars, the one that flees and the one in pursuit, and deploy a variety of cameras capturing pivotal moments of the chase from several vantage points as it passes, and edit between these strategically, in such a way as to make clear the continuity of the chase in time and space, and not only does the overall sequence become much more exciting and intense, but it displays on screen something no one participant could witness: the event in its entirety, and its impact upon all.

Another function of editing is to suggest themes by linking images together. Sergei Eisenstein was a pioneer in the use of "conceptual montage," which he considered to be most effective when contrasting images were combined in sequence, forcing viewers to supply the idea that connects them. The most obvious example from his work appears in the film *Strike* (1925), where towards the ending the frame displays workers standing in solidarity and being bludgeoned by the army to force them back into the factories, and cuts back and forth between these images and those of cattle led to slaughter, bluntly forcing the idea that in the eyes of those who commanded the attack, factory workers were considered mere commodities, like cattle. An even more effective example, that is at least slightly more subtle, and that combines both continuity editing and conceptual montage, can be found in a concluding sequence from Francis Ford Coppola's *The Godfather* (1972). Two series of events, apparently simultaneous, are displayed on screen in alternation: we witness Michael Corleone (played by Al Pacino) becoming the literal godfather to his infant niece by participating in her baptism, and at the same time as he affirms his oaths as godfather to his niece, we see his henchmen murdering his rivals, thereby consolidating his power as the figurative godfather, or head, of his mafia family. The juxtaposition of these sequences is not only ironic, but displays quite clearly that for him the religious sanction and sacred character of his role as a caretaker and protector of the family are inseparable from his capacity, secured through a series of assassinations, to operate effectively within that role.

Sound

The baptismal scene from *The Godfather* opens on a wide, establishing shot of the cathedral. As the organ plays, interrupted by the intermittent cries of an infant, the ritual begins. The priest recites the words of the ceremony in Latin and the organ continues to play as the screen reveals Michael's allies preparing for the assassinations. That the music and the sacramental words accompany these preparations highlights that they are part of the ritual through which Michael consolidates his power as head of the criminal family. As the actual murders take place, we hear again an infant crying and the sound of the organ intensifies. Its music is punctuated by gunshots, and the series of murders culminates as the priest asks Michael to renounce the works of Satan. He agrees: "I do renounce them." The continuous sound throughout the scene is what ties the contrasting images together. So it is not merely the juxtaposition of images, but the combination through editing of image and sound that clarifies the significance of what takes place. The images, here, are edited to accompany the rhythm of the music; but editing can also establish its own rhythm, whether fast or slow, and that can impact audiences visually in ways akin to hearing music.

The sound that accompanies motion picture sequences plays an essential role in establishing their significance and impact. Actually, it is misleading to speak of accompaniment, as if sound were a mere surplus component, and that to take it away would not fundamentally alter the experience. We do often think of film as a primarily visual medium. It was, largely, in its beginnings, due to the technical difficulties involved in simultaneously recording picture and sound, and then playing them back synchronized. Sound has since then become thoroughly integrated into the motion picture experience. It plays an indispensable part in creating the impression of the independent reality of the world evoked through cinema. While the two-dimensional images of things on screen are clearly not the same as the realities they depict, high-quality sound can be indistinguishable from the real thing. If the frame functions to separate the world depicted on screen from the world of everyday life, the soundtrack immerses audiences into the textures and moods of a story. A good soundtrack can bring images to life, giving them a sense of immediacy and presence the image alone could not achieve. It is often easier to overlook visual flaws in the imagery than badly captured sound. We can remain immersed in a story captured on grainy film or low-resolution video, as long as the sound quality is high. A beautifully shot film, by contrast, can quickly lose our interest if there are extraneous noises or if the sound mix is bad. Good sound is essential to the impact of cinema.

It is an interesting question why hearing and sight are sufficient to create the impression of an independent world, while the other senses of touch, taste, and smell are not only unnecessary to the experience but can prove to be a distraction. There have, of course, been attempts to introduce other sense modalities into the cinematic experience. William Castle rigged seats with electric buzzers that would cause them to vibrate at strategic moments during selected screenings of *The Tingler* (1959); other entrepreneurs developed mechanisms with names like "AromaRama" and "Smell-o-Vision," to introduce an olfactory accompaniment to the experience of film. More recently, theaters have experimented with seats that move in ways that match the action on screen. None of these have had much success, except as novelties. The innovations that have endured are improvements in the quality of the sound, and enhancements to the quality and size of the picture. This is, likely, due to the fact that both sound and vision not only allow us to discern objects at a distance but also give some sense for where they are relative to us. So they can give us the experience of something that is happening, but that we are not directly involved or implicated in. We can remain at a distance. Touch and taste require contact. For our sense of smell to achieve something similar to the spatio-temporal orientation of hearing and sound we need to be able to move our entire bodies. We'd need to follow a scent. 3D and virtual reality displays allow the objects depicted to seem much closer than when the image is fixed on a flat screen in front of us, yet they remain primarily audio-visual experiences. If and when touch, taste, and smell are fully integrated into the virtual experience, it will arguably have become an entirely different medium, that can no longer be thought of as primarily cinematic.

While the organs for perceiving sound and image are distinct, in our experience of cinema they are integrated. It is a thoroughly audiovisual experience. This is also true of our everyday experience with sound. The philosopher Martin Heidegger offers an insightful phenomenological description of hearing in *Being and Time*.

> What we 'first' hear is never noises or complexes of sounds, but the creaking waggon [*sic*], the motor-cycle. We hear the column on the march, the north wind, the woodpecker tapping, the fire crackling ... It requires a very artificial and complicated frame of mind to 'hear' a 'pure noise'.
>
> (207)

Our ordinary experience of hearing is similar to our ordinary experience of looking. We don't see colored and textured shapes. We see objects. We see dogs on the grass, trees in the field, the mug of coffee on the table. Similarly, we don't hear pitches and timbres. We hear *things* through the sounds that they make.

When filmmakers design the sound for a film, they add sounds captured from a disparate variety of sources to create the various noises called for by the script. Yet when they are successful we don't hear the original sounds captured by the Foley artist. They may have recorded the sound of a baseball bat hitting a side of beef, and combined it with the sound of a breaking pencil, but we hear the boxer's punch connecting with his opponent's chest and breaking a bone. We have the impression of a world, and of events taking place in that world that we observe and listen to. We hear, for example, the chattering of a telegraph cut short as the mercenary gunman rips its wires from the wall, in *Once Upon a Time in the West* (1968); we hear the ethereal glissando of the musical saw that the handyman plays to impress the butcher's daughter in

Delicatessen (1991); we hear the roar of the Tyrannosaurus Rex, triumphant after hurling the lifeless Velociraptor against the wall near the end of *Jurassic Park* (1993). The origin of the sound is not what matters but whether it combines with the image to make the right impression. Brian de Palma's film *Blow-Out* (1981) features a sound artist working on a slasher film, in search of the perfect scream for a pivotal scene. The actress, hired for her looks, can manage at most a pitiful squeal that doesn't come close to conveying real terror. Recording sounds outside at night, the soundman accidentally records evidence of a crime. While investigating further, he meets and falls in love with a woman who was involved. Attempting to expose the criminal by recording a confession, he ends up recording, instead, the moment that the criminal murders his lover. The irony of the film is that in the audio of her death he finds the perfect scream for the film. When we hear it synced up with the images from the slasher film, we have to agree with the protagonist who mutters, in guilt and anguish, "it's a good scream, a good scream." It fits the scene precisely. Apart from the sound artist and the director, no one watching their "masterpiece" would ever suspect that it wasn't the scream of the victim on screen.

Heidegger's observation that we hear things rather than sounds holds true for much of ordinary experience. It seems not to be how we hear music, where, perhaps as a result of the familiar experience of listening to the radio and other recorded songs, most of us are able to hear the music as such rather than hearing it as sounds made by various instruments. Listening to a tune on the radio, we don't hear the drummer, the guitarist, the bassist, or the singer. If we know the band, it might seem that what we hear is them playing the song. What we hear, though, is the song, which includes lyrics and a beat and a bass line and guitar riffs. While we can differentiate between the sounds with a bit of attention, we don't normally notice their separation.

Even if the experience of listening to music is different than hearing sounds, it doesn't require listeners to be in what Heidegger calls the "artificial and complicated frame of mind" that allows them to hear "pure sounds." That's not what it's like to listen to music. We don't hear pure sounds. We hear rhythms, melodies, and harmonies. We don't hear the separate beats. We feel the rhythms they generate not merely as auditory phenomena but as an encouragement to tap our feet or nod our heads in time. The steadiness of the rhythm sets the tone and a mode for how we hear the music as a whole. We don't hear each note, but hear the unfolding melody of which each note is but a moment, whose felt quality is a result of both the tune as it has developed so far and as we anticipate it to unfold into the future. The same note can be heard, for example, as a relatively low sound within the spectrum of the song or as a high point, depending on what comes before it and what after. It can be heard as a point of tension, or a point of resolution. Likewise, we don't hear the separate instruments unless we listen for them, which means we have stopped listening to the song. We hear the harmony that the different sounds and different notes create through their overlapping integration.

The phenomenologist John Russon has argued that these musical dimensions of rhythm, melody, and harmony characterize the temporal dimension of experience generally. Just as we don't hear simple notes when we are listening to music, we don't normally have the experience of detached objects, isolated from their context. I don't normally encounter my desk, my book, my pen, and my computer as objects whose significance is separable from the ongoing rhythm of my activities. I sit down at my desk, and reach for my pen, I open the book to where I'd left off, I read, and make notes in the margin, and when an idea strikes me I'll type up a note in the document containing thoughts for my chapter. I am dimly aware that shortly before three o'clock I'll have to set this work aside and go to a meeting. I may also feel a bit drowsy from lunch, and wonder whether I ought to make myself another cup of coffee. We are, ordinarily, caught up in the rhythms of nature and of routine; we presume this background as we are caught up in the melodic ups and downs in pursuit of those projects we put as our primary focus; and yet our mood and our attention as we carry out such projects is modulated by our simultaneous participation in the projects of others and through the impact of unfolding events we cannot ignore. "It is in this original making sense, this music to which we are bodily attuned, that all of our reality is given birth. We *emerge* in this matrix, this manifold, of rhythmic epiphany" (Russon, *Bearing Witness to Epiphany*). Apart from whatever music might be playing on the soundtrack, the events I witness on screen also set up their own rhythm, melody, and harmony, and my experience of them is shaped by and contributes to my own primordial musicality.

The primary components of a film's soundtrack include not only music, but also voice and other sounds that add texture and bring our experience of the reality on screen to life. Each of these can be experienced in two fundamentally different ways. They can be heard as proceeding from the world depicted on screen, which means that in principle they could be heard by the characters who belong to that world. Or, they can be heard as separate from that world, in which case they will impact how that world is experienced, but only the audience can hear them. Film scholars call the sounds that emanate from the story world of the film "diegetic," and sounds that are separate from that story world "non-diegetic." Diegetic sound includes what is meant to be heard by audiences as belonging to and emanating from the world depicted on the screen. It includes everything that could, at least in principle, be heard by the characters that populate that world. Dialogue, for example, is diegetic. Music that is playing from a source on screen, such as a car radio, is diegetic. The sounds we associate with objects on screen – a dog barking, the echo of footsteps, waves crashing – are all diegetic.

Voiceover tracks can sometimes be considered diegetic, and sometimes non-diegetic. When the voice we hear is that of a character on screen, giving the impression that we are hearing out loud thoughts she hasn't vocalized, that is sometimes thought to be semi-diegetic, because it does proceed from the world of the story, but it isn't something that the other characters nearby would be able to hear. By contrast, the musical score and the voice of a narrator who is not a character of the story are both non-diegetic uses of sound. We hear music in the background, for example, that orients or accentuates the feelings we associate with what is taking place on screen, but is music meant only for our ears as an audience. It is meant to impact our apprehension of what we see happening on screen, to shape the way we feel about it. We aren't given grounds for inferring that it is heard by the characters, or that the music is playing in the background of the events taking place. Other sounds besides music and voice can be included in the soundtrack. Sometimes these noises are intended to amplify the diegetic sound, or to cue audiences that something is about to happen. If there is no source for them within the story world depicted in the film, such sounds are also non-diegetic.

It is sometimes said that there is no visual analog to the distinction between diegetic and non-diegetic sound. An image is either there in the story world or it doesn't appear. Strictly speaking that is true because every image that occurs within the film is part of the story told by the film. This is so even for images that no character in the film witnesses, such as the famous image of a burning sled with the logo "Rosebud" at the end of *Citizen Kane* (1941). While no one in the story seems to notice, the realization that the tycoon's enigmatic final word referred to a toy from his childhood is nevertheless a part of the story that is told to the audience, and, of course it could have been seen by someone from the story. Still, the same thing is arguably true of sounds. Even the non-diegetic sounds, which don't emanate from the world depicted on screen, are nevertheless crucial to the story being told. They may, after all, be intended to let audiences know about or share in the mood of the characters on screen. Just as the framing of an image shapes how audiences interpret it, non-diegetic music and sound might be considered to be part of the "auditory frame" that gives the image its significance.

There remains a fairly clear difference between something that belongs to the world depicted in the story and something that is part of the telling of the story but not part of the world it is about. So we could say that while the things shown on screen belong to the story world, the way that they are framed belongs to the telling of the story. The "Rosebud" sled clearly belongs to the world of *Citizen Kane*, even if it is not seen (or if its significance goes unnoticed) by the characters in the world. Arguably, though, even some of the images included in films are not part of the world depicted in the film, even if their inclusion enhances the story by modifying how audiences interpret the story. In Sergei Eisenstein's film *Strike*, for example, the image of a spy is intercut with the image of a monkey. We aren't meant to think that there is an actual monkey present. Rather, the image gives us a sense for his character. Sometimes characters imagine things that aren't real. We are shown what they imagine, but it isn't any more a part of the world depicted on screen than their random thoughts we might hear in a voiceover. Like a subjective voiceover, these imagined images would at least tell us something about the character. In some films, we are meant to suppose that nearly everything we see on screen is merely a visualization of a story someone is telling to someone else on screen. In *A Princess Bride* (1987), we see a story about a doting grandfather reading a book to his grandson who is sick in bed. One might say that, strictly speaking, only the actions and words of the grandfather and the boy belong to the story world. Everything else that takes place in that story is, presumably, the product of the boy's imagination. In that case, we might consider the images themselves – apart from those that show us the grandpa and the boy – to be analogous to semi-diegetic sound.

Sound, unlike the motion picture image, is not restricted to the limits of the rectangular frame. Whether it is coming from a single speaker, stereo, or a surround sound setup, it fills the room, surrounding the audience. Part of what reminds us that the image is an image is the fact that it comes to an end. There is a frame, so the image has its limits. That means that while the image can only offer a selective orientation onto the world, the sound can exceed its boundaries. To show us something that exceeds the boundaries of the frame, the camera would need to move and adopt a new framing. Yet the soundtrack can let us hear things we cannot see. We can hear what is off-screen. Off-screen sounds are distinct from non-diegetic sounds. Non-diegetic sounds do not belong to the world depicted on the screen. Off-screen sounds remind us that the world depicted on screen extends far beyond the boundaries of the screen.

Like the screen, sound can have a perspective and orientation. Different volumes of sound can indicate relative distance, and changes in pitch can indicate movement. Stereo and surround sound technologies allow the world of sounds to have an orientation, so that audiences can hear sounds coming from one or the other direction, or in front or behind them. Yet the perspective and orientation of the sounds that fill a particular scene or series of shots can be independent of the orientation of the camera.

This is particularly notable in musical numbers. In several scenes throughout the film *Moulin Rouge* (2001), the camera weaves in and out among dancers and singers, with rapid edits capturing a variety of perspectives on the intricate choreography. Yet the music plays throughout at the same volume, where no element takes priority over the song even if the camera happens to highlight one or the other performer or musician or perspective on the room. In dialogue-heavy scenes in most films, actors are recorded independently so that they can all be played back at roughly the same volume. The camera may point in different directions to highlight this or that character, or may move in close to capture facial expressions, or expand its perspective to indicate where the characters stand in relation to each other. The sound, throughout, remains stable. The voice of someone speaking doesn't suddenly get louder when the camera frames her in a close-up, for example.

Perhaps most important among the many things we hear in films are voices. Notably, the early successful feature-length sound films were known as "talkies." While the nickname is likely due to the fact that the most important technical hurdle they had overcome was synchronizing dialogue with picture, it may also indicate that from an audience perspective their most notable accomplishment was to let the movies speak. Soundtracks and sound effects had already been possible. What was missing were the nuances of expression made possible through the inclusion of voices. The importance of the voice is not limited to its capacity to deliver information. Silent filmmakers could already communicate a great deal of information, and present intricate plots, through the creative use of framing and ordering. The over-reliance on dialogue to communicate information is, even now, considered to be the mark of incompetent filmmaking. In cinema, as in life, speech is both expression and action. More important than its capacity to deliver information is the voice's ability to express character in a more nuanced way than is possible in silent film.

One can, of course, say a great deal through gestures and the face. Yet to first hear someone speak, regardless of what they actually say, can provide much greater insight into who they are, how they see themselves and how they relate to others than is possible through bodily comportments alone. A small person can have a commanding voice. A voice can express both disgust and lust. Voices can be charming, whiny, shy, suspicious, welcoming, hesitant, or bold. The film *Singin' in the Rain* (1952) highlights the power of the voice when silent film heroine Lena Lamont has her talkie debut. On screen in silent films she is seductive and beautiful. As soon as we hear her nasal and whiny voice, she appears to be arrogant and insecure. It is a cliché to say that the eyes are the window to the soul. Only new lovers really feel it to be true, when they gaze into one another's eyes and see not the other's soul but their own fascination mirrored. In public settings, the voice is far more expressive than the eyes. That is why the most important feature of sound design in cinema is to ensure that voices can be heard and understood. Michel Chion, a French composer and critic who has written several books on cinematic sound, wrote that

> in actual movies, for real spectators, there are not all the sounds including the human voice. There are voices, and then everything else. In other words, in every audio mix, the presence of a human voice instantly sets up a hierarchy of perception.
>
> (The Voice in Cinema 5)

When watching films in a foreign language, the cinephile always prefers to read subtitles over the dubbed version since a vital feature of the performances is lost when we cannot hear the actors' voices in their original language.

Good cinematic dialogue does more than merely communicate information between the characters and to the audience. Dialogue is action. With the introduction of sound, filmmakers were able to put on display a far wider range of human activity than what could be shown in silent film. At the most basic level, talking to each other is something we do. Even in everyday life, conversations are almost never simply about communicating information. Conversation is interaction. It can build trust, or it can amplify antagonism. It can be a form of play, and it can be a form of seduction. It can be extremely tense or combative. Talking is also a way of doing things. We can lie. We can tell the truth. We can form allegiances or create enemies. We can make promises and commitments which we may or may not intend to keep. We can ask questions, and provoke doubts. Often the most important thing about cinematic dialogue is what is not said, what is held back, or what is said by saying something else. That is what is usually called "subtext." While dialogue can be expository, supplying the audience with information that is needed to appreciate the plot, this works best when it is also motivated by the needs of the characters, so that it advances the plot as well. Good dialogue, filmed well to reveal the range of the participants' reactions, can be every bit as entertaining as a so-called action scene, precisely because it is action. It can also, like Platonic dialogues, provoke questions and evoke thoughts in the audience regarding the implications of what is both said and left unsaid.

Genre, story, and representation

There is a difference between the story that a film has to tell, and the way in which its filmmakers tell it. We considered the formal techniques of film (the framing and ordering of the images, as well as the use of sound) first, because it is by the use of such techniques that stories are told at the cinema. When we walk out of a film, though, and someone asks what it was like, we might tell them we loved it, or hated it, or that it wasn't half bad. If asked to elaborate we won't usually talk about the style of the film. We'll tell them, if it wasn't obvious, what genre it was, and then we'll tell them the story. We won't tell them about the cinematography, or the editing, or the sound, unless any of these were either awful or utterly distinctive. Sorting out what to say about the formal elements of a film usually requires repeated viewings and careful analysis. What stands out on a first viewing is the story it tells and our emotional response to it. If pressed further, we'll talk about what we think it might mean. Even where a film tells an entertaining story and is competently produced, we'll often walk away unsatisfied unless it seems to have something to say, unless it leaves us with something to think about. Of course what it leads us to think might well be problematic, and worth challenging.

Genre

We often go to the movies in the hopes of a certain kind of experience. We want to laugh out loud, or maybe to laugh a little and cry a little, to feel a sense of wonder, to be excited, or frightened. Certain film genres are organized primarily with such expectations in mind. Comedies are supposed to be funny, or at the very least light-hearted.

We are disappointed if they don't make us laugh or smile. Melodramas are meant to make us care and feel for the ups and downs of the lives of their characters. Science fiction and fantasy films can be adventurous, scary, or funny, but above all, they should appeal to our capacity for imagination and wonder, at possibilities that exceed our current grasp. Action and adventure films offer vicarious thrills. Part of what appeals about horror films is the sudden rush of fear and terror that leads to laughter and relief when we recall that we are not truly in danger.

The word genre just means "type" or "kind." To generalize is to put things into a group based on certain shared characteristics. When a certain kind of film has been successful, other filmmakers, naturally, attempt to repeat that success. When a handful of similar successes develop into a trend we have the beginnings of a genre. Yet genres are not always or for the most part defined by an expectation of a specific kind of emotional response. Some types of films turn out to be appealing because they address subjects that many people find fascinating, or they tap into beliefs, concerns, and obsessions shared by a wide number of people. The popularity of films that appeal to such interests can lead to the development of genres focused on a specific subject matter. They, usually, feature a range of familiar character types and elements that allow that subject matter to be dramatized.

Some such genres have emerged quickly and then faded into obscurity. It is an open question how long the appeal of the enormously popular genre of comic book superhero films will last. Other genres have been around since nearly the beginnings of cinema and remain important today. One of the most popular and enduring American genres has been the Western film. These films are usually set in the Western parts of North America, and purport to show "how the West was won" – or how the lands that had formerly been inhabited primarily by native Americans came to be occupied by the citizens and regulated by the laws of the United States of America. The appeal of such films has spread far beyond the U.S.A., in part because the issues they examine are universal. They function almost like myth. They tell stories that address questions we can't help but care about and provoke concerns we can't help but find troubling. The places we inhabit weren't always as they are now. No matter where we live, other peoples have lived there before us. Even if our neighborhoods are welcoming, there are places we know that we can go where we won't feel safe. Yet the places we do feel safe can feel restrictive to others. Westerns deal with the tension between security and freedom. Is lawlessness the same as freedom? Or does genuine freedom require the order that comes from settled and enforced law? Westerns address the fact that the enforcement of law can often be one-sided, protecting and enabling one group while oppressing the lives of others. Western settlers weren't moving into empty lands, they built their homes in places that had been inhabited for centuries by native peoples. Westerns explore the conflicts that arise in the process of colonization. If some early Westerns depicted these conflicts in black and white terms, depicting "noble" cowboys threatened by "savages," later Westerns tended to be more nuanced in their portrayals, suggesting that audiences were more willing to consider the troubling aspects of the past. John Ford's classic *The Searchers* (1956), released in the early years of the civil rights movement in America, tells a story of revenge that is at the same time a vivid examination of the insidiousness of racism. Westerns explore other conflicts that, in different forms, have continued to plague the United States, such as those that arise when small businesses (such as family farms) are overrun by big business (in the form of big cattle ranchers).

The enduring interest of the subject matter and concerns addressed by Westerns is indicated by the fact that variations on the genre have appeared in many countries around the world. The Japanese filmmaker Akira Kurosawa adapted stylistic and thematic elements of Western films, especially those of John Ford, in several of his samurai films set in ancient Japan. Kurosawa sued Sergio Leone (successfully) when he stole the plot of Kurosawa's *Yojimbo* (1961) to create his own Western film, *A Fistful of Dollars* (1964), starring Clint Eastwood. The success of that film spawned an industry of Italian-produced Western films, which later became known as "spaghetti Westerns." There have been Soviet Westerns, East German Westerns, French, Latin American, and Australian Westerns. The genre has evolved quite a bit over time, and has been adapted for various uses. The questions that the genre explores, dealing with the legal and moral issues surrounding land use, the political and philosophical issues regarding the relationship between so-called "civilization" and "savagery," and the relation between freedom and law, continue to fascinate and vex. So the genre is not likely to disappear anytime soon. Other genres that appeared early on in the history of cinema, and appear to have a lasting appeal, include the musical, the crime film, and the coming-of-age or youth film.

Each of these genres belongs to the larger cinematic category that is the focus of this book: fictional narrative films. They can be contrasted with two other broad categories of film, documentaries and experimental films. Although fictional narrative films are sometimes called just "narrative" films, that label is a bit misleading. Documentaries, at least, always also tell a story. It is just one that is purported to be true. Of course fictional narrative films can also be based on true stories or historical events, but the key word here is "based" – they are always to some extent fictionalized. They use actors, for example, rather than the original characters. Even if, as in Clint Eastwood's film *The 15:17 to Paris* (2018), some of the characters are playing themselves, they are playing themselves while replaying the past, acting out what they had once lived through. Neither they nor their depictions can possibly be the same as they were then. No matter how faithful a film based on facts is intended to be, there will always be some differences. In any case, the perspective from which the story is told will be unique to each telling. This point of contrast is complicated by the fact that some documentary films – such as Errol Morris's *The Thin Blue Line* (1988) – include re-enactments, using actors, of some of the events that they describe. Even early documentaries, praised for their authenticity, such as Robert Flaherty's *Nanook of the North* (1922), staged certain events. The title character, for example, was asked to recreate for the camera some of the traditional Inuk hunting and fishing practices that were no longer typical among his people. While there has always been some controversy regarding the legitimacy of re-enactments and staging in documentary, they are sometimes indispensable. They remain among the arsenal of devices through which documentarians attempt to depict certain aspects of reality. Some experimental films are explicitly non-narrative. They function, for example, more like animated abstract paintings than like cinema. Yet some clearly experimental films are narratives and manage to tell some kind of story, however oblique. Maya Deren and Alexander Hammid's famous *Meshes of the Afternoon* (1943), for example – which seems at first like a vision of a dream or a nightmare – can't be easily reconstructed into a straightforward series of events in which the dream elements are disentangled from the reality. It still tells a story, of sorts. Some narrative fiction films – such as Guy Maddin's *The Forbidden Room* (2015) – would be difficult to distinguish from experimental films.

Story and narration

A question that has preoccupied some film theorists and philosophers is how to understand the way films – particularly fictional narrative films – tell stories. A fictional narrative film is just a film that tells a fictional story. "Narration" refers to the way that the story is told. We often assume that for a story to be narrated there needs to be a narrator, a person or a persona who is telling the story. In fictional literature, it is not always or even usually true that the author is the narrator. Herman Melville is the author of *Moby Dick* (1851). Its narrator is a man named Ishmael, a fictional character in the book. Often, though, the narrator of a fictional novel is never identified. We read descriptions of people, places, and events, without any indication that anyone in particular is describing them. The story is just told, and the reader is never told who or what is telling it. It often doesn't make much sense to identify the narrator with the person who actually wrote the book. The style of the writing might, after all, have been deliberately constructed to sound different than the author would sound if she were speaking or writing as herself. Some books read as if they present an objective account of events; others seem much more subjective, biased in favor of a particular character. Some narrators may be unreliable, yet we can presume that the actual author knows what they are leaving out or lying about. The attitudes expressed in a text might themselves be fictional, and quite different from those the author actually adopts. Just as we should not assume that the author of a novel shares the attitudes or biases of any of its fictional characters, even if one of those characters is narrating the book, we also need not assume that the attitudes expressed or implied by the anonymous narrator of a novel are those of the author. Perhaps most importantly, the text of a novel usually reads as if the people and events it is describing are real, and as if it is providing a true account. Yet the author, presumably, doesn't believe it to be literally true. They are (or at least might be) making it all (or most of it) up. As a result of such considerations, literary theorists have generally supposed that we should attribute the storytelling "voice" to a fictional or implied narrator, distinct from the author who wrote the book. While the implied narrator of a novel may appear to be either omniscient or naïve, objective or biased, truthful or deceptive, we cannot presume that any of these applies to the actual author. All that matters is that they know enough about the story they want to tell to create the impression for the reader that they need to make it work.

For similar reasons, some film theorists have held that to understand films we need to posit an implied or fictional narrator to stand as the agent responsible for the story it tells. Yet the case of film is more complicated, in part because of the fact that unlike the case of literature it doesn't always make sense to suppose that films even have an "author" who might be distinguished from the implied narrator. It is also complicated by the fact that the primary medium of film is not words, but images, framed and arranged in a particular way to let the situations and events of the films be seen rather than described. Films, like literature, sometimes include an explicit narrative voice. It can be the voice of someone who is introduced as a character within the film, but it can also be that of an anonymous narrator, included to introduce the film and provide audiences with important details at pivotal points in the story. Strictly speaking, however, what any such narrator explains is only a small part of the story unfolding on screen. Films show far more than they tell. In fact, what a given film shows may be inconsistent with what its ostensive narrator tells. That doesn't necessarily mean that we should rely on what the film shows, since what is shown can be misleading as well. The Japanese film *Rashomon* (1950) shows several contradictory versions of the "same" event, each of which appears to be narrated by a different fictional character in the film. It never shows, and no one ever tells us, what *really* happened. The film as a whole, in fact, raises doubts regarding the possibility of such a showing or telling. There are different ways of describing any series of events, and different ways of showing it. There is no one way to show it all, to make all of its aspects clear. To make sense of the story of any film requires that audiences consider both what they are shown and what they are told, and decide what to make of it on the basis of the evidence (see Carroll, "Narration").

While the explicit use of narration within a film implies a particular perspective, the images shown within the film need not share that perspective, and needn't be attributed to any particular perspective at all. Often what we are shown, after all, is just the most convenient angle or camera movement from which to portray a given object or event. Such films seem to be objective, since they don't seem to privilege any perspective in particular. It doesn't always make much sense to suppose that all of the shots in a film belong to the unified point of view of a single narrator. Each provides us with pieces of events that we put together in order to understand the story as a whole. Perhaps all we really need to posit is a filmmaking team, working from a script and aiming to tell a story clearly. What they may have in common, likely as a result of the sensibilities of the team's leadership, is a style. Even where the shots of a film seem to favor a particular perspective, we needn't attribute that bias to either a particular person considered the auteur behind the film, or to a fictional narrator. It may, rather, represent a cultural or industrial bias, such as a predisposition built into the Hollywood studio system to privilege the male perspective in films.

David Bordwell begins his groundbreaking work on the nature of film narration by distinguishing between theories of narration that emphasize *diegesis* (or telling) and those that emphasize *mimesis* (or showing). Neither account, according to Bordwell, is adequate for an understanding of cinema, which makes ample use of both. Both what is shown and how it is shown – including the decision on the part of the filmmakers whether or not to include an explicit narrator – shape the way that audiences make sense of the film as a whole. While he makes use of a couple of technical terms, Bordwell's account of how fiction films tell stories is fairly straightforward, and doesn't require there to be a single perspective behind all of the various cinematic elements. A story is told, but we needn't posit a teller. It is, rather, the audience that is tasked to synthesize the various pieces together, to make sense of the story as a whole. He defines fiction film narration as "the process whereby the film's *syuzhet* [i.e. plot] and style interact in the course of cueing and channeling the spectator's construction of the *fabula* [story]" (*Narration in the Fiction Film* 53). The film's telling of its story is successful if the elements of the film are organized and presented in a way that allows the audience to piece them together in a way that makes sense and feels satisfying.

The story that a film has to tell can be distinguished from its plot. It should, though, be noted that different authors define the differences variously. In their bestselling textbook, *Film Art*, David Bordwell and Kristen Thompson define plot as the ordered sequence of film elements presented to the audience. Plot, as they define it, includes not only the scenes through which the characters and events that play a role in the story are depicted, but also non-diegetic elements, such as music, that can impact how audiences make sense of what is presented. The plot of a film, for example, might begin with a murder, even if, in the story, chronologically, it comes last, and what is shown after is intended to help audiences understand how and why it happened. The title credits and the music that might accompany this opening scene are also part of the plot, and may give audiences some indication of how they ought to feel about the murder. The story, which we come to understand and appreciate fully only at the conclusion of the film, may include events that are not explicitly presented on screen as part of the plot, but that we infer, since they explain and help to motivate the actions and events that we are shown. Perhaps the most important element of story, though, is character, since it is characters and their motivations that drive the story forward. The plot may include things that happen for no reason or by accident, such as the sudden and unexpected car crash at the beginning of Krzysztof Kieślowski's film *Blue* (1993). Yet the story of the film concerns the journey of self-discovery by Julie. She survived the crash that killed both her daughter and her husband, who, as she later discovers, had been cheating on her. In stories, nothing happens for no reason, because everything that happens has an impact on the characters or how we understand them, and anything that doesn't has no good reason to be included in the telling of the story.

The most familiar story pattern is the three-act structure. While it may seem to be overly formulaic, its wide applicability and appeal are due largely to the fact that each moment in its structure can be understood in terms of characters and the motivations of their actions. When the plot of a film follows the three-act structure, it is almost indistinguishable from the story. Following an introduction to the characters, the story proper begins with an inciting incident. What counts as an incitement, of course, depends on the character. Something happens to a character, and she must respond. Or, as a result of the accumulation of unfavorable circumstances, she discovers that she can't keep living in the way that she has been. Or she does something, and it has unintended consequences. In any case, she has to do something about it. Whatever she does, or fails to do, creates a new situation which creates new challenges. That is the end of the first act. The second act examines how she faces the challenges generated in the first act. Each new action creates new complications or opportunities, to which she must respond anew. This period of "rising action" may go through several cycles, and we may find that the character undergoes significant changes or developments in the process. The rising action leads to some kind of crisis, a problem that can't be solved in the way that she's been trying to this point. How she responds to the crisis generates a change in her situation. The final act is one in which she and we come to appreciate the significance of that change. Of course, with the introduction of more than one main character, and with the added complexities of real situations, the story itself can become considerably more complicated than is suggested by this abstract structure. Another essential complication is the fact that characters themselves don't live in a linear fashion. What happened in the past and what they anticipate for the future can impact how they interpret and respond to situations in the present. Careful narration, which includes both plot and the formal techniques through which it is presented, can communicate a great deal of this kind of complexity.

Representation

To understand the impact and significance of film, we need to consider not only how films tell stories, but which stories get told, whose stories they are, and who gets to tell them. Currently, despite recent advancements in diversity within the film industry, the majority of mainstream films are still directed by (white, heterosexual) men ("Inclusion in the Director's Chair"). An unfortunate result has been to limit the scope and perspective of popular film narratives. This is not to say that filmmakers – and artists generally – cannot and do not step outside of their lived experiences when they create new work, but rather to acknowledge that they may not be consistently mindful of their own limits and biases. This is, arguably, especially important in cinema because of films' special capacity to shape our understanding of reality. Films cause audiences to think about what is, should, and could be real. It is, therefore, important to recognize when, why, and how certain populations are included or excluded from their representations.

In 1985, the illustrator Alison Bechdel created a comic strip panel featuring a set of three rules to follow when deciding which movies to watch. They should have at least two female characters, who at some point in the film have a conversation, which must be about something other than men. Perhaps surprisingly, a large number of classic (and even recent) films fail the test. This set of rules, which has come to be known as the "Bechdel test," may appear to set a somewhat arbitrary standard. It doesn't really guarantee the films that meet it are any good, or that the depictions of the women they include have any merit. It doesn't say, for example, what kind of conversation the women are supposed to have, other than that it is not supposed to be about men. Some films, such as *Run Lola Run* (1998) or *Gravity* (2013), feature strong female protagonists. Yet they fail the Bechdel test since for reasons peculiar to the story there is never an occasion for two women to have a conversation about anything. The test also doesn't offer anything to address shortcomings in cinematic representations of race, ethnicity, class, and sexual orientation (see Koeze et al.). Still, part of the appeal of the test is that it sets the bar extremely low. Yet, according to the website bechdel-test.com, of nearly 8000 films examined only about half actually qualify. At a minimum, the test serves to raise awareness of the need for women to be represented in films as having other interests than men and as being more than just a love interest. It also serves to highlight an important problem. Women – and characters belonging to other marginalized groups – are often not depicted as individuals with independent lives and concerns.

The problems hinted at by the need for the Bechdel test extend far beyond the inadequacy of gender representations in cinema. Representations of race and ethnicity, sexual orientation and expression, class, age, and ability, are other areas that have attracted concern. It is not enough merely to include representatives of diverse groups. Too often those who are included conform to popular and harmful stereotypes. Even where representations may be considered to be positive, intended to work against stereotypes, other factors may mitigate against the potential to change perceptions.

Take, for example, the Marvel film *Black Panther* (2018), directed by Ryan Coogler. Its director is black. It features an almost entirely black cast. It depicts a (fictional) African nation known as "Wakanda," whose clothing, jewelry, and makeup are at once futuristic and inspired by traditional styles worn by native peoples from a variety of real nations from the continent of Africa. The characters – both men and women – are powerful, intelligent, and complex. They do not conform to familiar cinematic stereotypes for depicting characters who are either racially black or "ethnically African." The film imagines an African nation that was never subjugated by European colonialists, whose peoples were never subject to the horrors of forced migration and slavery. *Black Panther* was not only wildly successful in the box office, it has continued to inspire and empower audience members who had never seen people who looked like them playing superheroes, and especially doing so in a way that could draw attention to the vitality of a cultural heritage that was distinct from that of the European cultures that have come to be characterized as "white."

At the same time, the film could not have been made as one of Disney's Marvel superhero films unless it also appealed to a global audience. This includes, of course, "white" audiences, as well as those who may not consider themselves to be white but who also don't identify as black. While some members of this audience might find its character depictions, costumes, and imagery interesting or even fascinating, they wouldn't specifically identify with them any more than with characters in other Marvel movies. They wouldn't feel the excitement of seeing, for the first time on the big screen, powerful heroes, both women and men, who looked like them. They couldn't have that experience for the first time, because it is their experience nearly every time they watch a film. The box office success of the film suggests that many still found it thrilling. Some celebrated the film as a sign of progress. They considered its success to be a hopeful sign that in the future major studios would trust a more diverse group of filmmakers with the resources to tell stories on that scale. Others, though, pushed back against what they saw to be the "political correctness" of Hollywood. Some of the same people who complained on social media about the reboot of *Ghostbusters* (2016) featuring female leads, and who were angered by what they considered to be the politics of *The Last Jedi* (2017), also threatened to sabotage the critical ratings of *Black Panther* on review aggregation websites such as RottenTomatoes.com (Gaudette). Some didn't care whether or not the film featured black characters, but only wanted it to be full of action and fun to watch. Given that the film was not intended to stand alone, but to play a pivotal role in the unfolding of the massive franchise known as the Marvel Cinematic Universe, the filmmakers could not afford to alienate any part of the audience. A full consideration of the representational significance of the film would need to take into account the impact of commercial considerations such as these upon the shape of the film as a whole.

Notably, the film was released during a period when, in the United States, an increased awareness of instances of police brutality directed mostly at young black men had given rise to the "Black Lives Matter" (BLM) movement. While the movement has been popular and influential, it has also generated severe criticism from those who think it unfairly stereotypes law enforcement officers and who interpret the slogan to imply that *only* the lives of black people matter, or that other lives matter less. Erik Killmonger (Michael B. Jordan), easily the film's most charismatic and powerful character, is angry at the world – at the oppression and injustice faced by black people of various nations – for reasons that would be recognizable to proponents of the movement. In the film, however, he is the villain. While he seeks to use the advanced weaponry of Wakanda to fight against what he characterizes as white oppression, in the end he is defeated and the Black Panther, T'Challa, decides to share Wakanda's technology in the struggle against poverty, illness, and injustice faced by everyone. It is, almost, as if the overt conclusion of the film is that – to employ the slogan critics of the Black Lives movement use in an effort to invalidate its concerns rather than to express solidarity – "all lives matter." This message, at least, establishes that T'Challa is not a partisan for a particular race but is a full member of the team of superheroes known as the Avengers whose aim is to protect humanity. It also establishes that while this film includes diverse representations its ultimate message is one of unity. It allows, above all, for the film to be seen as non-threatening by the widest possible audience.

While this may be the overall message of the film, it needn't be considered to invalidate the importance of its representational qualities. The message conveyed by the representations in a film isn't always consistent with the message suggested by its story. The story of *Black Panther* was told in such a way that no one in the audience should feel alienated, but that doesn't mean its representations of "blackness" and of African traditions – and even of the importance of the message of the BLM movement – were not empowering for those members of the audience who saw them. In spite of the fact that in the end Killmonger didn't win, and that he also had some serious flaws that signaled why he had to lose in a superhero film, Michael B. Jordan's nuanced portrayal ensured that the character's concerns were aired powerfully, and his righteous anger unmistakably expressed. That alone is remarkable in a popular film of this magnitude, and may account for some of the enthusiasm with which the film was received upon its release.

Black Panther doesn't merely represent race. It also highlights the nature and significance of the difference between race and ethnicity. Film scholar Robyn Wiegman points out that

> where ethnicity provides the means for differentiations based on culture, language, and national origins, race renders the reduction of human differences to innate, biological phenomena, phenomena that circulate culturally as the visible ledger for defining and justifying economic and political hierarchies between white and non-white groups.
>
> (161)

Studies of the history of cinematic representations of race have shown the gradual transformation of Jewish identity in American films from a primarily racial to an ethnic category, and that similar transformations have taken place in depictions of other European immigrant groups such as the Irish and the Italian. Early films depicting Jewish, Irish, or Italian characters emphasized visible characteristics such as skin, hair, and facial features to establish identity; later films focused more on features that could be performed, such as customs, accents, gestures, and speech. Since the focus shifted away from physical features as a way of designating characters as non-white, the effect was to expand the range of possibilities for representing whiteness. Representations of blackness have not undergone a similar expansion. The same is largely true of representations of Latinos, of Asians, and of Native Americans, all of which tend to emphasize stereotyped physical features and stereotypical character types, while largely disregarding the historical, cultural, and linguistic factors by which individuals define themselves (Wiegman).

The distinction between race and ethnicity is represented clearly in *Black Panther*. While others may see the main characters in the film as "black" or "African," the characters see themselves as essentially Wakandan. Race is often falsely assumed to be an objective biological property, that defines who one is regardless of whom one thinks oneself to be. By contrast, ethnicity is clearly intersubjective. It is not merely a matter of how a group of people is seen by others, but of how they define themselves. It is not something that one can simply adopt at will, either, because to belong to a specific ethnicity requires that one be seen as such by others who share it. Killmonger, who grew up outside of the Wakandan community – and had always been seen as black by others – only gained acceptance as a Wakandan by participating in a ritualistic duel in which he defeats T'Challa. While Wakanda is a fictional nation, and the ethnic characteristics that define it draw upon features of a variety of actual national and cultural features native to Africa, its depiction in the film highlights the fact that no one is, in fact, generically "black." Race, like ethnicity, is a socially constructed category. If "blackness" is applied to a group of people by others on the sole basis of easily discernible bodily characteristics, the question of who identifies themselves as "black" is far more complicated. People tend to define themselves primarily by the families and communities to which they belong. Likewise, we might add, there is no such thing as a generic "African." The African continent has been home to a vast number of different peoples, living in distinctive geographical regions, with their own distinctive customs and practices, as rich in their own way – even if not as rich in super-powerful metals – as the fictional nation of Wakanda.

It is, perhaps, understandable why filmmakers would rely on stereotypes. To tell a compelling story requires the creation of characters who the audience can care about or at least understand well enough to appreciate their motives. One easy and quick way to create empathy for a protagonist is to make them be the kind of person that the majority of the anticipated audience can be expected to identify with. A perhaps more powerful way to get the audience to care about the aims of the main character is to make their enemy or antagonist appear hateful or unlikeable. Drawing upon widely held stereotypes, and depicting the antagonist as a type of person who is already vilified by popular media and culture, is an easy way to accomplish that. Of course, the problem is that filmmakers are not only drawing upon stereotypes but are reinforcing them for their audience. One of the reasons to push for and support a more diverse group of filmmakers is because their experiences are more likely to give them the capacity to create nuanced and interesting characters that engage audiences because of their richness and not because it is easier to rely upon popular stereotypes and clichés.

It is not, then, enough just to consider who gets included in films and how they are represented. We also need to reflect upon the role that their representation plays within the film as a whole, and whether the films they are included in challenge or conform to the larger cultural understandings of the categories they are taken to represent. Finally, we need to consider the larger impact on the film industry of films that are made by people who traditionally had been excluded.

All of the elements we have considered – from the question who makes films and how, to the question how they tell stories and represent characters by shooting and arranging bits of film and combining them with sound – all of these contribute to the overall impact and significance of a film. They give a sense of what matters and of how things hang together as a whole. Attending to each of these details, writing them down and reflecting upon them to consider how they affect our experience of what unfolds there on the screen, is the first step in considering what the film might have to say about philosophical questions.

Part II
Appearance and reality

3 The appearance of reality

Arrival of the Train

Cinema begins with the arrival of a train. This little film by the Lumière brothers, depicting a locomotive rolling in at the Ciotat station, was by some reports so startling that people panicked, fainting and scrambling out of their seats to get out of the way. It wasn't actually the first motion picture. What's more, as noted by film historians such as Tom Gunning, the stories about its impact on audiences are almost certainly exaggerated (Gunning 114–15; Bottomore). They have, nevertheless, contributed to what has been called the "founding myth" of cinema. Even if *Arrival of the Train* (1897) was not the first film, the stories surrounding its reception signaled powerfully that something new and fantastic had arrived upon the scene. Like all good myths, they offer a gripping indication of the originary experiential significance of this new phenomenon.

Moving picture entertainments had already existed in a variety of forms. The *Arrival of the Train* (a film "remade" several times by the brothers, and "plagiarized" by several others) was not even the first film attraction presented publicly by the Lumière brothers. Their short films, drawn from scenes of everyday life, were appealing for many reasons. Made up of photographs, they preserve a record of the past, and yet unlike photographs they manage to bring these scenes to life. Audiences were

Figure 3.1 The train arrives.

fascinated by little ephemeral details such as leaves fluttering in the trees. A large part of the appeal of such films seems to have been their ability to record and replay passing moments in time, allowing audiences to notice and cherish details such as these, that often escape us and fade away from memory.

The stories about *Arrival of the Train* suggest a different fascination. From their beginnings, motion pictures, as little as photographs before them, were hardly mistaken for reality. They are, or were then, black and white (or grayscale), reducing the rich colors of the world to monochrome. They were not just silent, but could be positively noisy, except where the accompaniment of a piano or an orchestra managed to drown out the mechanical sounds of the projector. They were, and still are, flat, reducing the spatial depths of the world to a two-dimensional plane, and the sensory richness of the world to what is visual (only later adding a synchronized soundtrack), to a rectangular window of flickering shadows and lights. What is novel about the train film is the sudden shock that was reportedly felt by audiences. As the image of the train got larger and the train seemed to come closer, they reportedly had the feeling that it might escape from its confines and emerge from the screen.

It is, though, just a feeling. It is hard to believe, and there are good reasons to doubt that audiences actually jumped from their seats and scrambled to exit the theater. If they had, as recent film historians have noted, there would have been injuries and police reports. There weren't. Much more likely, some were startled. They surely knew better, but the shock they felt was real. We might call it the shock of the real, the feeling that what they were seeing was real, even when they knew it wasn't. In fact, the point of the stories is precisely to call attention to this contradiction between the unanticipated feeling that the film induces and the knowledge that it is just a movie. The stories are themselves surprising precisely because those who hear them know that motion pictures aren't real, that while they may be drawn from reality by means of a mechanical device, what that device produces is merely an image painted in light. So the effect of the stories is to suggest, paradoxically, that while they are *obviously* not real, they can nevertheless *seem* to be.

Film theories and philosophy

There is (or was, for much of the time since the beginning of cinema) a long-standing debate among film critics and theorists regarding the distinctive characteristics and capacities of film. Central to this debate – between "realists" and "formalists" – is the question of how film, as a medium, relates to reality. "Realists" held that what made film unique was its direct connection with the real. Because film, for the most part, is made up of sequential photographs, created by pointing a camera at something in the world, it seems it should be able to capture and preserve reality as it is, in all its changing detail. It can take the fleeting moment and hold on to it, so it can be experienced again and again. The influential French film critic André Bazin compared it to the way ancient Egyptians preserved their loved ones as mummies, but suggested that film did even better: it could keep things alive ("Ontology of the Photographic Image" in *What Is Cinema, Vol. 1*). By contrast, "Formalists," such as Rudolph Arnheim, insisted that film transforms reality, that when it is captured on film, reality becomes something other than it was. It is experienced differently. The sensory richness of the world is reduced to the auditory and the visual. Textures and depths are eliminated, and we are left with a soundtrack accompanying a two-dimensional, framed image, whose range of colors and qualities of light are radically changed from what we experience in everyday life (*Film as Art*). What is distinctive to cinema, for the formalists, is not that it captures reality, but that it transforms it (sometimes into art).

In fact, the dominant approach to filmmaking, an approach we often associate with Hollywood but that is pursued to varying degrees in most major film traditions throughout the world, is neither strictly realist nor formalist. While compelling and influential films exhibiting the "realist" and "formalist" tendencies have continued to be made throughout the history of cinema, it wasn't long after film's beginnings that the most popular approach to filmmaking was one that neither emphasized the unfiltered reality of its depictions nor the artifice involved in their portrayal. It focused, rather, on dramatic storytelling by way of motion pictures. The so-called "classical" (or "classicist") style of filmmaking puts the artifice of film to use, employing the various techniques we have considered under the headings of "framing" and "ordering" in order to immerse the audience into the unfolding experience of an emotionally gripping and (at least) plausible story. Films in the classical style can't be too formalist. The framing and editing, for example, shouldn't call attention to itself in such a way as to detract from the audience's absorption in the situations unfolding on screen. They shouldn't, either, be strictly "realist," in the sense of seeming to show us something real that just happened to be captured on camera (Bordwell et al., *The Classical Hollywood Cinema*). Films in the classical style don't simply let reality unfold; they present it in the way that draws most fully on the audience's attention and emotional engagement. While they needn't be "realist," they do need to be "realistic" in the sense that audiences can suspend disbelief enough to relate to and care about their characters and the situations they find themselves in. While classical films may not deliver "reality" as it is, they are often celebrated (when they are successful) for transporting their audiences into a new reality, for providing a window into another world and allowing their audience to experience it vicariously.

We should note, though, that the debate as a whole – between realism and formalism, on the one hand, and between these and the classical style – takes something basic for granted: that "reality" is well understood. That reality is just what is there, before the camera captures it. Realists claimed that film captures and preserves reality, that films allow audiences to experience things as they really are. Formalists held that film manipulates reality, transforming what it presents. Classical films deliver audiences into a new reality, they create cinematic worlds that are similar, in some respects, but to varying degrees different from the real world that their spectators inhabit in their everyday lives. The realists presuppose, then, that reality is such that the camera can capture it and that the encounter with reality can be evoked upon the screen. Classical films seem to make new realities appear, and formalists insist that what we get on the screen is not reality but its distortion by the camera. All of this presumes, once again, that the distinction between reality and its distortions by the camera is, more or less, clear.

Philosophers have tended to be suspicious of such assumptions. What people tend to consider real are just the things that surround them, understood in the ways they are usually thought of, as self-contained entities we can interact with. Philosophers have consistently argued that we need to look beyond our ordinary ideas about reality, beyond the opinions drawn from our everyday experiences and educations regarding how things are. They tend to consider that the answer to the question "what is reality?" is not at all obvious. If it seems to be, that is part of the problem: that the way things seem to be is not always how they really are. We are often mistaken in our assessments of specific situations, and it is not impossible that we are wrong about most everything. We are sometimes baffled by the worldviews of others, but they are likely to be as baffled by ours. While one or the other of us might be right, the fact that at least one of us is wrong implies there is a difference between how things seem to us as a whole (between any given "worldview") and the way things, on the whole, truly are. At the very least, we only see a side of things, how they appear to us, given our histories, background, educations, and experience, and on the basis of the specific character of our cognitive and sensory apparatus. Philosophy, arguably, begins with just this insight, that things may not be as they seem, and with the question of how they really are.

Thales, for example, the Milesian philosopher, initiated the ancient Greek quest for the true nature of reality (around 600 BCE) by claiming the apparent multiplicity and variety of things was in fact the result of a common, underlying, material substance. He identified this underlying substance with water, which makes sense given both that water is essential for life, and that it is something we can see undergoing changes from solid to liquid to gas. Others considered there to be more than one underlying substance and that changes resulted from their combinations and separations. Parmenides followed shortly with the even more radical insistence that change itself was merely appearance, that the true nature of reality is to be unchanging and eternal. Heraclitus responded that what was unchanging was the process of change itself. He compared reality to a flowing river, which remains the same even as its waters are constantly changing. Pythagoras considered that the unchanging truths about reality could be discovered mathematically. Democritus held – in a theory that anticipates the discoveries of modern physics – that what remains the same are unbreakable atoms which he considered to make up everything. These mostly invisible atoms combine to make up the things we perceive all around us, generating the diversity of appearances by entering into varying configurations. Plato's so-called theory of the forms attempts to account for both change and identity, by positing that the underlying essence of things does not change, while appearances do. His student Aristotle distinguished, likewise, between the unchanging structure that gives a thing its identity, and the variable and contingent properties that give to individuals their differentiated appearances.

During the Middle Ages – beginning with the decline of classical culture in the fifth century and until the Renaissance which began around the fourteenth century – higher learning was largely confined to the clergy. Christian and Islamic philosophers considered the existence of God, asking how to conceive of a being held to be responsible for the creation of everything, including, according to some, the very fabric of space and time in which alone things can come into being and pass away. Others considered the existence of concepts, asking how our conceptions relate to the realities we conceive. Are concepts real, so that our very capacity to think them entails an insight into the true nature of reality, or are concepts merely words, meant to help us make sense of and bring order to our various experiences? Much later, at the time of the birth of modern science in the seventeenth century, René Descartes claimed that the senses are deceiving, that what appears to us is false, and that to discover the true nature of reality we need to employ reason. He argued that there were two fundamentally different kinds of realities, mental and physical, and that what constitutes the true identity of a person is her mind rather than her body. Subsequent philosophers have asked how minds and bodies could ever interact if they are essentially distinct. Philosophers ask a range of questions regarding the nature of reality, our knowledge of it, and how we should act in consequence, but at their heart is the basic observation that how things really are is not what they appear to be.

That things aren't what they seem to be, though, isn't obvious. In spite of the eighteenth-century philosopher Immanuel Kant's insistence that human beings have a rational interest in questions regarding the ultimate nature of reality, he also knew (and thought it proper) that for the most part we are caught up in the concerns of everyday practical life and experience. Philosophy doesn't come naturally. That much should be obvious from the fact that the way things seem to be is what, to all appearances, they are in fact. We can, of course, make mistakes. We might be fooled by optical illusions or magic tricks, for example. Still, we discover the trick and correct the mistake by investigating further, by comparing how things seemed to us at first with how they seem to us after taking a closer look. We don't, generally, begin to doubt everything just because on this or that occasion we made a mistake. We might consider that a dream is real, at least while we are sleeping. When we wake up, however, we realize it was only a dream and consider that how things appear to us then, while awake, is how they really are. Appearances are convincing, and it takes special work to cultivate the insight that things aren't as they appear. To say that someone *appears* to be telling the truth means that there are reasons to think that she is and it isn't at all obvious she isn't. What things seem to be is what we consider that they are, unless there are compelling grounds for thinking they aren't. So, while philosophy begins with the distinction between appearance and reality, it is not an easy or obvious distinction to make.

It is, though, in the cinema. For the most part, in the course of our everyday lives, we take appearances to be real. We don't, though, when the appearance is on screen. When we go to the movies we have what we might consider to be a philosophical advantage in the sense that we do, then, naturally distinguish between appearance and reality. We distinguish between what we see on screen and what we consider to be truly real. Yet cinema's appeal comes from the fact that we respond to it in some ways as if it were. We care about the characters, caught up as they are in situations that resemble those we are familiar with from everyday life, and we recognize what we see on screen in roughly the same way as we recognize the things of our everyday experience. So while films present an appearance that we know is not real, they draw their power from its appeal. When they work, they manage to present an appearance that we recognize to be unreal, but that nevertheless draws us in, convincing us to take an interest in it and care about what happens, as if the situations and events and people it portrayed were in fact real.

Unlike everyday life in which the difference between what seems to be and what truly *is* does not appear obvious, when we are watching a film the distinction seems natural. We know that what we are watching on screen is an appearance. Yet the film doesn't grip us unless we find it compelling, unless we accept it, for the moment, as if it really were. To enjoy the film we must, as they say, "suspend disbelief," which seems to mean that we should allow ourselves to be caught up in the experience of what is on screen as if it were something truly real. At the same time, we shouldn't react to what we see in the way we would if it were. This seemingly paradoxical relationship to what is seen on screen is illustrated powerfully by the stories surrounding the reception of one of the earliest films.

The Arrival of the Train, along with other early films by the Lumiére brothers, is often regarded as a signature example of the realist tendency in film. Yet what is fascinating about this film is its reputation as a film that not only evoked reality, but also seemed so real to its audiences that it caused them to leap out of their seats in fear. If the stories that surround the reception of the film were accurate, it would seem to have presented an appearance that was indistinguishable from reality. In fact, however, the stories are likely exaggerated, and the point of telling this story is, in part, to remind audiences that the alleged reaction to this film is inappropriate. Films may seem real, and that makes up much of their appeal, but sophisticated film-going audiences should and do know better than actually to react to them as if they were. A closer look at this film and its reception shows that what was from its inception the distinguishing mark of successful cinema is neither its reality nor its artificial character, but the use of artificial means to create an experience that seems to be real but that we know is not.

In philosophical terms, what cinema manages to make appear is, precisely, the distinction between appearance and reality. This, we might say, is film's most basic affinity with philosophy. Film evokes, naturally, an awareness of the distinction with which philosophy begins. In its capacity to evoke and explore this distinction between appearance and reality – to put us in the presence of something that seems real but isn't, and to thereby provoke us into a consideration of just what it means to be real – film is (or does) philosophy.

Mistaking film for reality

The early film *Arrival of the Train* creates the impression for audiences of a reality unfolding on screen, one that could almost be mistaken for an event taking place in the very same room. Subsequent films such as *The Countryman and the Cinematograph* (1901) by the British inventor and filmmaker R.W. Paul (shamelessly copied almost shot for shot the next year by the American Edison company) dramatized the power of this illusion by depicting an uneducated "country bumpkin" who cowered and ran

Figure 3.2 The countryman fears for his life.

away in the theater when he saw the train "approaching" on screen. Jean-Luc Godard, whose film *Breathless* will be the focus of the final part of this book, includes a similar scene in his 1963 anti-war film *Les Carabiniers*. In that film a poor farmer, tricked into enlisting as a soldier arrives in a city and watches a film for the very first time. Not only does he throw up his arms to protect himself from a train that seems to be arriving on screen, he also moves around the theater in an attempt to get a better look at a woman who is undressing on screen. These films at once remind their audiences of the power of the cinema, that it can fool those who don't know better into thinking it is real, and at the same time congratulate those audiences for being wiser, for being unlike the ignorant "bumpkin" who can't distinguish between the cinematic appearance and the reality it depicts.

R.W. Paul's film, in which the audience watches as the "countryman" stands in a theater, watching a film about a train and responding inappropriately, illustrates that to watch a film appropriately requires that the audience be capable of differentiating between what appears on screen and what is truly real. We, the audience, see the man and see that he sees a screen, just like the one on which we see him. We also see that he mistakes what he sees for reality, that he seems to think the train will run him down, and we, who know far better, are amused by his mistake. The film amuses because it demonstrates just how silly a mistake it is, by showing us, on screen, that there is an obvious difference between reality and the screened image.

The way it shows this seems simple enough. What we seem to see is, simply, a man who doesn't know what film is, and can't tell the difference between an image of a train and a real one. In fact, what it shows is somewhat subtler. The film doesn't merely indicate the difference between appearances and reality by poking fun at someone who can't tell the difference, but shows precisely the nature of his mistake, and thereby highlights what is distinctive to cinema.

In the short bit of the film that still survives, one can see the man, wearing what appears to be the wrong kind of attire for a night on the town. He stands near the edge of a movie theater, close to the screen and ahead of where an audience would normally be seated. There is a curtain, pulled to the side. We see on screen an image of a young woman in a white dress, dancing. She dances in a lavish building whose walls are decorated in much the same way as the walls of the theater. Both the image of the theater and the image of the screen are in black and white. So it might appear at this point to the audience of the film as if the dancer is on a stage, in the theater with the countryman. If we look closely, however, we can see that it is not a stage but a projection on a screen. It bounces slightly relative to the theater wall, and the edges of the projected room extend somewhat beyond where the stage would be, reflecting off of the simulated pillar that would have marked the stage's edge. While this is something we can see if we pay close attention, it is apparent that the man does not notice it.

That the screen is not a stage becomes much more obvious to the audience a moment later, but at just that moment we can see that the man is not looking. He dances in the aisle along with the woman in the white dress, and in his exuberance turns away from the screen for a moment so that he is looking away as we see the room and the dancer disappear and the screen go blank. Then the scene changes to reveal an entirely new setting: a railway upon which a train is moving forward, at an angle that leads it to approach the side of the screen closest to the countryman. He turns, and is at first apparently more excited than startled. He looks to where, presumably, the audience is seated and points out the oncoming train. As it appears to come closer, however, he begins to worry. He throws his hands out, attempting perhaps to signal that it should stop, and then, irrationally, to protect himself as he fears it will go off its rails and collide into him.

Rather than simply demonstrating the failure of the countryman to appreciate that what is on screen isn't real, this bit of the film highlights for its audience the distinction between the reality of what takes place on a stage and what appears on a screen. It is this distinction that the countryman fails to appreciate. This is at least in part because he failed to notice the cut: he was looking away when the screen went black between the dancing and the train sequences. The cut reveals clearly to the audience that the screen lacks depth, that it is just a wall, reflecting light. What it shows is illusory. It is by convention – a convention that can be broken – that there is no interaction between the audience and what takes place on stage. (That the countryman appears not to know or care about this convention suggests that he has little more familiarity with the theater than with the cinema.) The separation between events on screen and their audience is not merely conventional. It is, we might say, metaphysical. They belong to different realities. Or, they are "real" differently. The stage and what takes place upon it exist in the same space as the audience, but are set apart. By contrast, what takes place on screen is, we might say, a world apart. It isn't happening then and there. We might say it isn't happening at all but has already happened. It is a past (or imagined) event that the audience is only, just now, getting a chance to witness. If it can be said to exist at all it is in an imaginary (or perhaps merely remembered) time and space.

This is what the countryman fails to notice, and what this film suggests is necessary to appreciate cinema: that what it shows seems to be real, but isn't. To appreciate it is at once to be caught up in the experience, accepting it as if it were real, and yet knowing all along, and acting in accordance with this knowledge, that it is not a part of the reality the audience inhabits. For this to work, what appears on screen does have to be something that will captivate the audience, and yet it also needs to indicate its distance from everyday life. It would be a very different kind of experience if the audience genuinely could not tell the difference between what they see on screen and what they encounter in their everyday lives. One can, of course, imagine that someday (perhaps not far off) a three-dimensional immersive or virtual reality experience would be (virtually) indistinguishable from the experience of life. In that case, the reaction of the countryman, throwing up his hands or screaming in fear, would be both reasonable and (likely) inevitable. That isn't what takes place in the cinema, in spite of the stories surrounding the *Arrival of the Train*.

In both the case of what we see on screen and on the stage, we often do have feelings about them and associations with them that resemble those we'd feel and experience in everyday life if the things we saw were everyday occurrences. When the countryman sees the young woman dancing, he's not wrong to share her joy. He's not wrong to appreciate her youth and beauty, just as he would if the young woman were dancing in the same room. Where he makes a mistake is in standing up and dancing with her. Even if she were there on stage, as he seems to assume, he would be expected to appreciate the performance from a distance, seated and observant, only applauding when it's finished. If it really were a stage he could, of course, not only stand up in the aisles but climb up there with her. There would be nothing to prevent him but agreed upon social norms, and, perhaps, a stage manager or usher. It is, once again, only convention that separates the world of the audience and the performance on stage.

Similarly, in the case of the train, he's not wrong to marvel at the technological power of locomotion, or even to feel some trepidation as it seems to approach. He might even, for a moment, be startled by its sudden appearance. He should, though, know better than to consider it might really be a train suddenly appearing in the space he'd taken for a stage. He should know better because real things like trains don't suddenly appear out of nowhere; if they do suddenly appear, assuming they hadn't simply been hidden, they must not be real, they must be merely apparent. What is on screen can't enter the space of the audience, and the audience can't enter into its space. It is not nothing, but it isn't what it seems to be, and isn't what it's felt to be. To appreciate it for what it is, is to understand that what we see on the screen isn't part of everyday life. Its separation from everyday life, moreover, is not merely a matter of convention. It is a matter of metaphysics. It belongs to a different kind of reality.

Specifically, as noted, the kind of reality we get on screen is the reality of an appearance. It is, however, a distinctive kind of appearance, different from the kind we encounter in the theater. In the theater, we see actors on a stage, and we are meant to consider them as if they were the characters they play. On screen, we see images, of people and places and things that actually appear to have taken place elsewhere and in another time than that of the audience's ongoing experience. Indeed, in some cases, they seem to belong to another world entirely. The people and places and things that these images depict seem to be real, in much the same way as the theater and its inhabitants are real. At the same time, however, as they seem to be real, they also show that they do not belong to the ongoing reality to which the spectator belongs. The film demonstrates that what it shows is not real, both in the sense that what it shows are images, and in the sense that what they are images of, are people and things belonging to a different time and space than the one the spectator inhabits. That time and space, moreover, have never been, at least not in the way they appear. Another way of putting this is that what appears on screen is not just an appearance (something that seems to be real but isn't) but an appearance in which the very difference between appearance and reality itself appears. It shows what seems to be real, and also demonstrates that what it shows is not part of the reality of the audience. That is to say: it shows it isn't real. In order to clarify this paradoxical nature of cinematic appearances – that what it shows both appears to be real and also shows it isn't – we should first be clear about the nature of appearances generally.

The nature and variety of appearances

The first thing to notice is that the distinction between appearance and reality is more complicated than might appear, since appearances are themselves real. Appearances may be false, but they are not nothing. Appearances must be real, since if they weren't they wouldn't even appear. Yet their reality is not what it seems to be. In part, this is because appearances seem to stand on their own, but are in fact dependent realities. Appearances depend on two things, generally speaking: a perceiver and some set of conditions that cause that perceiver to perceive the appearance. In the case of movies, the locus of the appearance is what we see on screen. Members of the audience are the perceivers, and what causes the appearance is the projection of light through a filmstrip (or, these days, from a digital projector or an LCD screen) as well as the filmmaking process responsible for producing images on that filmstrip (or disc or tape or hard drive). What appears in the cinema seems to be real things: real people doing things, making sounds, in real settings. What appears, in fact, are shadows and light, sometimes colored, sometimes black and white, as well as sound, from an orchestra or piano in the early days, or, later, from a recorded soundtrack emanating from speakers. Of course, shadows, light, colors, and sounds are real too, but what makes them appearances is that what they show audiences seems to be something it is not.

So appearances are, first, not what they seem to be. Second, they are dependent realities, that depend, both, on the conditions that make them appear, and, equally, on there being someone or something they can appear to. Appearances are those realities whose metaphysical status was perhaps best described by the eighteenth-century Irish philosopher Bishop Berkeley. He proclaimed, famously, that *esse ist percipi* or that "to be is to be perceived" (24). He considered that what we take to be the material world around us is in fact merely a rich set of internally consistent perceptions, what might as well be an elaborate dream, except one from which no one ever wakes up. Strictly speaking, this doesn't mean that Berkeley held there to be nothing but appearances, since he did assume that in addition to perceptions, there exist perceivers, or souls. He also held that God exists, and considered him to be the ultimate cause of the elaborate and internally consistent dream shared by all (that we call reality). Berkeley's insight is, then, consistent with what we have seen so far regarding the nature of appearances: that they are dependent realities and are not what they seem to be. For Berkeley the appearance that is the world is dependent in just the ways we've noted: it is dependent on perceivers and dependent on a cause (God) who is ultimately responsible for the perceivers perceiving. It is also not what it seems to be, because it seems to be a material world existing outside of us in time and space, but is in fact merely a collection of perceptible ideas.

Rather than admit, at this stage, that nothing at all (apart from souls and God) goes beyond appearance, we should note that some things, at least, are obviously mere appearances. A rainbow, for example, is an appearance. It isn't what it seems to be. It isn't a colored semi-circular object floating in the sky. It is, rather, an optical phenomenon, something seen in the sky as a result of the reflection and refraction of the sun's light due to rain and water droplets dispersed in the air. The appearance of rainbows depends on a set of conditions, its cause, and on beings with eyes who can see them. Colors likewise can be said to be appearances. What seems to be red, say, an apple, is a real organic object whose surface manages to absorb some light from its surroundings but reflects back just the light of a frequency we perceive as red. Shadows, as well, are appearances. They seem to be dark objects, moving on the wall or on the ground, but are in fact the result of obstructed light, light that is partially blocked by an object or opaque substance that stands between a light source and the surface where the shadow appears. To see a shadow is not to see a real thing in the shape of the shadow, but is to see light in the process of being obstructed by something in such a way as to suggest that shape.

Theater also presents an appearance, insofar as what we perceive upon the stage seems to be dramatic action, such as that of Romeo kissing Juliet in fourteenth century Verona, but is in fact a performance, played out by actors on a set pretending to be the star-crossed lovers. Of course, in addition to being an appearance of dramatic action, theater also presents us with the reality of actors on a stage, in the same space as their audience. The actors and the production team are responsible for the appearance, but what appears as a result is drama. Films are appearances too, but different from those of the theater. What we see in the film isn't what it seems to be: people, objects, situations, all taking place in a world. It appears as it does only as a result of conditions outside of itself (such as the projector and the filmmakers and the camera and the objects it filmed) that do not appear within the film itself, and it exists as a film only for an audience. Unlike theatrical productions, though, films are, we might say, merely appearances. They don't, for example, bring us into the actual presence of real trains, in addition to the appearance of trains, or into the presence of real actors in addition to the appearance of the characters they play. Usually (at least in the absence of advanced special effects and CGI) we can presume that there was a real train or a real actor filmed in some real place in order to create the cinematic appearance, but they are not accessible through the screen, and they no longer need be present during the appearance. Indeed, they may, as a result of cinematic technique, appear to be places they'd never been or doing things they never actually did.

We've already noted that the full appreciation of theatrical appearances requires the acceptance of certain conventions, conventions with which the ignorant countryman in R.W. Paul's film seemed to be unfamiliar. Someone who came upon a theatrical production, without knowing what it was, would also be presented with an appearance, but not the appearance it was meant to be. They would see something that seemed to them like something other than it was. They would, for example, seem to see people on stage acting strange, rather than people on stage acting. For theatrical appearances to work, their audiences must respond to them in roughly the ways specified by convention. We understand that those we see on stage are actors, and that the stage is just a stage. Yet part of what makes the drama engaging is the tacit agreement, or convention, to consider them as if they were the characters they play, and to treat the stage and set as if it were the arena in which their story unfolds. While stage conventions vary, and some of the most interesting theatrical innovations work by breaking with specific conventions, it is usually accepted that the performers and the audience are distinct and that they should not interact.

For cinema, as we've seen, this is not merely a convention, since it's not even possible for the audience to interact with the actors on screen. The fact is: they aren't there. We are not therefore required to distinguish between the actors present in the same room with us and the characters they play. We are presented only with their moving images. That means that we don't perceive them directly. We don't see the countryman (any more than we see the actor who played him), but see his moving image, and what that image shows is him in a theater, somewhere else than where we are when we watch. We may or may not consider the scenario that depicts him as fictional. Some might even think what they see there is a documentary. They might think they are seeing footage of a real event in which a man is frightened by a train he sees on screen. Even so, they wouldn't likely make the same mistake it shows him making, of thinking it is happening then and there where in fact there are only shadows and light, flickering on the screen. If they do consider he is an actor, and that what the film shows never really happened except as a performance, they might still laugh at the film because it depicts a situation that they find at least plausible (and if it was real it would be laughable). In that case, though, we might say that what they see on screen is roughly like an image of theater. They see images of actors, who they know to be actors, and then adopt the conventional attitude towards them that they would if they were actors on the stage. They would consider them as if they were the characters they play, and respond to the scenario they act out in the ways they would if it were a dramatic performance, with the difference that in this case that performance would, potentially, not be taking place on a stage, but on location, in a real setting of the sort where the scenarios depicted by the performance normally take place. If it was taking place on a stage – if, for example, a scene from the film depicted a theatrical performance – the stage it took place on wouldn't be a stage in the theater from which the audience watched it.

What we see on screen, then, are moving images, of people, places, and things. These are usually, but not always, recognizable as more or less similar to the people and places and things we encounter in everyday life. Images are not real. They don't even seem to be, except, perhaps, to someone like the countryman who may have never seen a moving image. What images seem to be is a likeness of something. What makes them images (as opposed to symbols or signs or icons, that may also resemble something they stand for) is that we seem to see through the image to that of which they are an image. That isn't to say that the image is transparent, or that we see someone or something through it as we would through a window. We don't, or we don't quite. Nevertheless, in seeing it, we seem to see something else. We see it as presenting to us the look or appearance of something other than itself, that of which it is the image. Images, in other words, are obviously appearances. They are dependent realities, which seem to show us something other than themselves: the situations, people or things of which they are an image.

That they are appearances distinguishes images from, for example, symbols. Symbols stand for something other than themselves, but that thing they stand for does not itself appear through the symbol. For those who understand them, they indicate that of which they are a symbol. Or they call to mind the idea that they symbolize. A symbol's meaning is not established by resemblance but by agreement. To understand a symbol is to be familiar with a convention: that some group agrees that symbol stands for something specific. Symbols don't, usually, resemble what they symbolize. At least, they don't need to. Images do. They show us what the thing they depict looks like.

For simplicity's sake (though the matter is far from simple and could easily be the focus of another book, and *is* the focus of several), we might consider here just two paradigmatic types of image: a representational painting and a photograph. To simplify even further, consider just two portraits, one a painting and the other a photograph. Both, presumably, resemble their subject. To see them as portraits is to see them as showing, to some extent, what their subject looks like (or at least what he or she might look like under certain conditions). To see the image as an image of something, other than itself, is to see the image as an appearance. Specifically, it is to see it as an appearance that is clearly not the same as the thing of which it is an image, but does show us how that thing appears, what it would look like if we were to see it.

Of course, to see the image is not the same as to see their subject. To see their subject in the portrait requires that we "look past" certain features specific to the medium, whether painting or photography, and that we do not attribute those features to the subject but to the way that subject appears through that medium. Precisely what those features are, that we must learn to "look past," in order to appreciate the image as an image, are not exactly fixed by the medium, because the nature of artistic media, whether it is painting or photography or film, is not fixed, but evolving. Media forms evolve both as a result of technical innovation and as a result of artistic accomplishments, and these can also be motivated by cultural and economic changes. So, for example, an early photographic portrait would be strictly monochrome, or black and white, but no one would consider that the person it depicts, or their clothing, or the background against which they stood, was monochrome. By convention, we accept that the early photographic image does not resemble what it depicts in that respect. Nevertheless, by exhibiting gradations of brightness and shadow the successful portrait does manage to show us what someone looks like (or looked like), at least from a certain perspective and in a certain light. The conventions that govern painted portraiture are even more complex. The fact that a painting is colored does not always entail that its subject has the same coloring. If the portrait is done in an abstract style, the shape of the face in the painting might not even closely resemble the shape that the actual face would appear to have under ordinary perceptual conditions. Nevertheless, if it is to be a portrait, it should manage in some way to capture the look of that face, such that to see the painting (properly) would amount to seeing something of what that face looks like.

A photograph is a still image. A photograph of someone is obviously not the same as them. Yet, in looking at the photograph, we seem to see something of the person whose image it is. Take, for example, the Polaroid photograph that Leonard (played by Guy Pearce) scrutinizes towards the end of the film *Memento* (2000). As Lenny looks at the photograph, he *sees himself*, at some point in the past. While he suffers from memory loss, he can't actually remember the event depicted in the photograph. Yet he clearly recognizes himself, as well as the emotional state he was in when the photograph was taken. He seems happy. He seems proud of having accomplished something. The still image, though, is not enough to tell him what he was proud of, what he'd just done. It captures the look of a moment, but doesn't give us its context. Lenny has to rely upon such photographs in lieu of his memories, but to say what they mean he has to add captions. This one is missing a caption, and Teddy, the cop, is there to tell him what it means. He doesn't like what Teddy tells him, so he burns the photograph, destroying its memory.

Cinema can not only capture a moment, or a look, it can capture a movement, bringing it to life. It can provide images of events. It can depict a story. All Lenny has are his Polaroids and the notes he has written to himself on the photographs and in the tattoos on his body. We, who have seen the film, know what he refuses to acknowledge. We know what will happen as a result of his destruction of the photograph. He had just killed a man he thought had killed his wife. Teddy told him that he'd already

Figure 3.3 Polaroid of Lenny in *Memento* (2000).

killed another man for the same alleged crime, and that this photograph was the proof. The photograph alone was not enough to tell the story, to tell what happened and why. Still, images can only show us how things look from a single perspective at a specific moment. They can't show us how that moment came about or why. If he would just caption the photo so he could remember this, it might end his cycle of vengeance. Having burnt the photo, he won't have any way of remembering that he had already accomplished his revenge quest. So he'll begin his search for his wife's killer yet again.

Moving images are, traditionally at least, made up of still images, but these are projected in a rapid sequence so that the individual images are not perceived distinctly, which results in the appearance of movement. The actual film is not the same as the filmstrip (or the DVD, or Blu-ray or any other recording medium). The film itself is what appears on screen and what is heard on the soundtrack. It is what the audience experiences when they watch the film in a theater. We have already distinguished between appearances – what is perceived in the appearance – and the conditions that make that perception possible, which include both a perceiver and a set of conditions that leads that perceiver to perceive what they do in the ways that they do. The medium upon which the film is recorded belongs to the conditions for the possibility of the cinematic appearance, the cinematic moving image. The film itself, an appearance, is what is seen and heard by the audience when the film is played or projected.

That film presents a moving image serves to account for its distinctive character as an appearance. To experience what is on screen as an image is to recognize that it isn't real, or that it is real only as an image. Yet what appears by way of the perception of an image does seem to be more than just an image, it seems to be a reality in its own right. What appears by way of a moving image seems to be an event drawn from life itself: real people engaged in real actions in real settings. Even if the real people who appear seem to be actors, playing a part in a fictional story, they nevertheless seem to be real actors. Even if the setting they play against seems to be a set, it nevertheless seems to be a real set, located somewhere real. In some moving images the reality we seem to encounter, that goes beyond the image, is simply the reality of those conditions that produced the image: actors being captured on camera, framed and arranged in a certain way by the filmmakers. In that sense, the encounter reminds us that it is merely an image, reminds us that it is something made. In other cases, though, what we seem to encounter through the image draws us in, taking on what seems to be a life of its own, as if the fact it happened to be captured on film was irrelevant to it. We don't completely forget that what we see is just an image, as evidenced by the fact that we only react and don't attempt to interact with the situation we witness there. We may laugh and cry, or give a sudden startled scream. We may become caught up in and caring about what we see on screen. Yet we remain in our seats. We are not confronted by a situation we can do anything about. We are merely witnesses to the image of a situation that may or may not have taken place.

We have contrasted images with, on the one hand, theatrical performances, and with symbols, on the other, by noting that it is by convention and not resemblance that we take the performance to stand for a dramatic action and the symbol to stand for what it means. It should be noted, though, that there are conventions that govern our appreciation of images, too. Some of these are conventions with which one must be familiar to appreciate the image *as* an image, and others that affect our appreciation of what they depict. An example, as noted above, is when a moving image depicts actors on a stage: to find ourselves caught up in and appreciating the drama, we should at once recognize it as an image of actors and at the same time focus not upon the actors but see through them to the characters they play. It is not always a simple matter to sort out the differences between the different levels at which conventions can be operative in an audience's appreciation of appearances. There are, also, different kinds of images, and the line between, say, an image and a symbol that resembles what it symbolizes is not fixed.

The fact that to appreciate an image, whether it is a photograph or painting or a moving image such as film, requires some familiarity with the medium and its historically evolving conventions, technologies, and techniques has implications for the creators as well as the appreciators of images. Recall that appearances are dependent realities, and that they depend upon both a set of conditions that produce the appearance and on a perceiver to whom it appears. Where appearances are not natural, like rainbows, but are deliberately produced, like a painting or a photograph or a film, the producer needs to consider both the perceptual capacities of its audience and the conventions they will draw upon in their appreciation of it, that may shape and modify their perceptions, but will certainly affect their interpretations.

To create a successful appearance through the image, its creator must know both how it will be perceived, and how it is likely to be understood. An image produced with ultraviolet light, for example, will not function as an image. It will not show what something looks like to an audience which lacks the capacity for perceiving ultraviolet light. At the same time, a painting might not function as an image at all for an audience utterly unfamiliar with the conventions it employs. In such a case, audiences might complain that they don't understand the painting, or that they don't know what they are looking at. Not only painting, but photography and cinema also require for their appreciation an awareness and acceptance of certain conventions. We have seen that a part of what the film about the countryman accomplished was to call attention for its audience to the fact that to appreciate cinema, one must be familiar with the difference between the cinema and the theater, and that the countryman was not.

What makes the cinematic moving image – say, that of Leonard Shelby in *Memento*, frantically writing a caption at the bottom of a Polaroid so that he'll remember what it is supposed to remind him of when he has forgotten the moment he took it – what makes this moving image obviously distinct from a still image – such as the uncaptioned Polaroid he'd had taken just after completing his revenge – is that moving images are images of events. While still images seem to show us what a person, place or thing (or a group of people and things in place) looks like, moving images seems to show what they do, or how things happened. They show us, for example, the Lumière train rolling in, people milling about on the station, some getting on, some getting off, some waiting for those who've arrived. They show us the moment when Lenny, looking in the mirror at clues tattooed on his body realizes that his friend Teddy is the man he'd been looking for, and writes this on his photo. Or, they show him holding a gun to Teddy's head, while Teddy begs him to realize he is making a mistake. Even where nothing happens on screen, as when the camera stays still for a moment on a close-up of one of Lenny's Polaroids, what the camera shows us is a pause, which is also a happening, a situation unfolding through time, even if just for a moment. In this case, what it seems to show us is that Lenny is looking at the photograph, and to show *that* is quite different than to show what the picture shows, which is what its subject looks like. A moving image of a picture is thus not the same as the picture. Still images *can* suggest an event, by depicting its culminating moment, but moving images show the event. More precisely, they appear to show what it would be like to perceive that event from a specific perspective.

Cinema, then, presents a distinctive kind of appearance. It is the kind of appearance that shows what it would look like to perceive an event from a specific perspective that is nevertheless not identical with the perspective of the perceiver to whom it appears. When we watch a movie, it is as if we are perceiving an event unfolding in front of us, and we feel about it much the same as we would if we were in the presence of that event. Other media than film can of course do something similar, yet cinema is distinctive in the degree to which it can evoke in audiences the experience of what at once seems to be real but is at the same time clearly separate from the reality of their life. Other art forms, such as literature and poetry, for example, can describe events in ways that lead us to think and feel roughly as we would if we'd heard about them actually happening. Yet they don't literally make these events appear. We don't perceive them, but draw upon our memory and imagination to make sense of their accounts.

Painting, sculpture, and photography do give us something to perceive, but they can at most suggest its movement indirectly. What they may make appear is a moment drawn from an event, but not an event itself. None of these art forms has the same power, at least to the same degree, to evoke the experience of being confronted by a reality that is illustrated by the founding myth of cinema. We don't, for example, jump out of our seats when we read the description of a train, or even if we saw a painting or a photograph that suggested its emergence from the frame.

It is, perhaps, theater that comes closest to the power of cinema in allowing us to perceive and feel confronted by actions unfolding in time. Its power to evoke the realities it depicts, however, requires that we adopt the convention of accepting that the people and things we see on the stage stand in for characters and things in a reality apart. The audience perceives the movements of the actors on the stage directly, but those movements are meant to evoke events that the audience cannot perceive. To experience the drama requires that the audience consider the actions of the actors as if they were the actions of the characters they play, taking place somewhere else than in the theater where the audience sits. The people, things, and events that we witness on screen in the cinema, however, are by their very nature set apart. What we see on screen are moving images, which show us what it would look like to perceive the events of which they are the images. We encounter through those images something that seems to be real, and yet is not there with us. Even if what they show us are obviously actors playing parts, they are not playing those parts in our presence. It may require, as we saw in the case of the countryman, some familiarity with the conventions of cinema to notice and recall that the events we see happening on screen are not taking place in the same space as the theater, that they are not happening to us, and we cannot interact with them. Yet we do tend to think about and respond to those events emotionally as if they were, even though we know that they aren't.

Yet the cinematic moving image does not put the entirety of the event on display. It shows only a part of it. We have a specific perspective upon the countryman, for example, as he reacts to the image of the train. We see him from the viewpoint of another member of the audience, someone seated in the theater, since the filmmakers placed the camera where the audience would be. The film may suggest that there is an audience, occupying roughly the space from which the camera would have recorded the image, but that audience does not appear within the film. We don't see the audience itself, so we cannot see how they react to the countryman's inappropriate reactions.

As a matter of fact, there may not have been an audience. The event may have been staged specifically for the camera, yet it does seem as if there is an audience and that the film could have shown it. In general, it always appears that there is more to the events that films put on display than the portion of these events that appears on screen. That the events films show us seem to have more to them than what is shown suggests that these events are at least to some degree independent from how they appear. It may be that this impression is false. It may be that what we see of those events is all there is to them, since they were filmed specifically for the camera and there is no other perspective from which they could have been perceived. Yet this is not how things appear. Films show us what it would look like to experience those events from specific vantage points, but they also make it seem that there is more to the events they show us than what appears on screen.

Films show us what it would look like and be like to experience the events they portray from a variety of specific perspectives. We do not actually adopt those perspectives. We retain our own perspective, and can look away from the screen and around the theater or around the room from which we view the film. The film does not bring us into the situation in which the event occurred, and yet that situation does seem to appear, indirectly, through the image. What seems to appear in an appearance is something real. Moving images, then, seem to show us something real, an event whose reality is independent from the image itself.

The reality of cinematic appearances

It may seem, though, like a mistake to suggest that moving images show us something real. After all, the most popular films are fictional. They depict situations that aren't real, and in many cases couldn't be. Usually, they don't even seem to be real in the sense of seeming to show us something that really happened somewhere. They don't actually show us something real, other than the reality of the appearance, but they do seem to show us something that isn't merely an appearance. That is, as we have seen, the nature of appearances. Appearances seem to be something they aren't. It is not that the cinema always gives us an image of something actually real, but that it shows us situations that (at least to some degree) seem to be. They can seem to be real, as well, in different senses. For convenience we might characterize these as seeming to be *simply real*, seeming to be *realistic*, and seeming to be artificial but displaying the *reality of the artifice*.

The first sense is the most obvious, and fits the film we started out with, the *Arrival of the Train*. It seems to show us a real train, arriving in a real station. It seems to be a direct moving image of reality, which shows us what it would look like to be there in the station watching the train roll forward from a specific vantage point. The reality depicted there seems to extend beyond what is shown to us on screen, and seems to be something that could have been filmed from another perspective.

The *Countryman and the Cinematograph* is more ambiguous. It could, potentially, also be seen as depicting a real situation. If there were a man like the countryman who really did fear for his life as he saw a train on screen, then it would be in principle possible for a camera to have captured his reaction. More likely (and in fact) it is fictional, and would be seen as such. There are, though, a few ways in which this fictional film might appear. It might be recognizably fictional, but seem real enough for audiences to make sense of and respond to it emotionally in the ways they would if it were.

They'd smile, perhaps, at the dancing young lady, and laugh at the man's mistake. It would seem realistic. Someone who was unconvinced by the acting, or who found the situation implausible, might see it as an image of a real actor, acting badly, or of a real performance, whose scenario was poorly conceived or directed. Note that here while the film itself seems artificial, what seems to appear through the film is the reality of the artifice: it would then seem, for example, to be a moving image of a situation in which amateur filmmakers and performers made a poor attempt to make a film about an uneducated bumpkin who doesn't know what film is. Of course, it might have been precisely the aim of the filmmakers to call attention to the artificiality of the situation, in which case it wouldn't have been a failure but an aesthetic choice. In that case, the reality that seems to appear through the image is the reality of the film production process, the reality of the filmmakers' decisions.

In the first case, of what seems to be simply real, the image appears to show us a reality whose existence is independent of the fact it was filmed. It is as if the situation it shows us is one that would have taken place whether or not it was captured on camera. The train would have arrived, and for those who (mistakenly) consider the *Countryman* film to be a documentary, it would seem that the man would have been startled, even if his reaction hadn't been filmed. The difference between the image of the event and the event itself is still, more or less, clear, even if one who lacked experience with motion pictures might be confused. Yet what seems to appear through the image, what the image appears to be an image of, is an autonomous event. It seems to be something that really happened, and would have happened whether or not it was captured on film.

In fact, the reality is never quite as simple as it seems, since the reality seems to be independent, and yet the camera is always present and the way that it is captured on camera has an impact on what the reality seems to be. The features of a film conducive to this appearance of an independent reality can vary, and have to do as much with style as with subject matter. They depend in part, for example, on an audience's general awareness of the film technologies existing in different historical periods. While a current event shot with a handheld and shaky video camera may seem to be real now, it would not seem so if it was supposed to be footage of the Second World War (since video cameras didn't exist back then, and most audiences, presumably, know this). Situations that seem real on camera often have a sense of contingency. They seem spontaneous and unpredictable. This can be the result of a choice to use unrecognizable actors, or actors whose performance is heavily improvised. It may also result from shooting the film in a public space, where some of what appears on screen is in fact spontaneous and unpredictable. Or it can be the product of a shooting style that emphasizes long takes, with minimal editing. Situations shot with multiple cameras, placed all too conveniently so as to capture reactions and close-ups of the people involved, where the footage is then edited together to produce a seamless experience, will not seem to be independently real in this sense, even if they do seem to be realistic.

In the other two cases – the realistic and the artificial – what the moving image seems to show us are dependent realities, situations that seem to have been created precisely so that they might be recorded on film. In both, the appearance delivers what seems (at least to a film-savvy audience, upon a moment's reflection) to be artificial, something made for the sake of the film and not something that would have existed independently of the creation of the film. In the first of these, however, which fits most popular films that end up in movie theaters, the film is to varying degrees realistic. Traces of artifice will remain and it may be quite obvious for audience members who stopped to consider, that what they were witnessing through the motion picture was not something that ever really happened in the way it seems to on screen. In spite of this, they tend to look past the artificiality and are caught up in the seeming reality of the situations the film depicts. They certainly would know, as they know in the case where they see something on screen that seems really to have happened, that it isn't happening then and there where they are. They know it isn't something they have to or even could interact with, because they are only perceiving its image and not confronted by its presence; and yet, what they seem to see through the image is realistic, and seems to them similar enough to the kinds of situations that actually happen or can happen, that they respond to it as if it were. They are caught up in the experience and they think about it and respond to it emotionally in roughly the same way as they would think about and respond to a situation that they'd heard about, say, on the news or in a documentary, but couldn't do anything about.

In the final situation, the artificiality is overt. It calls attention to itself so that the audience is explicitly aware of its traces, and is not as likely to look past it and become fully absorbed in the situation the film depicts. The reality that shows up through the image is the reality of the artifice. This might be a failure on the part of the filmmakers, or it might be deliberate. In the case where the artifice seems deliberate, it might be that the filmmakers are not as interested in convincing an audience of the reality of what appears on screen as in calling attention to their own virtuosity as manipulators of imagery, or in framing and arranging the elements so as to communicate ideas about them. It may be more subtle: they may be telling a story that is realistic, and that absorbs the audience, but also employing a variety of noticeable techniques in order to emphasize certain elements or to create a mood or a rhythm. Of course, they may have aimed to tell a compelling story and failed because of poor technique. In that case, the technique would stand out as problematic, rather than calling attention to itself as something to be interpreted. What would then appear on film is, for example, an unconvincing performance, anachronistic costumes, a bad set, and a blatantly inconsistent set of events. The film would fail to seem like anything other than artifice. It might still hold interest, but the interest would be in the artifice, and likely not so much in the scenario that was badly presented by its means. The reality it would display is the reality of the conditions that produce it, including both the reality of the set and the actors and props as well as the (unseen but apparent) reality of the decisions made by the filmmakers. Tommy Wiseau's infamous film *The Room* (2003), arguably, has just this quality; what draws audiences in is not the story that the film was intended to tell but the inadvertent documentary of a passionate and charismatic but largely incompetent filmmaker attempting to make a barely veiled film about himself. In his *Disaster Artist* (2017), the director and actor James Franco brings *that* story to life, in both heartbreaking and hilarious fashion.

In all three cases, then, the image *seems* to be of something real. In one case it shows us what appears to be independently real, in another it shows us what may be recognizably unreal but is nevertheless realistic, and in the final case it shows us what seems to be the reality of the appearance, seems to show us something of the process of its production or the artifice of its makers. Of course, these are not mutually exclusive categories, and, because they have to do with how things seem, they may overlap in various ways.

The appearance may be ambiguous. It is notable that one cannot always say with confidence which of the three it most seems to be, and a film that at first seems to fit one may later seem more obviously another. In particular, without knowing in advance how the film was made one cannot always be sure whether a film depicts something real or something merely realistic. This uncertainty may in fact heighten the sense of its urgency for the audience, and so filmmakers may employ a variety of techniques in an effort to undermine the tacit assumption on the part of the audience that what they are watching is fictional. In fact, though, even where the camera captures events that really took place, they may be framed and edited so that the end product on screen seems to be a moving image of events that never actually took place, at least not in the way that they seem to. Or events may be staged, and seem to be real. A film can seem to be shot on location in a documentary style, for example, and that style itself may merely be artifice, as in the case of so-called "found footage" fiction films such as the horror flick *The Blair Witch Project* (1999) and the superhero feature *Chronicle* (2012). Likewise, a documentary film can be shot in ways that make the audience wonder whether the events it portrays are fictional. Even in the case where the artifice seems obvious, as when the characters seem to be obviously actors playing parts badly, it may have been that it was deliberately shot just to seem that way. In the realm of appearances, things aren't always or exactly what they seem to be.

The point is not, though, that we can't be sure. With respect to appearances, it is not a question of being sure, but rather of how things seem. If things seem a certain way, they really do seem that way, whether or not they are in fact. If it seems to be ambiguous, that is really how it seems. That is the nature of appearances: they deliver a perception of something that seems to be a certain way, and we cannot tell on the basis of the perception alone whether what we perceive is really the way it seems. What we can say, on the basis of our reflections on the nature of appearances so far, is that there is more to appearances than appears in them.

Cinematic appearances result, roughly, from an interaction between the audience and the images that are projected upon and then reflect off of the screen. How things seem owes both to the technology and techniques that produce this projection, and to the perceptual faculties and understandings of the audience. At least in part how the audience sees what is on screen, and what it seems to them to show, will depend upon their past experiences in and outside of the theater. Also, what appears on screen will depend in part on the history of cinema, as not only those who watch the film but those who make it will have seen other films, and will take into account what they expect their audiences will understand and appreciate on the basis of their own experience with movies. In general, though, an audience's experience of the film will either focus upon what it shows or how it shows it, and which of these it focuses on depends both upon their own (active or passive) manner of attending to the film and to the features of the film that serve to draw their attention in one or the other of these directions. When their attention is focused on what the film shows, it seems to be a moving image of something real. It can seem to be independently real or it might seem like a reality fabricated for the sake of the film. If it does seem to be fabricated, or artificial, audiences can either focus on its artificiality or look past it to be caught up in the experience of the (seeming) reality it depicts.

There is, of course, more to appearances than, as they say, "meets the eye" (or the senses and awareness, more generally). There is a perceiver, whose manner of perceiving contributes to how things appear; and there are conditions in place that can be considered responsible for the perception. The way that the perceiver perceives is partly the result of her physical constitution, and partly the result of her background, and may be equally shaped by her conscious activity. The conditions responsible for her perception are her immediate surroundings, whose nature and whose impact upon her may be described and accounted for in various ways, such as from a physical or psychological or historical perspective. These two sides are not easily separable, since some of the conditions responsible for the perception include factors internal to the perceiver, such as the fact that the perceiver has sense organs, but also the fact that she has the inherited or acquired capacity to recognize and distinguish between the things that surround her. For someone watching the Lumiére brothers' famous film who'd never seen a train, for example, it wouldn't seem that a train was about to emerge from the screen; it might not even seem like some unfamiliar thing was getting closer, but might seem instead that a small object was getting progressively larger. To see it *as a* train requires, at least, that the perceiver have some notion of trains. The appearance is not, then, simply the result either of external conditions of the world or internal conditions of the perceiver's bodily or mental state, but of the interaction between these. This interaction between the perceiver and the conditions of the world gives rise to an appearance, a way things seem to be.

Cinema and reality

Films, as we have seen, deliver the appearance of reality, whether it is the reality of an independent situation, the realistic depiction of a fictional world, or the reality of the filmmaking process. Recall that at least the first two of these descriptions of what appears in the cinema match almost precisely how proponents of "realism," and of the "classical style" characterized film's distinctive potential: in terms of its capacity to show us reality as it truly is, and in terms of its ability to immerse its audience into an emotionally gripping and realistic story. The third possibility, that film can also reveal to us the reality of the filmmaking process itself, is what makes it possible for "formalist" filmmakers to make use of a variety of filmmaking techniques to manipulate and shape reality or to comment upon it. Realism, formalism, and classicism can, then, perhaps best be understood as attempts to characterize what is distinctive to cinema in terms of the kind of reality it renders apparent.

What should be clear now, however, is that none of them deliver more than an appearance. In none of its modes – whether a film seems to be more realist, or formalist, or classicist – does film actually confront us with reality as it is in itself. It is a mistake, for example, to say of a "realist" film that it puts us in direct or indirect contact with reality as it exists independently of cinema. Rather, each of them can be said to show us, in different ways, what we consider reality to be like. Film does not give us reality. It shows us what it looks like to us and can thereby indicate something of what we think about it. Film shows us how things seem to us to be. It gives us an appearance of reality. At the same time, because we recognize the appearance it delivers to be an appearance, and not real, film has the capacity to highlight for us the difference between reality and appearance.

On the one hand, we consider reality to be what is out there, existing independently of any relation to it we might happen to possess. Realist approaches to filmmaking emphasize this sense. It is widely accepted that realism is a style, and that there is no guarantee that what a realist film depicts is somehow closer to reality than a film created in another style. A realist film can be fully fictional, but the techniques associated with realist filmmaking all have the aim of putting emphasis upon the independence of the reality being filmed. If there are actors, they tend not to be stars, whose presence would make obvious that the situation on display was an act, and so it would not seem to be a real situation, unfolding independently. Realist films tend to begin and end abruptly, in *media res*, as if to suggest that the situations they depict are indifferent to the interests of the observer or the filmmaker, who might prefer to have a beginning which needs no explanation or that shows her what she needs to know so that she can understand what happens next, and would likely want the film to end at a point where all of the conflicts raised within the film have been resolved. Realist films tend to include long takes, wide shots, and deep focus, suggesting that the aim is to let a situation develop without imposing upon it any kind of framing or timeframe; or, they can be more haphazard, making use, for example, of a handheld camera to suggest that the filmmaker just happened to be present, wielding a camera, and managed spontaneously to capture an event that would have taken place regardless.

Films in the classical (or "Hollywood") style depict scenarios that seem to be unfolding independently of us, but that nevertheless seem tailor-made to elicit our interest. They tend to tell stories, of people we can relate to, and whose troubles concern us. The techniques used in classical style filmmaking are all employed in the interest of immersing the audience into the story. Cutting and framing, for example, serve both to follow and direct the spectator's interest. An object framed in close-up focuses the attention of the audience upon its details; a face shown in close-up of a person intently looking, will lead audiences to wonder what she is looking at and the natural next shot in the classical style would be to show them. The reality depicted in the classical style is a human reality, a human world, something we naturally take an interest in and feel ourselves a part of.

Formalist films make realities appear, but the interest we take in them is in how they appear. Elements are framed and arranged deliberately, in ways that lead us not only to notice what they show, but also to consider why they show it and why they show it in the way that they do. At least two distinct but related senses of reality can be emphasized in this way: insofar as the emphasis is on the significance of the arrangement, this can suggest that reality has a meaning; insofar as the emphasis is on the fact that the arrangement is deliberate, this can suggest that reality is a construct, that what it is is what we make of it and what we make of it is what we are encouraged to make of it by agencies such as filmmakers.

When confronted by a film that seems to be real, our natural response is to believe it, to accept the independence of the reality it depicts. Classical films, by contrast, require viewers to suspend disbelief, so that they may be caught up in and care about the story they depict. The appreciation of a formalist film does not require belief, but generally does demand careful attention and thought. Such films suggest the sense of reality as an object for reflection, whose meaning can be contemplated. Or, in the case where the emphasis is on the filmmaking itself, it can suggest a sense of reality as a construct, as something whose significance does not lie in itself but in how it is presented to us and interpreted by us.

Human reality and appearances

Appearances both show us something that seems to be real, and are realities in their own right, dependent on a set of conditions for their appearance. We focused upon the distinctive kind of appearance that is cinema, which by seeming to show us something real, also shows us what we take to be real. The various senses of reality that cinema draws upon – of reality as independent, of reality as relational, of reality as a construct, and reality as meaningful – can be reconciled when we think of reality not as a thing-in-itself to be conceived in distinction from how it appears to us, but rather as appearances themselves along with the conditions responsible for producing them. It is independent when it is understood as a whole which includes us. It is relational when it is understood as conditions under which intelligent beings such as us come to understand it and themselves both as a result of their individual experiences and in the course of history; insofar as the realities we come to understand are social, and insofar as we come to understand ourselves as a product of those social realities, it is a construct. It is meaningful insofar as we can grasp how it all hangs together and makes sense.

Because film can reveal reality to us in all of these ways, and because its presentations are at the same time recognizably not real but appearances, it is especially well suited for enabling our reflection on appearances generally in relation to reality. Filmmakers working in the realist style can give us a sense for the independence and autonomy of reality as a whole. Filmmakers working in the classical style can lead us to reflect upon social realities, realities in which we are ourselves implicated. Filmmakers working in the formalist vein can encourage us to reflect upon the realities they depict, to consider situations as meaningful and as having multiple meanings according to how they are framed and arranged. Films can also present appearances that complicate the distinction between these senses, and encourage us to reflect upon their relationships.

Human reality, reality as it appears to us, is not made up of things or facts or even situations. Our reality is made up of stories (contextualized by histories), in which things and facts and even the situations they comprise appear as components, but what matters is how they figure in the unfolding of the narrative. What matters is how situations present problems requiring action and set up the terms under which those actions can achieve their objectives.

Cinema, in its beginnings, was concerned simply to allow the moving images of these elements of reality to appear, to present a moving image of situations. A train arrives in the station. A man kisses his wife, or a couple feeds their baby. Or, as with Georges Méliès, another early filmmaker who had begun his career as a stage magician, to use the power of cinematic editing and compositing to combine such real elements in unexpected ways, creating the impression of impossible things made real. That was, initially, enough to fascinate audiences. Cinema went beyond the condition of a mere novelty or stage attraction when filmmakers learned to make use of the power of editing to tell stories, stories about people facing difficulties who rise to the challenge and act.

Theorists reflecting upon this new art form in its early days debated whether its distinctive aesthetic potential was to be found in its capacity to capture and preserve reality in its richness, or in its ability to transform the realities it captures. The primary subject matter of popular cinema – the kind that became the dominant art form of the twentieth century – was hit upon early and independently of debate between theorists. It was what people wanted to see in the cinema: human interest stories, in which the formal devices of cinema were largely hidden and subordinate to the presentation of emotionally gripping accounts of the actions of characters that audiences could care about. There were filmmaking artists who explored the formal features of cinema without the mainstream focus on narrative, but their works are best understood in relation to modernist developments in painting and music and the other arts. Popular, mainstream cinema, unlike many of the other more traditional arts in the twentieth century, has tended to subordinate the modernist urge to explore to their limits the essential features of the medium to its more powerful impulse, established early on and consolidated by the growing importance and impact of a film industry, to focus on telling compelling stories about people.

The dominant subject matter of cinema, then, is human reality, reality as it appears. Human reality unfolds in the form of stories, and insofar as we consider the ultimate reality to be what reveals itself to itself, this occurs through the telling of stories. Not just any stories, though. The stories in which we discover ourselves need not be true, but they need to be truthful in the sense that they reflect our sense of what reality is like. We must be able to suspend disbelief in the face of them. They need to be such that they do in fact show audiences something about themselves and about the human condition.

In the following chapter, we will examine how the contrast and relation between appearance and reality have been explored within the history of philosophy. We will see that the broad conception of human reality as a reality that appears, developed in this chapter by considering the nature of cinematic appearances, is in fact how reality has come to be construed within the philosophical tradition that culminated in the work of Immanuel Kant in the late eighteenth century, and in subsequent thinkers who were inspired by and responded to his insights. We will take a closer look at the history of Western metaphysics, focused on the question of how the relationship between appearance and reality has been characterized from the time of the ancient Greeks until the twentieth century.

4 The philosophy of appearance

At first it might seem we are at a philosophical disadvantage in the cinema, insofar as what confronts us is merely an appearance, something not real that can nevertheless seem to be real enough. In fact, as we have seen, from a philosophical perspective this is not so different from our ordinary situation, even outside of the movie theater. We are confronted with what we take to be real, but is in fact just our take on reality. We don't encounter things and situations as they really are, but as they seem to us to be, from our perspective, given the nature of our perceptual faculties and the character of our upbringing and the quality of our attention. In other words, in everyday life we are also confronted with appearances and not reality. In that sense, we have an advantage in the cinema: at least there we know that what we are seeing is an appearance. What is more, because what we see on screen seems to be real, reflection upon cinematic appearances can help to clarify how reality seems to us generally. How reality seems to us, what it looks like and what we think about it, is not the same as what it really is, but is an appearance. We should say, in fact, that it is not just *an* appearance but is appearance as such, in roughly the sense that philosophers have in mind when they contrast appearance with reality, when they contrast the way things seem with the way things are. We are thus not so much at a disadvantage in the cinema as we have the advantage of recognizing the appearance it delivers to be an appearance and not to be reality. Film, an appearance, has the philosophical potential of rendering apparent the nature of appearance, and thereby illuminating the contrast between reality and appearance with which philosophy begins.

Film, in fact, offers what we might consider to be a distinctly modern approach to philosophy. While, as we have seen, philosophy begins with the contrast between appearance and reality, or between the way things seem to be from the way things really are, it was for a long time considered that appearances can be best understood from the side of reality. Appearances were considered deceptive, and the task of philosophy was to go beyond appearances and to clarify the true nature of things through dialectic or reasoning or some other method, and to account for and explain appearances in terms of what was thereby discovered about reality.

The modern approach to philosophy, whose beginnings coincided with the rise of modern science in the sixteenth and seventeenth century but which, arguably, was only fully clarified in the eighteenth century with the work of Immanuel Kant and through the ideas of his successors, was to adopt a different starting point. Rather than employing a variety of methods all aimed at elucidating the ultimate nature of reality as it exists independently of how it appears to us, modern philosophy begins by attempting to clarify the process whereby it appears to us in the first place. As Kant insisted, we can make no progress in philosophy if we ask whether the way things appear conforms to the way they truly are, because we have no access to anything at all except insofar as it appears to us. We cannot compare how things seem with how they truly are, because the only way we could ever know how things truly are is on the basis of how things seem.

What Kant proposed, and was heralded as a novel and revolutionary approach to philosophy, that has to varying degrees informed all subsequent philosophical work of importance, is that we begin with appearances. We should begin with how things seem to us, and consider on the basis of how things seem to us what reality must be like in order that it could appear to us in that way. The impact of this shift was that reality could no longer be understood as something essentially other than appearance. Rather, the only reality that can mean anything to us is the reality that appears, along with conditions that, as we can infer from appearances, make this appearance possible. Film, which by its very nature lets appearances appear, lets them be seen *as* appearances, is naturally suited for the exploration of reality as it is understood within this modern philosophical tradition. To clarify the importance and impact of this new way of thinking about the relation between appearance and reality, in what follows we will outline the history of the philosophical conversations that led to it and the insights regarding reality that can be developed from them. We will see that our relationship to appearances generally corresponds closely to, and can be illuminated by, what we have already seen about our relationship to cinematic moving images.

A history of metaphysics: from substances to subjects

Metaphysics begins with the distinction between appearance and reality. Philosophers throughout the ages urged that appearances are deceiving. The way things seem to us is not how they really are. They considered that the true nature of reality was something to be sought out behind or beyond the surface of things, and that the way to arrive at this transcendent truth, a truth intimated by myth and religion, was through reason. As the ancient Greek philosopher Plato has his teacher Socrates put it in *The Republic*, it is as if for our entire lives we are trapped as prisoners inside a cave, contemplating shadows flickering on the wall. Unaware of anything else, we mistake the shadows for reality. We do not look to the light that casts them or the objects they reflect, or to the conditions that create the darkness making them possible. What is worse, we actively resist efforts to lead us out of the cave, to witness these conditions for ourselves. The shadows in this allegory stand for appearances, and the pathway out of the cave, allowing us to see things as they truly are, is philosophy. By asking questions about the basic assumptions that inform the way things seem to us, we can be pushed to see them as they truly are.

Contemporary readers of Plato's *Republic* have been struck by the similarity of the situation of the prisoners inside the cave and that of the audience in a cinema. They also sit, captivated but not held captive, by images that seem to be real. To do philosophy with film does not, though, require us to get up and walk out of the theater, like the prisoners who are dragged from the cave by the philosopher. It requires that we ask questions about the apparent realities we see on screen, and consider the importance of what they show us for understanding how to think about the realities outside of the cinema.

Philosophers in the time of the Greeks rightly recognized that appearances are dependent realities. Shadows, for example, depend on the light and on the objects that obstruct it. Not only do the things we experience in the world all around us depend on other things for their existence – since they come into being at a specific time and pass away as a result of the impact of forces that surround them – but the way that they appear depends upon us who perceive them. By way of contrast with the dependent and malleable nature of appearances, the Greeks tended to construe true reality as something that is independent and autonomous, and not subject to change. What is truly real, they considered, should be what it is on its own account, should be unaffected by anything else outside of itself, and regardless of how it is seen or understood. For familiar examples of such independent realities, they pointed to numbers and mathematical or logical truths, which, allegedly, are always the same, and can therefore always be relied upon to help us count up the many and make sense of changing appearances.

Forms

Plato himself never wrote down his own views regarding ultimate reality, so we need to be cautious regarding the positions we attribute to him. In the dialogues he did write he has characters, such as Socrates, entertain (and also investigate and criticize) a variety of hypotheses that amount to what has been called Plato's "theory of forms." While most (if not all) of these characters were drawn from life, the specific words he puts into their mouths are almost certainly (for the most part) fictional. The central thesis of this theory is that ideas (or forms) are real. Not all ideas, of course, since we all have purely subjective notions we've arrived at through our senses or our imagination or faulty reasoning. Ideas arrived at in the right way, though, the ideas we arrive at when we scrutinize our preconceptions and sort out inconsistencies, are not merely thoughts in our heads but reflect the structure of reality as it exists beyond appearances and independently of us. Mathematical truths are examples of this. Someone who hasn't studied math might start out with several false opinions about the properties of numbers or shapes. He might have acquired these beliefs by chance, or possibly as a result of hearing them from someone else who didn't know better. To learn math, though, is not merely to acquire a new set of opinions based on the authority of instructors. Rather, it is to discover what must be true of anything at all insofar as it can be counted.

According to the "theory of forms" there are many such true ideas, ideas that reflect the way things are, independently of how they may seem. The apparent realities we encounter everyday are dependent on these true ideas, which is to say that these apparent realities are what they seem to be only insofar as they measure up to these ideas. Our very capacity to recognize apparent realities depends upon a prior grasp of the true ideas of which they are imperfect copies. This is, once again, most obvious in the case of mathematical ideas. When I look at the pen I use to write down these words, it seems to me to be a single thing. In fact it has various parts, and is made up of materials that could take on different shapes, or that could be broken into pieces. Its unity is an idea; but the material realities of the pen do in fact approximate that idea insofar as they hang together and share a purpose. I can, though, only grasp it as a unity (as *a* pen) because I already have in me the idea of a "one." This idea is not something I learn from experience, even if it may require some experience and instruction to make its implications explicit. It is, rather, an idea I bring with me to experience, given that to make sense of my experience I have to be capable of differentiating between things that are not the same and aware that some of the sensory qualities I experience as distinct (such as colors and textures) nevertheless belong together as the various properties of a unified thing, like my pen.

Since such ideas are not drawn from experience, and yet we must draw upon them in order to make sense of our experience, Plato has his characters propose that our grasp of them puts us in touch with the way things are independently of all experience. Given that such ideas make it possible for us to understand and sort out the variety of changing appearances and yet they remain themselves unchanged, the theory of the forms supposes that they reflect the underlying eternal structure of reality. This underlying structure of reality not only includes mathematical ideas, but is sometimes supposed to include a much wider variety of ideas, that together make up the essence of everything we are capable of recognizing and meaningfully referring to within experience. Sometimes Plato's characters speak, for example, as if there might even be eternal ideas corresponding to objects like beds (or pens) – because not only do I recognize my pen to be one thing but I also recognize it *as* a pen, and I recognize various objects as pens, and some as better and others worse examples of what it is (and ought to be) to be a pen. All these pens of different colors, shapes, and sizes, it seems, must have something in common, an essence, that transcends their sensible and material properties. Perhaps, then, there is an idea of the perfect pen that in some sense had always existed, even before there were pens. Or maybe what always existed is the possibility of making legible marks, and pens were invented to satisfy this possibility, the idea of which preceded its realization.

It may not in fact make much sense, except by way of a hypothesis or thought experiment, to suppose that there exist eternal ideas corresponding to artifacts, to tools that, like pens, are made by human beings, who might never have gotten around to making them. Plato's characters have much greater confidence when they assert the independent existence of standards in accordance with which the value of artifacts and actions and assertions can be measured. They speak, for example, of the ideas of justice, and of beauty, and of piety. The most important such ideal is the idea of the Good, which Plato's characters speak of as if it were the highest idea, the idea that makes all the others possible. We recognize many things to be good or bad, and consider some things to be better than others. That implies that we have a standard, call it our idea of what is good, that underlies such assessments. Of course, someone might claim that my standard of goodness is biased, that I consider as good only those things that serve my own interests or the interests of those like me. This criticism of my particular standard of the good presupposes another, higher standard regarding the good, according to which, at the very least, a standard cannot be good if it is biased. If I am honest, and am able as a result of this criticism to see that my standards are biased, I will at the same time recognize that they are not fully good. So the effectiveness of this criticism of my standard, and of any criticism of any standard of value or goodness, depends upon the fact that our ultimate standard, the idea of the Good (with a capital "G" to indicate that it is in principle the same idea for everyone) is shared.

We can always look for inconsistencies and biases in any particular conception of what is good. All such inquiries, though, presuppose an implicit ideal regarding what counts as a good standard, one that entails, at least, that it should not be inconsistent or biased. At least upon reflection we are all capable of discovering that any given narrow or biased standard of goodness is not the true "Good;" and we arrive at such insight regarding the imperfect goodness of particular standards precisely in light of our prior grasp on the higher, universal idea of the Good. This standard for standards, which has the negative implication that we will not accept any standard as good if it is inconsistent or biased, but which is considered by its advocates to have positive qualities as well, is not simply one we learn from the imperfect process of coming up with standards. Since this ideal makes such inquiry possible, we must possess it prior to any particular assessment of this or that action or idea.

Plato's most famous student, Aristotle, worried that an idea of "the Good" broad enough to apply to every possible good was bound either to be abstractly empty or beyond the grasp of humans. "Even if," he writes, "there is some one good that is attributed in common, or is something separate itself by itself, it is clear that it is not a thing done or possessed by a human being, and something of that sort is being looked for now" (*Nicomachean Ethics* 8–9). It is not clear, for example, what every apparently good thing might have in common – except perhaps that it is *a thing*, and that its existence is not incompatible with the existence of other good things. If there is some quality that permeates all good things in ways specific to their natures, and at the same time transcends them, existing on its own prior to their existence, then it is hard to see how finite beings like us could begin to make sense of it in any other way than by considering what is specifically good about each thing. Aristotle thus held that forms or ideas – including the idea of the Good – don't exist at all anywhere beyond the finite things they enable us to make sense of. They exist, rather, in things themselves.

The good that we *can* make sense of, and that we can actually discern in things and activities, is what they are good *for*. A pen is good for writing. Writing is good for communicating ideas. Communicating ideas is good because it makes learning and collaboration possible. Each of these is a relative good, it is good for something, and it is therefore only good for someone who wants or requires it. If, Aristotle reflects, we are to speak of "The Good" – a good for everyone that is more than merely relative – it would have to be something that everyone wants, and something they are aiming to get at in all that they do, and what the things they want are ultimately good for. There is, he considers, just such a good. He calls it *eudaimonia*, a word commonly translated as "happiness," but which refers to a life that fulfills its potential, or a life in which one flourishes. Happiness (understood as human flourishing) is "The Good," at least as far as human beings are concerned: it is the only ultimate good that we can grasp and that we all agree is good. By "happiness," Aristotle doesn't mean a temporary state of satisfaction or pleasure but a good life as a whole, because, he points out, we can't truly call someone happy unless they live their lives well and things turn out well for them in the end. We do things and we want things because we think they will contribute to a fulfilling life. That's why people want to learn and collaborate – and so that's what pens are ultimately good for – because they consider that learning and collaboration will be either enjoyable on their own or will give them what they want or need to live a satisfying life. Note that if happiness is "The Good," the idea in terms of which we consider anything good, this idea does not need to exist anywhere outside of or beyond those good things themselves. It is, as philosophers sometimes say, an "immanent" form or idea, it is a feature we discern within things themselves and not a "transcendent" form, that exists somewhere beyond them.

Likewise, the idea or form of a pen is just "what it is" to be a pen. Let's say a pen is a tool graspable in one hand that delivers streams of ink in flowing lines suitable for creating legible shapes on a suitable surface (such as paper). A given object is a pen just insofar as the materials that make it up are organized in such a way as to realize this function. This form of the pen is its essence, and it is accidental (which is to say, not essential to its being a pen) whether the surface of the pen is colored red or green or black or whether it is made of a feather or of metal or of plastic. The form of the pen does not exist at all unless there are pens; it does, though, exist, given that there are pens. It is not merely an idea. It is something real, and really exists, *in* actual pens, and is something that all pens have or they wouldn't be pens.

Substances

For ideas to be real, and not *merely* ideas – and for convenience let's say that a form is an *idea that is real*, and not merely an idea in someone's head – for forms to exist there have to be things for them to exist in. They have to be the forms of actual things. The form of an actual thing is its organizing principle, that which makes it the kind of thing that it is. It is the fact it can fit in my hand, and its material components are structured so as to let ink flow through it cleanly and make legible marks on paper, that makes my pen a pen. For Aristotle, though, what really exist are actual things, like people or pens, and it is only because these exist that forms can exist in them. Aristotle's *Metaphysics*, the book from whose title we get the word "metaphysics" – which has come to mean the philosophical inquiry into what it is to be real – is largely devoted to the question how best to characterize the nature of such actual existing things. Aristotle's word for an actual existing thing is "*ousia*" – a Greek word that has come to be translated as "substance."

He examines, in the *Metaphysics*, the merits of various definitions of substance. He also considers the question whether there must be an ultimate substance, a reality responsible for everything, a being who causes everything else without itself being caused: an unmoved mover, or God. For the purpose of this brief summary the key to all of it, the essential feature of substance, whether of individual substances or an ultimate substance, is, according to Aristotle, that it is itself by itself. It is what it is on its own terms. It doesn't really need something else in order to be itself. It is not, in other words, a dependent reality. It might undergo change, as a result of its interactions with other things, but a substance remains itself even as it undergoes change, and is itself what sets the terms for those interactions.

Living substances, like animals and people, are the best examples of this. A dog changes, but its essential structure, what makes it a dog, stays the same throughout its existence. This essential structure, the organization of the organism, which establishes and sustains its capacity to eat, grow, reproduce, and move about, and generally keeps it alive, is what Aristotle calls the soul or "*psyche*." Unlike many popular or religious conceptions of the soul, Aristotle's soul is not something that could live apart from the body. It is not a spirit or a ghost, which happens to be inside of a body. It is, rather, the form of the living body. To be a living being at all, it must have the right kinds of parts and these parts must be organized in just the right way as to sustain its capacity to carry out reliably the activities and functions that keep it alive. Having this structure in place, which is what Aristotle means when he says that the body has a soul, makes the organism relatively autonomous, insofar as this allows it to separate itself from its environment and actively orient itself within that environment, avoiding external threats and taking in from outside what it needs in order to continue in existence.

What establishes the organism as a substance, a being in its own right, is this relative autonomy. To be a substance is to be an independent reality, something that is what it is on account of itself. The organism sets the terms for its own existence. It is independent insofar as, so far as possible, it changes itself rather than being changed by other things, and defines itself in distinction from what is other than it. It moves itself, it reproduces, it grows and develops in ways appropriate to itself, all in ways that are defined by its nature.

The debate between Plato and Aristotle regarding what is ultimately real is thus not in fact a debate over the essential characteristic that differentiates what is real from what is apparent. Both Plato and Aristotle agree that what is truly real is independent, stands on its own, or is itself all by itself and not on account of something else. To be ultimately real is thus to be the kind of thing that Kant will later characterize as a "thing-in-itself" or what Hegel will call "the absolute." The debate between Plato and Aristotle, a debate that continued throughout ancient philosophy and intensified among medieval philosophers, is a debate as to which entities exhibit this independence and can therefore be characterized truly as realities in their own right or as "things-in-themselves." The Platonists (later called "realists") held that the true realities in their own right were forms or ideas, the underlying organizing structures that can be grasped in thought and that render intelligible the changing appearances we think of as real. Aristotelians (sometimes characterized as "conceptualists") held that forms do exist but only in actually existing things, or substances, and so they are not truly realities in their own right. As an alternative, "nominalists" held that ideas exist only in our thinking. They depend only on us. They reflect nothing that is ultimately real in the changing flux of appearances, but only serve for us as convenient ways to group what seem to be its common features. Of course, that implies that what is truly real, or substantial, are minds, or thinkers.

Descartes, writing in the seventeenth century, at the dawn of modern philosophy, made the existence of "thinking things" the foundation of his thought. The existence of everything else can be doubted, but no one can doubt the existence of his or her own thinking, since doubting is itself thinking. "I am, I exist – this is certain. But for how long? For as long as I am thinking" (*Meditations on First Philosophy* 65). Though he considered that many of our thoughts are confused and cannot be trusted, Descartes argued that at least some of our ideas reflect actually existing things outside of us, material realities whose properties can be described, measured, and quantified. He called these "extended things," because their essential feature is that they are spread out in and occupy space. There are, then, according to Descartes, at least two fundamentally distinct kinds of reality: thinking things and extended things. Each of these is, for Descartes, a substantial reality, possessing the quality of independence and autonomy and internal self-consistency that, since the time of ancient philosophy, were held to be the mark of what is truly real as opposed to what is merely apparent. Given that he considered there to be two essentially different kinds of reality, Descartes is described as a "dualist."

Another major seventeenth century thinker, Baruch Spinoza, was greatly influenced by Descartes' approach to resolving philosophical questions; yet he insisted that on this point at least Descartes had to be wrong. There couldn't be two essentially different kinds of reality, he argued, and his argument hinges precisely on the definition of what it is to be ultimately real that both of them inherited from ancient thought. What is ultimately real is independent and autonomous, it is what it is on its own, which is to say there could be nothing outside of it which is in any way responsible for it being what it is or how it is. Finite things, including the kinds of things (like animals) that

Aristotle considered to be substances, cannot therefore be ultimately real. To be finite is to be limited, and what has limits depends on things outside of itself. As a fish cannot live without water, the human being cannot exist without space to inhabit and air to breathe and food to eat, and so neither is simply itself by itself. So, Spinoza argued, what is ultimately real must be infinite (or all inclusive).

There can, then, only be one ultimate reality, one substance. Spinoza agreed with Descartes that thought and extension are essentially different. Yet he did not consider that they were two different kinds of reality. He held, rather, that the one infinite reality manifests itself or can be understood in two essentially different ways, both as "what is thinkable," and "what takes up space." We could call the one ultimate reality "God," but we could just as well call it nature. We might also call it the world, the sum total of everything that is or ever will be. What we think of as finite existing realities, such as beds and pens or fish and people, are just ways in which the world of nature is organized, localized manifestations of its ongoing activity. Such things, contra Aristotle, are not themselves substances, but merely modifications or arrangements of the one substance. Ideas, such as the idea of a pen or a fish or a person, do not exist in some other realm than this world of nature. They are the very same thing as the pen or the fish or the person, but just insofar as its reality can be grasped in thought. Spinoza thus held, here in agreement with Aristotle, that ideas are immanent to the world they make sense of.

Both Descartes and Spinoza arrived at their conclusions regarding what is ultimately real by reflecting upon ideas. They are both called "rationalists" because they insist that the mark of a true idea, an idea that reflects reality, is its internal consistency, a consistency that can be discerned through reasoning. A different approach to solving philosophical problems is employed by "empiricists," who consider that even internally consistent ideas are meaningless except insofar as they are grounded in experience. Even if, for example, reflection upon the abstract idea of a substance implies there can only be one of them and that it is infinite, experience only ever shows us finite multiplicities. Experientially, we only ever experience this or that quality – such as whiteness or hardness or sweetness – and the qualities we do experience are always limited in scope. The British empiricist John Locke argued that if we do have an idea of substance, an idea that truly makes sense to us experientially, it is at most "an uncertain supposition of we know not what" that underlies our finite experiences (*An Essay Concerning Human Understanding* 29). David Hume went even further to claim that we had no clear idea of substance at all. He based this claim, notably, on the traditional notion of what a substance should be: an unchanging unity that underlies change. Since all we ever perceive is change, he argued, we cannot actually perceive substance. Since ideas that can't be traced to perceptions are illegitimate, our idea of substance cannot refer to anything real. Perhaps, then, Bishop Berkeley was right, after all. To be is to be perceived and all that is truly real are perceptions (and perceivers).

The rationalists considered experience to be a source of error, showing us only how things seem and not how they truly are, and so they employed reasoning to arrive at their ideas regarding ultimate reality. The empiricists, by contrast, held that reason only helps us to sort out our thoughts, but gives us no insight into the nature of true reality. They began, therefore, with experience and focused on the relative coherence of the appearances it generates for us, accepting that we are not in contact with and cannot know anything ultimate. Appearances may be illusory and fragmented, but they are the best we have to go with. The eighteenth century thinker Immanuel Kant revolutionized philosophy when he posed the question not what is ultimately real, independent of how things appear to us, but how we experience things and what makes appearances possible.

We do have the experience of a more or less coherent world made up of things that endure and interact with one another, and whose movements exhibit law like regularities that can be discovered through inspection and investigated scientifically. This is how things appear to us, or what Kant called "the phenomena." This is just another word for what we have been calling "appearance." We find ourselves in a physical world, at a specific place and time, surrounded by specific objects with determinate properties that are not up to us. That world appears to extend indefinitely far beyond our own horizons both spatially and temporally. Though this is how things appear to us, Kant accepted, like most of his predecessors, that it is not necessarily how things are in themselves, independently of how they are experienced by finite conscious beings like us. We cannot know what things are in themselves, since all our knowledge begins with experience, and to contrast the appearance of things to us ("the phenomena") with the reality of things-in-themselves, he called the latter "the noumena." We experience objects in space and time, but that does not mean either that reality is made up of objects that resemble how they appear to us or even that space and time are themselves real. In fact, it had long been accepted among thinkers in the Judeo-Christian tradition, still very much a part of the philosophical conversation to which Kant was responding, that God is infinite and eternal, and does not therefore experience events sequentially or objects as distant. Whether or not one accepts the existence of God, if it is at least conceivable that an intelligent being might not know the world as we do, then it is possible that space and time, and even physical causality, do not belong to the way things really are in themselves, but are only features of how they appear to us.

Whatever might be true of the thing-in-itself, the fact is we can't know it. By definition we cannot know it through experience, since Kant defines the noumena, or the way things are in themselves, by way of contrast with the phenomena, which is how we experience things. He goes further to show that where philosophers have attempted to overcome the limitations of experience through reason, they end up producing contradictory arguments: they prove that God exists, or that there is no God; that we are free, or that everything happens deterministically, according to necessary causal laws; that the universe had a beginning in time, that it has always been there. The only way to avoid getting caught up in insoluble riddles of reason, he argued, is to stand fast within the limits of the human condition, accepting that we can only know how things seem to us, that we are stuck as it were with appearances – of which we can only ever have a finite and fallible conception – and cannot know true reality.

If knowledge required us to compare our representations of the world with the reality of things as they are apart from any possible experience of them, it would be unattainable. If, on the other hand, knowledge requires only that we compare our representations with the world as we experience it, then it is easy to see how we can have it. While we cannot know the way things truly are we can have genuine knowledge of how they appear to us. We cannot know the thing-in-itself, but we can know a lot regarding how things are and must be for us. Kant called such knowledge "transcendental" to distinguish it both from the kind of alleged "transcendent" knowledge of ultimate realities that rationalists aimed for and also from the kind of haphazard and contingent experiential knowledge to which empiricists considered us limited.

Subjects

Kant's "transcendental philosophy" aims to identify the conditions that make it possible for us to have experience at all. We might call these the conditions of subjectivity, because to be a subject of experience is to have an object of experience. I cannot be a subject, which is to say I cannot be conscious, unless I am conscious of something. What transcendental philosophy aims to identify are the conditions that must be in place for a subject to be aware of an object. It aims to describe what is true for any possible object of experience. Every possible object of experience, for example, appears somewhere in relation to the subject, and it appears at some moment with qualities that can change from one moment to the next. If there were not a difference between the subject and its object, and if the object itself were not capable of undergoing change, then the subject could not become aware of that object as something specific. If the subject is not aware of something specific, then she can't really be said to have an object. She would not then be conscious of something and could not really be said to be conscious.

Compare this with the experience of watching a film: if every frame of a 90 minute film were blank, an audience member who'd had the patience to sit through it might complain in the end that nothing had happened and might ask for a refund. Still, even in that case there would have been *something* there: a bright and steady rectangular light on the screen for 90 minutes. That bright light on the screen has salient qualities, distinct from what came before it and what might be there later. But if there had been no theater and no screen, and if the film took no time at all, one couldn't say anything about it because there wouldn't even be anything at all to have noticed. Regardless of the specific content of the film, there are conditions that make it possible to experience any film at all. Such conditions might include, for example, a screen, light, and a distance between the screen and the viewer's eyes. Kant's transcendental conditions are more general, insofar as they aim at what makes it possible to have any experience at all, whether of watching a movie, typing on a computer, drinking coffee, or even the experience of drifting in and out sleep, which does after all take time and involve some awareness of one's own body as a differentiated mass. Whether or not space and time exist independently of human consciousness, they necessarily exist *for* consciousness, as the form under which any possible object is experienced. Every possible object of experience, in other words, appears in time and space; and space and time are thus transcendental conditions for the possibility of experience. They make appearances possible.

Likewise, according to Kant, we couldn't have experience unless our sensations were grouped by us into objects. We cannot experience, for example, red as such. What we can experience are red patches, or red shirts, or red blood. When we open our eyes we see *things* with properties. When we listen we hear the sounds made by things: the notes of the piano, the voice of the American woman speaking French, the honk of a car. We don't simply sense. Our sensations are localized, grouped together, and – this is perhaps Kant's most important insight – it is *we* who do the grouping. Our experience of the world, according to Kant, has both a passive and an active dimension. Experience is passive in the sense that I don't simply decide whether an object is red or black and white or blue, or whether the sound it makes is loud or soft. At the same time it requires that I actively differentiate between objects, noticing that some qualities belong to one object and others to another. Grouping sensations together is the work of understanding, and not merely of sensation. When we see a red pen, for example, we are interpreting a variety of sensations as belonging together in a single object, a pen. When we listen to music, we consider each note as a continuation of the melody developing in the notes that came previously. For Kant, this does not mean that I first experience the sensations and then I group them together. Experience just is the awareness that comes from the grouping, which means that at least some of the activity of the understanding occurs below the level of consciousness.

Of course, to notice a pen requires that I already have the concept of a pen, and that is something I could only learn from experience. Kant pointed out, however, that not all of my concepts come from experience, because we can't have experience unless we order our sensations in certain specific ways. As noted, I wouldn't have experience unless I interpret sensible qualities as belonging to specific things – and so the concept of a "thing" must be something that I have prior to any possible experience. The concept of a "thing" is just the concept of a substance, the concept of a unity that undergoes change. So while Hume was right to say that we cannot derive the concept of substance from our experience, Kant's response is to point out that it is a concept we must already be working with in order to be capable of having experience in the first place. Likewise, to experience sensible qualities as the qualities of things is to distinguish between the substance and its properties, and so the concept of a "property" is also one I must bring with me to experience.

Another example of a transcendentally necessary concept is that of a "cause." While this is yet another idea that Hume had argued we cannot learn from experience, it is, according to Kant, a concept whose employment renders experience possible. It is another concept that we bring with us to experience and that makes it possible for us to have experience. If changes were random, if what we experienced in a given moment had no connection at all with the next, we would not be capable of learning from or gaining knowledge of experience. It would all just be a jumble. Nothing would make sense. We wouldn't really be having experience at all. It would be as if we were watching a movie but each frame of the filmstrip came from a completely different film. We wouldn't be able to say what happened because, really, nothing would have. For things to happen, there have to be continuities in what we experience. What is sensed in one moment has to be in some way connected to the next, and we have to be capable of discerning the connection. We are always, actively, attempting to make sense of the changes we experience in the world and to make sense of them is to see what happens in one moment as somehow responsible for what happens in the next. It is by making sense of what happens that we have experience, and become experienced. To make sense of things in this way requires that we make use of the concept of a cause. Causation is not, as Hume had thought, something we learn from experience. Rather, understanding sensations in terms of causality is what makes it possible, in the first place, to have experience and to learn from experience.

The impact of Kant's radical new approach to philosophy was to shift the metaphysical focus away from the nature of transcendent reality and towards the conditions of appearance. We cannot know and therefore must not concern ourselves with the way things are in themselves, apart from how we experience them. We can know a great deal regarding how we experience them. Metaphysics, according to Kant, should be focused on the reality that appears, on things as they exist for us, rather than on the impossibly elusive reality behind them.

Kant's greatest successor, the nineteenth century German philosopher G.W.F. Hegel, saw that the real implication of Kant's philosophical revolution was that we should no longer characterize ultimate reality as if it were merely a substance, or a thing – even a complex thing like a world or a universe, or an infinite and all encompassing substance as Spinoza had construed it – rather, we should characterize reality as something much more like a subject. In his Preface to the *Phenomenology of Spirit*, Hegel writes that "everything turns on grasping and expressing the True, not only *as Substance*, but equally *as Subject*" (10). Reality is not just some thing, not even a "thing-in-itself." The only knowable realities, and thus the only realities we can meaningfully speak of, are those that appear, and they cannot appear except to subjects. To characterize ultimate reality as a subject does not mean that one should think of it as *merely* a subject, as if it were simply a thinking thing isolated from the world and alone with its thoughts. As we have already noted, there cannot be subjects without objects. A subject always stands in relation to a world, of which it is partially aware, and in relation to which it is capable of acting. So to accept the reality of subjects is at once to accept the reality of objects and of the conditions under which that subject is aware of those objects. What is more, according to Hegel, to be a subject is to be aware not only of objects, but of oneself as distinct from those objects, and, he held, a subject can only become aware of itself as a subject as a result of interactions with other subjects. So the true subject of reality is not just some individual person, or a disembodied mind, and to say that reality is subjective is not to make the absurd claim that what exists are merely the thoughts of some individual, or even of a community. Rather, the true subject of reality is humanity, and human beings only exist in a world, and they have come to know themselves and that world gradually in the course of world history.

Hegel's own word for ultimate reality, the absolute or the thing-in-itself, is *Geist*, usually translated as "Spirit." Spirit, we might say, is reality as a whole (like Spinoza's infinite substance) but only insofar as it has come to be aware of itself in and through the course of human history. Reality becomes aware of *itself* precisely because human beings are a part of reality, so their coming to know about themselves and their world is precisely the way in which the substance of reality becomes a self-knowing subject. As human beings come to understand their world and themselves, and as they begin to organize themselves and reshape that world in accordance with that understanding, we can say that it is reality itself that is coming to understand itself, and to actively reshape itself. Of course this activity of Spirit, this process whereby reality comes to understand itself, is fraught with misunderstandings. Human beings at first do not understand themselves very well and misunderstand (and mistreat) each other with disastrous implications. Hegel's philosophy was optimistic, though. He attempted to demonstrate that we can in fact trace the ways in which specific misconceptions have been overcome through reason throughout the course of human history and thought. Some interpret Hegel as an optimist who held that, in the long run, reason would win out and human beings would come to comprehend both the world and each other, and organize their societies and their ways of life in accordance with this comprehension. He was in fact generally more cautious, insisting that we can only comprehend the rationality of historical events after the fact.

It is, however, this (apparently) optimistic view of human history that, towards the end of the nineteenth century, the German philosopher Friedrich Nietzsche rejected when he proclaimed, infamously, that "God is dead." He added: "and we have killed him!" (*The Gay Science* 120). Though, as he pointed out, not everyone had yet heard the news, it was becoming increasingly apparent to many that there is no agency operating behind the scenes of the world as we know it to bring about either a moral or rational order. Nietzsche agreed with Kant and Hegel that the only world we can know is the world of appearances. We cannot somehow get behind or beyond the apparent world and arrive at knowledge of an ultimate substance or "thing-in-itself." He was less convinced that reason plays a central role in the structuring of appearances.

If reality is in some ways subjective, as is suggested by Nietzsche's maxim that "there are no facts, only interpretations," he is unconvinced that the multitude of interpretations are in any way compatible. He doesn't consider that an intersubjective consensus will be arrived at regarding the real, or that even any one subject is likely to possess an internally coherent self-interpretation, much less of reality as a whole. He disagreed with Kant that there were universal categories every subject must apply to experience, and disagreed with Hegel that our ways of making sense of ourselves and of actively participating in the organization of the world were progressively becoming more rational. Many of the ways we make sense of the world, he thought, were pathological and destructive and there is no guarantee they are improving. As he writes in *Beyond Good and Evil*,

> It is no more than a moral prejudice that the truth is worth more than appearance; in fact, it is the world's most poorly proven assumption. Let us admit this much: that life could not exist except on the basis of perspectival valuations and appearances; and if, with the virtuous enthusiasm and inanity of many philosophers, someone wanted to completely abolish the 'world of appearances,' – well, assuming *you* could do that, – at least there would not be any of your 'truth' left either!
>
> (Basic Writings of Nietzsche 35)

The metaphysics of appearance

Regardless of their disagreements regarding the overall coherence of ultimate reality, what is shared by thinkers in the broadly Kantian tradition (including Hegel and Nietzsche, as well as the subsequent traditions of pragmatism, existentialism, and phenomenology) is the premise that what is ultimate should not be defined in opposition to appearance, but rather in terms of it. Reality, according to this tradition, is not to be understood as a substance whose essential feature is independence, something that is what it is on account of itself and regardless of how it is conceived or how it appears. Reality is, rather, to be understood in relation to the subject (or subjects) for whom it appears, and the world is to be understood in terms of how it appears to subjects, how it is experienced by them.

Subjectivity and its conditions

Reality is what appears, and what appears can only appear to a subject. There are two sides to this insight. The first is what we have characterized as the inescapably subjective character of reality. This is what is noticed when we emphasize the fact that whatever we want to call the ultimate reality does in fact appear, and that what it appears to is itself a part of that reality. Subjectivity, which can be defined as the being for which there are appearances, belongs to what is real, and it is inescapable insofar as a reality defined in opposition to subjects would be nothing to us at all. Reality as a whole, then, what we might call "the world," can be said to be aware of its own existence, since it includes subjects, who are aware of themselves and aware of many other things besides themselves. As Hegel puts it, reality as a whole does not merely exist "in itself" but also "for itself." That need not and should not be taken to imply a simplistic form of idealism, which is the view that nothing is real except for consciousness and its contents, or that, for those who define reality in opposition to appearances, there is nothing real at all and there are only appearances. We have already seen that for there to be an appearance there must be a subject to whom it appears and the conditions must be in place that make it possible for this subject to exist and for it to appear to the subject in the way that it does. So the claim that reality appears does not mean it can be reduced to appearances.

Not all of the conditions that make appearances possible (that must exist in order that there be appearances) will themselves appear. When I look at my hand, my hand is apparent. If we accept the (plausible) idea that there cannot be perceptions without something taking place inside the brain to make that perception possible, then my perception of my hand is correlated with certain neural activity. I am not, though, at that moment that I am aware of my hand also aware of what is going on inside my brain to make this perceptual appearance possible. My brain and various neural processes are, we might say, conditions for the appearance, but they do not themselves appear except indirectly, as a result, say, of scientific experimentation and theorizing. I am, likewise, not at the moment that my hand appears perceptually also aware of the electromagnetic waves (or light) that transmit energy and information from my hand to my eyes, or of the evolutionary process whereby eyes and brains developed. I am not at that moment cognizant of the learning processes that once had to take place in order that I be capable of recognizing my hand both as a hand and as my own. What does not appear along with the perception of my hand are the many conditions that keep me alive and capable of having a hand and of perceiving and recognizing it. For there to be subjects at all, there must be a world that contains within itself the conditions that make it possible for them to exist, and they wouldn't be subjects in that world unless they were at least partially aware of themselves and aware of the world as the arena for their activity.

Finitude and ambiguity

Given that reality should not be defined in opposition to appearances but rather as what appears along with the conditions that make that appearance possible, we can also consider how reality appears to those subjects for whom it appears. We have already noted that it doesn't ever appear as a whole. This is the other side of the insight, which we might characterize as the essential finitude of appearances. Reality always only ever appears incompletely. This finitude is not merely a fact about how reality appears, that its appearances always just so happen to be limited in some ways. It is a feature of appearances. It is how they appear.

What appears always appears to belong to something that exceeds it, upon which it depends. It is finite insofar as what exceeds it at once determines its limited scope. It appears to be finite precisely because the limits are themselves a part of the appearance. When my hand appears to me, for example, only one side appears at a time. I can see that there is another side to the hand, but I cannot see that other side. These limits that appear are, moreover, themselves indeterminate and ambiguous. They point in different directions, both outward and inward, but never both at the same time.

When I look at my hand, I can also see that it is connected to my arm, and that to my shoulder extending back towards my neck, but I can't see that. I can't see my own face, and can't see the eyes from which I see. When I pay attention to this internal limit, though, I lose sight of the other limit, which is that I can only see from one side and I can only ever see just so far.

In everyday life I always find myself somewhere, perceiving some things and not others. My situation is defined by a perspective, I am aware of the things that surround me, but only as far as my senses can reach. Some things, for example, are just too small for me to perceive; others are too far away. At the same time, I am aware that the things I do see have other sides (and insides) I cannot currently perceive, and that there are other things further away and out of sight. My perspective has limits that we might describe loosely as its horizon, and it always seems as though I could go to those limits and there would be more to perceive beyond the horizon. What appears to me outside of me always seems to be a partial glimpse of a world, a world that exceeds any perspective I may currently adopt, but that in principle remains open for further explorations. When I focus on my situation in the world, what appears to exceed and contain my perspective upon it is the world itself, which thereby appears to be the ultimate reality within which even I am myself merely a part.

I can, however, orient my attention otherwise, focusing not on the fact that my perspective on the world is contained within and limited by a world that exceeds it but on the fact that it is my perspective on the world and it is my perceptive attention which defines it. Considered in this way, what appears does not seem to be defined and limited by something outside of it, the world, but by the fact that it is an appearance to me, by the fact it is *my* view on the world.

My perspective, thus, has an outer and an inner limit. It is contained within a world that exceeds it. It appears for a subject that does not appear within it. It is also limited in its duration. What appears always appears within the present, and yet it is a presence that endures, in the sense that what appears to me now seems to be a continuation of a past and will continue into the future. Although my consciousness is interrupted by sleep, I generally wake up with a memory of having gone to sleep. I generally wake up in a place that is familiar and expect I'll be able to find my way from my bed to, say, the bathroom without any trouble. So there is a past and a future that are, as it were, folded into my present moment of awareness, at least insofar as I am capable now of recollecting a past from which this moment emerged and of anticipating a future into which it will develop. Yet this rough continuity of my presence to the world is one that also has indeterminate limits, which we might identify with my birth and my death. I am not, of course, aware of my birth and will no longer, presumably, be aware after death. I do, however, experience something like birth in the hazy and indeterminate way I recall having once found myself aware of myself in a situation whose features were not of my choosing. Death, too, exists for me, at least in the impression I have that the world of which I am currently aware in part will continue along as it has been even when I am no longer capable of awareness.

The essential finitude of appearances, the fact that appearances always appear to be finite, then, is ambiguous. What appears always appears to depend upon and belong to something that exceeds it. Outwardly, what exceeds it is the world, and I have the sense that whatever limited experiences I have belong to and are contained within the world. Inwardly, it is the subject, for whom appearances appear. The subject itself appears to itself as finite as well, insofar as its experiences seem always to be continuations from an indefinite past that will develop into an indeterminate future, and yet we can't get past our own beginnings, and we are always to some extent aware that we will come to an end.

Situations and events

The world appears to me, then, not as a whole, but always only from a limited perspective. We might call the reality revealed to me from this limited perspective my situation. My situation is defined at once by its perceptual qualities and by the possibilities it affords for action. We don't experience the world as made up simply by a series of objects or places or people. We experience objects in places, and for the most part we pay attention to them only as they provide us with the opportunities to do things. For the most part we are situated in the world among a range of familiar possibilities. I am in my office, and know where my books are. I have keys in my pocket and know how to get to my car so I can drive home or out to a coffee shop. My phone is nearby, and I can call or text a friend; when I do I know more or less how she will respond and am ready to reply. This sense of a familiar world, in which we are at home and have a range of things we know how to do and at the same time a sense for what we don't, this is what might be called our situation.

On the other hand, given that the situation for a given subject is always finite, and always defined by the limitations of the subject and by a limited grasp on what its world has to offer, there is always the possibility that something will happen, that the subject will change or something unanticipated will appear to disrupt the situation as it has been defined so far. That is what we might call an event. An event redefines the situation; indeed it may seem for those to whom it occurs as if it changes their world. It does represent a break with the parameters of what seemed possible in the world as they had experienced it so far. To put it in loosely Hegelian terms, the event contradicts the premises of their situation. I cannot, in the face of an event, simply continue as I have done so far, since I no longer find myself in the same situation, defined by the same realities and possibilities. To experience the event is to find oneself at once confronted by a situation whose parameters are not yet fully clear but that is very clearly not what it had been. From a metaphysical perspective we should note that situations and events are realities, and yet they are realities that do not exist on their own independently. They are not substantial realities, if substance is defined in the ways it traditionally was. They are realities for a subject. They are how reality appears to a subject.

Since our everyday and familiar grasp of the world is always partial, informed by experience and hearsay, perceptions and preconceptions, it always remains possible for something to happen that breaks with our expectations, challenges our assumptions, opens us up to new possibilities. In one sense, events happen all of the time. I spill my coffee, a dog barks as I jog by and I am startled, a friend tells me something I would never expect from her. Yet the notable events are those that challenge my sense of who I am, of what I am capable of or what is impossible for me, or more broadly, that challenge my worldview, my sense of how the world works as a whole. A political revolution or a major terrorist attack or a market collapse can function as an event on the world stage. On a more personal level, this can take place during a religious conversion, or when deeply held convictions are abandoned, when a friend betrays a confidence, a loved one dies suddenly, a marriage is destroyed, or someone falls in love.

To recall the previous chapter, the arrival of a train is in one sense not at all an event, because it is the kind of thing that happens everyday. It is, for those who live near a train station, a familiar occurrence. Each new arrival is just more of the same. It doesn't change anything. Yet there is, with each arrival, always also the possibility of something unexpected. The train may arrive early, or may be unexpectedly late. Someone might be waiting for a train and the person they waited for never arrives or someone else arrives who they didn't expect to see. The arrival of the train as depicted on film is an event for those for whom film was a novelty. The unexpected shock that arises from what is known to be merely a picture, is an event for those who encountered it, and the film's various screenings, bringing with them the discovery of the part of audiences of an experience of something that feels to be real but is known not to be, is a historical event, the appearance of cinema. Art, generally, can have the power to break us out of our usual ways of seeing, and the experience of it can have the impact of an event.

Interests and values

Situations and events are not neutral realities, realities to be specified in purely factual terms. They are not neutral realities because the subject for whom they appear is involved in them. The situation appears relative to the subject, relative to her interests and capacities. While the situation is never simply the product of the subject's choice, still her interests, her feelings, her mood, all have an inescapable impact on how it appears. Some things may seem threatening and others innocuous. Some distances appear within easy reach, because the path to traverse them is familiar. Places that may be near geographically may nevertheless appear impossibly far away for one who has no sense of how or why one might hope to arrive there.

One can always try to consider one's situation from the perspective of another, or to characterize features of that situation in terms that are independent from any particular perspective. That is what we attempt when we investigate scientifically, performing measurements and experiments. What makes this possible, however, is not that the scientist manages somehow to step outside of the interests and attitude that define her situation. Rather it is the result of adopting a new set of interests and a new attitude, which puts her into a unique situation. The scientist performing a measurement of, say, the weight of an animal is not in the kind of everyday situation in which one might encounter that animal. She encounters that animal, rather, as a body to be measured, as something whose weight is its essential feature. It may be that in order to encounter the animal in that way she needs to be wearing a lab coat, and the animal needs to be sedated. In those conditions, perhaps, she can adopt an attitude towards the animal that is appropriate for the task at hand, which requires her to consider it as an object to be measured. To the extent that she has any feelings about that particular animal, they are liable to distract her from the task at hand, putting her into a different kind of situation, one in which it will be difficult to produce the necessary measurements.

The result of successful measurements and experiments is to isolate certain features of the world from the various particular practical interests that might otherwise shape how they appear to this or that subject. In this isolation such features can be described in ways that are neutral, which is to say detached from specific situations. We call such neutral descriptions factual, and it is a familiar maxim of philosophy that one cannot derive values from facts. The reason for this, however, is not that facts are somehow more real and values intangible. Once we adopt the metaphysical approach that considers appearances to be real, values are just as real as facts. They are the values of facts as they relate to the subjects for whom they appear. It is just that facts are what appear when the interests and values that inform a perspective are detached from the situation that perspective makes available. In real, living situations, in reality as it appears, facts are not without value.

Real, living situations are informed by interests, and relative to interests things have value. My hand does not appear for me as an indifferent object, whose presence to me is merely a fact, and neither does the pen in my hand. The hand appears to me as me, as that whereby I am capable of many things, and the pen appears to me valuable insofar as I have an interest in writing, and perhaps for other, sentimental reasons. Other people do not appear for me as indifferent either, except perhaps in certain moods when I am not paying attention to them, and then they do not really figure as features of my situation, do not shape what appears to me as possible within that situation, and if they appear to me at all it is merely as features of my surroundings that I notice in passing. To experience another person *as* a person is not merely to encounter another object in my situation but to be faced with possibility, to be faced with interests that are not limited by my own, and by a perspective that differs from my own, that I may not share but whose validity I cannot immediately deny. It is to be confronted, also, by the fact that for her I am also an object, that she may or may not care about my presence, and that the objects that surround us are also available for her to interact with.

Stories and actions

We always find ourselves along with others in a world, of which we only have a partial grasp. On the basis of a limited range of experiences, we develop a sense for where we stand, whom we are with, and what is possible for us. The world becomes roughly familiar, and while we remain aware that there is more out there to be experienced, we form opinions about the kinds of things we can expect to happen, and the kind of people we can expect to meet. We never fully have the world in view, but only ever have a worldview. Our situations, however, and even our worldview, can be challenged when we find that another sees things completely differently, or directly challenges our right to behave as we have so far, or when something occurs that couldn't if our sense of our situation had been complete and accurate. Such events call our sense of our situation into question. They pose of us the question how we can respond. Our responses, our actions, then reshape our situation and shape who we become.

Our mostly retrospective sense of the significance of our lives, of what in them was significant, is characterized not by descriptions of situations but by responses to events. What we do in a given situation might ordinarily be called an action, but insofar as it is just the kind of thing we usually do it is not truly active. A genuine action is a response to a problem. It is what one does when what to do is not simply given in advance. I don't decide how to brush my teeth. I just brush them. I must decide whether to approach a stranger who I find interesting but intimidating. If I do, I have begun to act.

If someone asks, or if I consider to myself the question, what happened today, I search for the moments that stand out against the background, moments I didn't anticipate, that created a problem, and describe what ensued or how the problem was resolved. This is what forms the substance of human reality, of reality as it matters to us.

We *find* ourselves in situations, we *define* ourselves in response to events that create problems for our given situations, and as a result we place ourselves in a new situation that makes new possibilities available to us. This process of becoming defines how we appear to ourselves and is thus the essence of subjective reality, or reality as it appears to the subject. It is what we call history at the level of peoples or of humanity and story at the level of individuals.

Stories emerge when something happens to unsettle an established situation, when someone is faced with a problem they must act to resolve. The story begins with the action and concludes with its resolution, when the action in response to the experience of a challenge has resulted in a changed situation. In life it may be only after the fact that we can say something happened; a story may have begun before we are aware of it. Someone might strike up a casual chat in the coffee shop, like she does nearly everyday with various strangers. This time, though, it turns out to have been with someone who will later be significant for her. The chance encounter turned out to have been the beginning of an event that changed her life, set her on a different path, established her in a very different kind of situation than she'd been in before. The story she can later tell is a love story, the story of how she met this person and fell in love. We'll see now how the story about metaphysics that we've sketched so far in the present chapter compares with the account of the nature of cinematic appearances outlined in the prior chapter.

Film and metaphysics

Metaphysics considers the nature of reality. What is real? What does it mean to say something is real? Are there different kinds of realities? If so, how do they relate to one another? Is there an ultimate reality? Traditionally, philosophers were drawn to these questions because they felt there was more to life than what we could see or touch or feel. The things around us come into being and then pass away. We are born, we live a short while, and then we die. Even great civilizations fade away. Change is all around us, and yet we yearn for something stable, lasting, permanent, and meaningful. Even as we improve our lives and meet our basic needs, we wonder what it all means, whether there are truths deeper than those we need to make sense of the world around us and to live well. In philosophy, this quest for a deeper truth, born of wonder, meant using reason in an attempt to go beyond the ephemeral world revealed to us by the senses and imagination. Philosophers aimed to look beyond the deceptive veil of appearances to discover the true reality that lay behind it. Yet appearances themselves have depth. However we conceive of reality, appearances belong to it and they reveal it to us in a variety of ways.

The reality of film, as we have seen, is the reality of an appearance. The film is not the filmstrip, or even the changing patterns of color and light that project upon the screen. It is the images that these render perceptible for an audience, that depict to that audience a moving situation. Film is thus a dependent reality, something that can only exist given a set of conditions that make it possible. What makes film possible, what we might consider to be the reality behind the appearance, or the reality *of* the appearance, are all of the features we discussed in the chapter on the experience of film: the film industry and the technology of film production, the process of the film production, the finished product, and the audience which will perceive and interpret the film in a variety of ways, as influenced both by their own experiences and by the history of cinema as well as by the choices of the filmmaking team.

So film is not merely an appearance. There is a reality behind the appearance, and that reality is essential to it. The relation between cinematic appearances and the reality behind is not to be understood according to the model of an older metaphysical picture, as if appearances gave us an imperfect glimpse, a shadow, or an image, or some other kind of copy, of a reality that we cannot see directly. Rather, the reality "behind" or beyond appearances is to be understood as the conditions responsible for the appearance appearing in the way it does, to those for whom it appears. What lies "behind" cinematic appearances, for example, are filmmakers and the technologies of filmmaking. Cinematic appearances are, at the same time, the result of an interpretation on the part of their audiences. These interpretations are partly rooted in processes of perception that presumably much of their audience will share. They may be, to some degree, subjective and idiosyncratic, but also result from the fact that audiences come to the cinema familiar with a variety of things, and familiar with a range of films and cinematic conventions. The upshot is that film possesses the distinctive capacity not only to show audiences a reality that seems to exist independently of it, but also to highlight some of the ways in which its own existence as an appearance depends upon these various factors. The various senses of reality that film makes apparent correspond in fact to different ways of understanding the reality of film comprehensively. The reality of film is independent; at the same time it is relational; and it is, moreover, significant, in two senses: it facilitates the communication of meaning on the part of the filmmakers, and it offers meanings that can be discovered independently of any artistic intentions on the part of its creators.

If someone considered that I'd made a mistake in describing a particular scene in a film, for example, they could go back and check to see whether what I reported seeing was there or not. I can, of course, be wrong in what I say about a film. It has a reality that is what it is, independently of its audience. At the same time, it cannot be entirely independent of its audience since it is an appearance and if there were no one there to perceive it, it wouldn't appear. The objective features of the moving image are not enough to account for the way it appears. How it appears also depends on its audience, since it has to be at the very least perceptible, and beyond that must make at least some sense, so that audiences recognize what it presents. How they interpret the film experience, which is to say what it seems to them to be an experience of, owes in part to their own past experiences, both in and out of the cinema. It also owes in part to features incorporated into the film by the filmmakers in an effort to communicate something about the realities they make appear in the film. The reality of film is thus relational and significant. Film exists, as an appearance, only insofar as it is experienced and interpreted, so that the reality of film is the result of an interaction between an audience and the screen.

The reality made apparent in the cinema is human reality, reality as it appears to us. We, ordinarily, find ourselves caught up in an experiential situation that we understand in a particular way. Yet we take our understanding to be reflective of reality. So the reality we are caught up in can seem to be independent. Upon reflection, we can see that what we take to be real is just an appearance. We can see that the situation we find ourselves in, as it seems to us to be, is in fact a product of our background and experience. In that sense, the reality of film can seem to be relational: the reality that the film presents is what it is only for an observer. At the same time, we take an interest in film because it presents us with matters of significance, matters that we care about, that we take to be important even though the situations they appear in our not our own.

When we recognize that what we take to be real, or true, or worthy of concern, is in fact the product of our preconceptions, we can begin to reflect upon those preconceptions and so begin philosophy. Cinema has the capacity to encourage such a philosophical orientation by presenting us with values that differ from those with which we are familiar. At the same time, reflection upon cinema's capacity to generate such appearances, and upon the senses of reality it makes appear, encourages us to adopt the more comprehensive conception of reality as that which gives rise to all appearances.

Reflection upon the character of film as an appearance led us to see that what films make appear is a glimpse of reality: they seem to show us something real. They don't give us reality as it is, in itself, or reality as a whole, but give us a perceptual experience of something that seems to be real, from a certain perspective. The realities they make appear are both limited in scope and appear to be real in different and incompatible senses, and cannot therefore offer an adequate grasp of reality as it truly is, in contrast to how it appears. These various senses of reality can, however, be reconciled when we consider them as distinct facets of the reality responsible for generating cinematic appearances in the first place. This range of conditions responsible for cinema is what we might rightly consider to be the reality "behind" the appearance that is cinema, or, more simply, the "reality of cinema," in contrast with the reality that appears through cinema. This reality, the reality that gives rise to the appearance, can itself be best understood in terms of all of the different senses of reality that cinema exhibits, as each highlights essential but distinct aspects of this reality. Reality, as it appears through cinema, is independent, is relational, and is significant.

The next step should be obvious: that the reality ultimately responsible for generating cinematic appearances is in fact the reality responsible for generating all appearances, including the appearance of itself. It is what we have been calling "reality," the way things truly are rather than what merely seems to be. The conditions of cinema, after all, include the history of cinema as well as the history of the technology that produced it, the laws of nature that make that technology possible, and that make it possible to record reality using cameras, the social conditions under which cinema has arisen to prominence, the aesthetic background and education of the artists, as well as the audience, the film industry and the world of industry and commerce more generally, the actors, the settings recorded on camera … in short, what is ultimately responsible for any given film is the world as a whole insofar as in its history it has given rise to the existence of cinema, the existence of its audience and to the wide range of conditions that make it possible. Given, then, that the reality responsible for any given film must ultimately be granted to be "reality itself," the suggestion now is that we would do well to consider that reality itself can be understood along the same lines as we have understood the reality behind cinematic appearances. We should, in other words, think about the relation between "appearance generally" and "reality as a whole" (or between the way things seem and how they truly are) in roughly the same way as we have so far characterized the relation between cinematic appearances and the reality that produces them.

Audiences relate to cinematic appearances in roughly the same way as subjects generally relate to the appearance of the world. Audiences in the cinema are afforded a specific perspective upon the particular situations and events drawn from the world that appears through the film. It can seem to be an autonomous and independent world, but its appearance is in fact a dependent reality. It depends both upon the various factors that went into the production of the film and upon the factors that

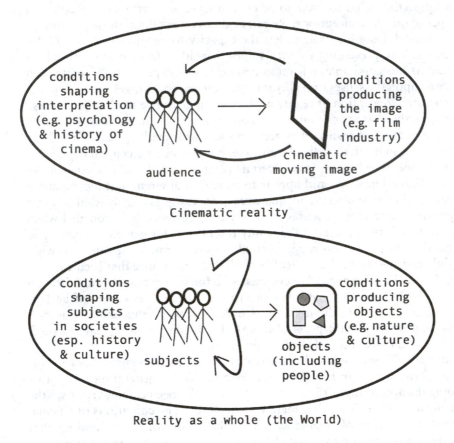

Figure 4.1 Comparing our relation to cinema with our relation to reality.

impact the audience's way of making sense of it. Likewise, the world as it appears to us can seem to be simply the way things are. It can seem that the various realities we encounter in the world, such as people and things, are independently existing entities. They appear to be understandable on their own without reference to anything else outside of them, and it seems as if the way that they appear to us is how they would be even if there were no one to perceive them. This is, however, a mistake. They are, like the events that appear in a film, dependent realities. They are dependent on the various historical and natural conditions responsible for their existence, and how they appear to us depends additionally on the conditions that have shaped our capacities for perceiving and understanding. Reality "as a whole," then, should not be understood as a thing, or as a collection of objects, or even as a "world," if this is conceived as something that could be what it was in the absence of subjects for whom it appears. Such a reality is inconceivable and would be nothing for us. Reality as a whole is better understood as what appears, along with the conditions that make those appearances possible.

This analogy between the cinematic experience and "reality as a whole" may seem, at first, to have a basic flaw: while we can exit the movie theater, we can never get outside of experience. In the case of cinema, we can step away from the experience of the film and investigate the conditions that produced the film. We can, for example, get "behind the scenes" and interview the director and other members of the filmmaking team, to find out what went into the making of the film. In the case of reality as a whole, by contrast, we can never step outside of or get "behind the scenes" of our experiences. We can't turn away from experience, but only away from some particular kind of experience and towards another one. In the case of a film, however, we can step away from the film itself and consider the various factors that contributed to it. Of course, even then, we only turn towards another appearance, an interpretation of those factors and of how they seem to us to have contributed to the film.

We can ask how the film got made. We can examine that question both from an industrial standpoint, focusing on the economic factors involved in its production, or we can look at it from an artistic standpoint, by looking at the range of choices made by the filmmakers. We can also read what the producer, the cinematographer, the editor, and the actors have had to say about their decisions and their process during the making of the film. We can find out what camera was used to shoot the film, and what equipment was used to edit it, and we can investigate the extent to which technological factors had an impact on the look and design of the finished product. We can consider the film in relation to the history of film, in order to find out the extent to which its approach to telling its story was continuous with films that came before it, and the extent to which it was novel. Additionally, we can pay close attention to some of the details, as we have begun to do in this book, or we can apply some of the critical methods of film studies to that finished product. We can also compare our own reactions to the film with the reactions of its contemporary audiences, and to the reactions of our own contemporaries. We might even perform empirical studies. We might employ the methods of, say, psychology or cognitive science to study what difference it makes when audiences process a scene that is shot with standard continuity editing as compared with a scene that includes jump cuts. Applying any or all of these methods is likely to help us notice and reflect upon the significance of details that would not be apparent on a casual or initial viewing of the film.

So we can turn away from the appearance of the film and consider some of the conditions responsible for that appearance. When we do that, however, we aren't turning away from appearances generally. When we consider what happened behind the scenes, we might be relying upon documentary evidence, the reports of witnesses, or the claims of those who were involved. We are still relying on appearances. We still have to assess whether the way things seem to have happened is how they really happened. When we employ the vocabulary and methods of film studies we may notice things we hadn't noticed on first viewing. We aren't, however, escaping the limits of subjectivity. We are, perhaps, broadening our perspective, or adopting a new perspective, one that may focus our attention differently. This modified perspective may allow details to appear to us that would not have been salient on a more casual viewing of the film. So when we turn away from the film to consider what took place behind the scenes, we are not leaving appearances behind altogether. We are comparing one appearance with another. Comparing how things seem to have happened behind the scenes with our experience of the film can sometimes enable a richer and more comprehensive encounter with what was there to begin with.

The upshot is that we are not really in such a different situation in relation to appearances generally than when we are watching a film. The important difference is that while watching a film we know it is merely an appearance; and when we consider the conditions it depends on it may seem that we are dealing not just with appearances but with realities. In the case of our ordinary experience of the world, it can seem the same way. We don't always realize that what we experience is not what it seems to be. Sometimes the awareness that we are dealing with appearances can be prompted by the fact that we notice inconsistencies in our experience. Take, for example, the case of a stick in the water that appears to be bent. This is one of the examples that Descartes employs to motivate the insight that perception alone cannot give us the truth about the world. When we see a straight stick in the water it can appear to be bent, and in order to correct the mistaken impression, we have to investigate the stick. We might, for example, pull it out of the water and see that it is straight; or we might run a hand along the length of the stick in order to feel that it is not bent. In these cases it is the appearance of the straight stick that helps us correct the impression that it is bent. We never get behind or beyond appearances to a reality that exists independently of the perspective from which it is perceived. We don't escape appearances, but we can reflect upon the fact that the appearances are inconsistent, and that can lead us to discover that the stick only appears to be bent when part of it is submerged in water. That discovery, that the appearance is conditioned, does not change the appearance. It still looks bent. Yet knowing that it isn't what it seems to be, and understanding some of the conditions for its appearance, does allow us greater insight into the reality of the world that appears to us.

Something very similar takes place in any investigation of the conditions of appearances. Each involves turning one's attention away from a particular appearance and towards another that can be compared with the first. In order to overcome the imprecision of a subjective assessment of size, for example, we employ a measuring stick. In order to overcome the imperfections of memory, we consult records. Scientific and historical studies allow us to step outside of how things appear in the context of everyday experience and reflect upon some of the conditions responsible for generating that appearance. We can investigate some of the conditions responsible for how we make sense of and interpret appearances using, for example, the methods of sociology, psychology, as well as of the humanities disciplines, including philosophy. In neither case, however, do we arrive at anything more than a partial and limited account, whose accuracy depends on a range of conditions that can never fully be incorporated into the account, and that is thereby always subject to revision. We never, in other words, arrive at anything more than an appearance. That is not to say, however, that every appearance is equally informative. The way things seem to an untrained eye is very different from, and far less illuminating than, the way things seem to someone who has had a lot of experience studying the objects under investigation. The difference is not that the latter has somehow gotten beyond appearances, but that she is more thoroughly immersed in appearances. She can compare a new phenomenon with ideas that have been formed as a result of careful study of other phenomena.

Philosophy begins when we distinguish between the way things are and the way things seem to be, between appearance and reality. The problem, then, becomes one of going beyond appearances, in an effort to arrive at a true conception of the way things are. This problem seems at once to be insoluble, though, if we define reality and appearance in advance as an opposition, such that reality can never be said to appear and where something appears it cannot be said to be real. It is in principle impossible, in other words, to compare the way things seem to be with how they really are but do not seem to be. We can, at most, compare how things seem to be on one occasion with how they seem to us later, upon further investigation. If, by contrast, we accept that we are confined to appearances, we can reflect, on the basis of appearances, on the conditions that make them possible. If we consider reality not to be something essentially other than appearances, but to be appearances themselves, along with the conditions that give rise to them, then we can gain insight into the way things are on the basis of our access to the way that they seem.

The broad outlines of this approach to thinking about our relation to reality should already be clear on the basis of what we have seen regarding the nature of appearances. An appearance is a dependent reality. It *is* only insofar as it appears, and therefore depends on both a range of conditions that make it appear and someone or something to which it appears. The way things seem to us, considered as "appearance" generally, should be understood in the same way. Things seem to us a certain way based on both the conditions of the world that have given rise to our experience and on our own background in accordance with which we make sense of that experience. The reality responsible for how things seem – the world as a whole – is not something that could exist "in itself" and apart from us. Rather than consider reality as apart, we should recognize that we are a part of that reality. Reality is that which gives rise to us, as well as to our experiences, and in that sense, through us, reality appears to itself.

The analogy between the reality of cinema and "reality as a whole" is useful precisely because while we cannot get outside of appearance "as a whole," we can get outside of a specific appearance and consider its conditions, at least insofar as *they* appear. We can never strictly get a glimpse at the structure of "reality as a whole," because we only ever have a limited perspective upon things. Yet we can reflect upon the structure of "reality as a whole" by way of analogy with the structure of a particular appearance. As we have seen, appearances are dependent realities. What they depend on are perceivers, for whom they appear, and the conditions responsible for creating the appearance and for shaping how the perceivers make sense of it. We can see how this works concretely in the case of cinematic appearances, and cinema has the advantage that what appears on screen both seems to be real but at the same time is recognizably not real. We think and feel about it roughly the same way that we would if it were real. Yet we do not respond to it as if it were a reality in our presence. That means that it not only delivers an appearance, but it is an appearance that, we might say, appears to be an appearance. So it naturally invites reflection upon the conditions responsible for the appearance, and in some cases, the film is designed to encourage such reflection.

The way things seem as a whole, which is appearance in the broad sense, is distinct from the way things are, but this does not mean that the gulf between them is essentially unresolvable. The way things seem is distinct from how they are because the way things seem is the result of an interaction between conscious beings (those for whom there are seemings) and the reality as a whole, of which we are a part. Because we belong to reality, and because our access to it is both limited in scope and oriented specifically around the ways it impacts us, our perceptions and conceptions of it will inevitably be partial and biased. We may hope to overcome some biases and misconceptions, broadening thereby the scope and clarity of how things appear to us, but it is a fundamental misconception to hope for a grasp of reality as a whole, independent of all perspective. At the same time, to know this is to be open to the insight that the world is always more than my view of it, and that insight is essential to motivating the pursuit of different and more comprehensive worldviews. It also leads to a recognition of the condition that because all worldviews are a view of the whole from the perspective of a part, they are all to some degree limited and partial.

To recognize this, that the way the world seems to us is not the way it is, but is a way of seeing it, is to adopt the same attitude towards reality as a whole that cinema naturally encourages, insofar as we are reminded in the theater that what we encounter there is merely an appearance. Having this attitude serves to stimulate an encounter with new ways of seeing the world, allowing us to have our worldviews challenged. We can find such challenges in the cinema, when we expose ourselves to works that engage with stories that are unfamiliar to us, or working in styles that differ from the conventional styles we are used to. To acknowledge that the way things seem to me is not the way that they are, but is a particular perspective upon the world, that it is shaped by assumptions that allow me to become aware of some things and not others, is at the same time to become open to the questions why I adopt just those assumptions and what are the alternatives to my perspective. To engage with such questions is just what it means to do philosophy.

In the following part we will take a closer look at a groundbreaking work of French New Wave Cinema, Jean-Luc Godard's film *Breathless* (1960), a film that has endured not only because it is entertaining, but because it and other films like it draw upon our natural fascination with some of the basic questions that arise from the human condition, of being both part of reality and capable of standing apart from and reflecting upon it, of having it appear to us in a variety of ways. *Breathless* at once draws upon techniques of realism and employs a variety of formalist devices in order to highlight the way that contemporary realities have been shaped by cinema and can be reshaped cinematically.

Part III
Breathless metaphysics

Introduction

The philosopher Gilles Deleuze, author of an influential two-volume work on cinema, argued that a crisis of conviction, following roughly in the wake of the Second World War, necessitated new forms of filmmaking. Audiences, he wrote, could no longer believe in the world. By this, he doesn't mean, simply, that they could no longer accept the fictions depicted in the cinema. Rather, he writes,

> the modern fact is that we no longer believe in this world. We do not even believe in the events which happen to us, love, death, as if they only half concerned us. It is not we who make cinema; it is the world which looks to us like a bad film.
>
> (Cinema 2: The Time Image 171)

The world, we might say, had become stranger than fiction. Or, perhaps, it simply seemed to lack a convincing plot. In the twenty-first century, in the era of the rise of the internet and the collapse of confidence in the possibility of independent and unbiased sources of information regarding global changes taking place at an increasingly accelerating rate, the situation he describes may seem perhaps overly familiar. There is no longer, for many of us, a satisfying or plausible story we can tell about the character and meaning of events, about the direction of history.

Deleuze considers post-war developments in cinema to parallel the revolutionary shift that we have already traced in the history of philosophy, beginning with Immanuel Kant's attempt to account for the sense that we are no longer in touch with and are incapable of accessing what is ultimately real. Or worse, that the idea of an objective reality is a fiction. To put the point in the philosophical terms outlined in the previous chapter, the worry is that there is nothing real behind appearances. Ephemeral and changing, and sometimes contradictory, appearances with their elusive meanings are all we can ever hope to encounter. While Kant himself considered that the proper task of reason is to sort out the apparent contradictions and tensions within experience, some of the philosophers who followed were less confident in our capacity to produce a system or story that could sort through the confusion. Against the positivist assertion that the world is made up of facts, Nietzsche insisted that "it is precisely facts that do not exist, only interpretations" (The Portable Nietzsche 458). Some interpretations are, surely, more well founded than others, and yet we can never get beyond the "fact" that we can never know facts except through experience, and our experience is always from a particular perspective that lets certain matters be seen and others obscured. When I compare my own experience with that of another, or when I compare my experience as a child with my experience now, I find that truth is elusive.

The response to this worry is to note that what is ephemeral and changing and elusive in its significance is nevertheless real, and so instead of looking for reality behind or beyond appearance, we can focus on the reality of or within appearance. In spite of seeming to be by definition more directly accessible, since after all it appears, characterizations of apparent reality can in fact be more challenging, given that it doesn't always adhere to the rules of continuity and non-contradiction we might have considered to be the marks of true reality. It can be, as we have seen, ambiguous. Insofar as metaphysics, from its beginnings, inquired into the nature of reality understood as what contrasts with mere appearance, this new form of inquiry, into the nature and reality *of* appearance, involves a redirection of metaphysics. In fact, although it has sometimes been characterized as the "overcoming" of metaphysics, this redirection of metaphysics has been going on for a long time in the history of philosophy, beginning, at least, with Kant. Deleuze's view is that this reconception of reality that began in the thinking of philosophers, was repeated independently and somewhat differently (and later) in the creative (and more popularly accessible) imagery of cinema, especially in Europe and then briefly and sporadically in America as filmmakers grappled with the changes that faced them in the aftermath of the Second World War. Among the most important of such filmmakers is Jean-Luc Godard. What is remarkable about his early output is the ease with which it manages to blend the subtlety and sophistication of the French intellectual climate he grew up in, with the accessibility and excitement of American popular film.

Born in Switzerland, Godard came to Paris in 1949 with the intention of studying film. Rejected from the most prominent film school, he got his real education in film at the Cinémathèque, run by Henri Langlois, where he was exposed to an astonishing and eclectic range of films from around the world. He met other young film enthusiasts, such as François Truffaut, Eric Rohmer, and Jacques Rivette at these screenings. All would later write about film for André Bazin's *Cahiers du Cinema*, and each of them would become celebrated filmmakers, whose output became known as the *Nouvelle Vague* or the French "New Wave" of cinema, that influenced other daring filmmakers throughout the world. He was exposed around the same time to the existentialism of Jean-Paul Sartre and Simone de Beauvoir, who were also regular attendees at the Cinémathèque. An avid reader, he loved literature, and wrote every day, but saw the cinema as a more powerful medium. "When we saw the movies," he said in an interview, "we were finally delivered of the terror of writing. We were no longer crushed by the spectre of the great writers" (Brody 19). He wrote about films in order to sharpen his thoughts about cinema, to prepare himself for the moment when he would make his own films. In another interview he recalled that "as a critic I already assumed myself to be a filmmaker" (Frodon 11).

He had already made a documentary and a few short films, and written various scripts, when his friend Truffaut completed his first feature film *The 400 Blows* (1959), which screened at the Cannes film festival to great acclaim. The success of that film presented an opportunity for Godard. He asked Truffaut if he could use a story idea they'd worked on together; then, with Truffaut's support he pitched the idea to producer George Beauregard, who raised money for the making of *A Bout de Souffle* (*Breathless*). What he accomplished with the film was far more than anyone had reason to expect. "After *Breathless*, most other new films seemed instantly old-fashioned … The film moved at the speed of the mind and seemed, unlike anything that preceded it, a live recording of one person thinking in real time" (Brody xii). *Breathless* was refreshing because it depicted for a post-war generation their sense that the established moral and aesthetic values that had defined both French society and French cinema were no longer applicable.

In the introduction to his first cinema book, Deleuze wrote that "it is not sufficient to compare the great directors of the cinema with painters, architects or even musicians. They must also be compared with thinkers" (*Cinema 1: The Movement Image* x). Without pausing to explain the distinctive (and notoriously difficult) conceptual framework that Deleuze employs to characterize the shift from pre-war cinema and its "movement images" to the "time images" that became viable after the war, and to trace its instances throughout an astonishing array of films, and without attempting to follow here his thinking directly – in what follows let us simply borrow his view that filmmakers can be considered as thinkers, and that their manner of constructing moving images reflects their insights into how things are and ought to be considered. On this hypothesis, the novel use of filmmaking techniques such as the direct address to the camera and the jump cut (neither of which were original to Godard, but which he made use of in distinctive ways) reflects new ways of thinking about the reality that appears in cinema.

Films *do* philosophy differently than philosophical texts. They don't, normally, present arguments. They don't, explicitly, define their terms or work to clarify concepts. They don't, literally, *think*, any more than philosophical texts or talks can. Films can, however, give us much to think about. In his fascinating book on the life and works of Jean-Luc Godard, Richard Brody wrote that "even now, *Breathless* feels like a high-energy fusion of jazz and philosophy" (*Everything is Cinema* xii). To listen to jazz live is not merely to hear the music but to be caught up in its rhythms, moved by its melodies, attuned to the richness of its harmonies. Transformed, for its duration, by the way the music flows, we are able to be in the situation differently, to forget about the preoccupations and worries that pull us in so many directions. Good cinema is like that too. On a first viewing, we are caught up, transfixed by its stylistic flow, drawn in by the dramas unfolding on screen. After the fact, we can sort out the specifics and pay close attention to the ways it managed to lead our feelings and thoughts, to the places of discomfort where we didn't know what to think, to what it called upon us to notice and what it gave us to consider. In what follows we will pay close attention to several of the specific techniques and stylistic decisions through which Godard and his filmmaking team tell the story of *Breathless* (1960), in an effort to highlight the places it provokes thought or calls attention to dimensions of experience and reality that might otherwise go unnoticed. We will consider, in short, the metaphysics of *Breathless*.

5   Cinema and reality

Our brief consideration of a central theme from the history of metaphysics has shown that in the aftermath of Kant it no longer makes sense to look for reality beyond or behind appearances. If there were such a reality, it would mean nothing to us. It would be, at most, an empty word, the name of a mystery. The only reality that we can or need concern ourselves with is the reality that appears, at least in part, and of which we are a part. It is what is there for us, the world we are caught up in.

This has two primary implications. The first is that the way things really are should not be construed as essentially other than or existing apart from appearances. The way things are should, rather, be understood in terms of appearances themselves, along with the conditions that give rise to them. Of course, these conditions themselves only ever mean anything to us insofar as they appear. We can turn our attention away from this or that appearance, and towards some of the conditions responsible for generating that appearance, but when we do, we do not leave appearances behind. We merely allow something else to appear, and are able to consider the implications of these new appearances for making sense of our initial experience. So to say that the only reality we can know anything about is the reality that appears is not exactly to say that there is nothing more than appearance. It is not to say, with Berkeley, that "to be" is just to be perceived, because while it isn't directly stated in that formula, even he understood that in order for there to be appearances there must also be subjects who have perceptions, along with the conditions that make it possible for them to perceive and respond in the ways that they do. Yet, once again, these conditions can mean nothing for us except insofar as we direct our attention towards them, and when we do we may lose sight of the original appearances, for which they serve as conditions.

The second implication follows from this fact. It is that reality does not ever appear in its entirety to subjects. We are only ever afforded partial glimpses of the world. We encounter the world from a limited perspective, and perceive that there is always more to be perceived. We sometimes find that our perceptions are mistaken. What we took to be there before us was something other than what it appeared to us at first to be on the basis of a limited perspective. That is why it is possible for appearances to contradict one another, for things to seem one way and also another with no immediately apparent way of reconciling the opposition. That is why it is possible for two people who are equally competent to perceive the world differently. We experience our finite situations to be fraught with ambiguity, and capable of being disrupted by events that call their overall sense into question. We experience ourselves as agents, enacting parts in ongoing narratives whose significance is informed by stories we have heard and told in the past. Of course, philosophers such as Nietzsche are not wrong to suggest that we are often hopelessly deceived in our interpretations of the realities that appear to us, and that we are even, for the most part, unknown to ourselves. It is, nevertheless, only by way of appearance that we can begin to overcome the limitations of appearance.

Godard's approach to cinema, an approach that he began to develop during the making of his 1960 release, *Breathless*, aims to reflect both the fact that film is a conditioned appearance, and that nevertheless there is no escaping the finitude of appearances. His films are realistic, precisely in that they reflect the artificial character of apparent reality. Reality is never, for us, just what it is. It is both a product of interactions between our bodies and the things outside of us, and, more importantly, we make sense of these things and they appear to us in ways that are meaningful only as a result of the capacities we have developed individually and collectively for understanding and reflecting upon our experiences. Reality is what it is for us as a result of the variety of conditions that gave rise to us and made it possible for us to make sense of ourselves and of our situations.

Reality appears in film in a variety of senses. Each of the various approaches to film-making that we have considered draws upon and reinforces distinct senses in which we, as audiences, tend to construe our own relation to reality as we experience it: reality is what is independent of us; reality is a human world, that we are a part of and can relate to; and reality is an object for reflection, whose explanation or meaning we seek to discover. Film has the potential to explore each of these senses, leading us to consider and reflect on reality in a variety of ways.

Films show us human realities, realities rooted in appearances. The realities cinema tends to explore are, moreover, realities on a human scale. Even when a film shows us realities we could not ordinarily witness, as when they are too large or too small for a human being to perceive naturally, it magnifies or reduces them to the size of the film frame. The frame upon which such realities appear is, at least in a traditional movie theater, large enough relative to its audiences to dominate their field of vision without at the same time extending beyond their horizon. What is seen within this frame are, generally, situations and things that can draw our interests. What tends to interest most are people whose own interests create conflicts, conflicts whose resolutions can be explored in narrative form. Yet while the attention and concern of audiences can be drawn in by such human conflicts that appear on screen, they do not find themselves caught up in them.

When we watch a film the intriguing situations of conflict or of problems and the stories of their resolution that appear on screen do not appear as our own situations, our own problems. Films allow us to maintain a distance from the realities they put on display. The realities that manifest themselves on screen are realities comparable to those we encounter in everyday life, but they are not our realities, and this, too, is manifest. This, too, is part of how they appear. Cinema does not merely deliver an appearance, but one that shows of itself that it is an appearance. It lets appearances appear.

Films can, however, do more than show us what seems to be a self-contained set of situations in a world that is also, apparently, set apart from the world in which we find ourselves. They can also seem to show us the other side of appearance, that this appearance is deceptive and that it is the product of conditions that do not themselves appear directly. We saw an example of this in the 1901 film *The Countryman and the Cinematograph*, which showed a man who couldn't distinguish between the cinematic appearance of a train on screen and the reality of a train in his presence. The effect was to make apparent, to the audience of this film, that among the conditions that make cinematic appearances possible are audiences savvy enough to notice, say, the edge of the frame, or the differences in detail that distinguish the image on screen from the reality outside of the frame.

Many subsequent filmmakers have employed the medium of film, not only to create an illusion of reality, but also to call attention to the features and impact of that illusion, to render apparent the conditions of cinematic appearances. Given the affinities we have already considered between the appearances generated by film, and appearance more generally, such films also have the potential to provoke thought regarding the conditions of the shared appearance that we call reality, the world as we find it. Jean-Luc Godard is among the most consistently inventive filmmakers, and has managed to make films that both entertain, and that explore through the medium of film both the nature of film and the intersubjective character of existence in the modern world.

Breathless, Godard's debut feature film, signaled the arrival of a powerful new voice in cinema, and a revolutionary approach to telling stories on screen. Along with Truffaut's *The 400 Blows* (1959), it marked the birth of the French New Wave. Yet *Breathless* is just one of many films that could have been chosen to explore through cinema the nature of human experience. All films raise some philosophical questions, and many films do it so well that it appears to be deliberate. In what follows, I have chosen to focus on the theme of metaphysics in relation to *Breathless* in part because it is a film that rewards close analysis, but also because its evocation of questions about the nature of human experience and the relationship between appearance and reality does not seem to be overly deliberate. It is, above all, meant to be an entertaining film about a car thief on the run, and his doomed romance with an American student in Paris. It provokes insights into the relationship between cinematic appearances and reality because it is a thoughtfully and artfully constructed cinematic appearance which was intended, at least, to challenge audience assumptions about what an entertaining film could be like.

Continuity and rupture

Breathless opens on a dedication to Monogram Pictures, a "Poverty Row" Hollywood studio known for its low budget Westerns and crime films. The piano notes of Martial Solal's breezy jazz score accompany the credits. The French title of the film, *A Bout de Souffle*, which means literally "at last breath," appears in white letters against a black background as trumpets repeat the piano motif. We know, then, already, some of what to expect: the jazz hints at its urban and modern setting. So it will likely be a crime picture, perhaps a film noir, featuring hardened tough guys and the women they love, who lead to their downfall. Its director, Jean-Luc Godard, once famously insisted that all you need to make a movie is a girl and a gun. Action and romance (more bluntly: sex and violence) have long been the staples of mainstream cinema. This, his first full-length fiction film, features both.

The first shot is of a newspaper, obscuring completely the face of the man holding it open. Its cover depicts a seductive model in swimwear, her head turned coyly to gaze at the reader. We hear a voice, presumably that of the man reading the paper, giving voice, apparently, to his thoughts: "After all, I'm an asshole." He berates himself in advance, for a plan he has yet to carry out, but then insists he must proceed: "I've got to, I've got to."

Figure 5.1 Our first look at Michel Poiccard.

He lowers the paper. Looking down, his hat covers his eyes. A large half-burnt cigarette hangs from the right side of his lips. He slowly looks up and then suddenly turns his head to gaze in the other direction as he blows out smoke and lifts his hand to remove the cigarette. Pursing his lips, he rubs the back of his thumb across them, back and forth, in a gesture whose significance will only later become clear. Then the frame cuts to a close-up of an anxious woman's face. She looks around, signals with a nod, and we cut back to the man, Michel Poiccard, who, remaining calm, directs his gaze casually to where she had indicated. An older couple, the man in uniform, exit their car to walk along the coastline of the French Riviera. The woman signals again, more urgently, and then stands lookout while Michel approaches the car, lifts its hood and connects some cables, hotwiring the vehicle. The engine starts up and he climbs in, preparing to drive off. He refuses his accomplice when she pleads to come along: "No. Ciao! Gotta make tracks, Max." Then he backs out and pulls away.

The editing of this opening sequence is surprisingly conventional for a film that has become famous for its innovative cutting style. We see a man looking, and then the film cuts to show us what he sees: a woman signaling to him, and we see that he catches her signal and then see the easy target she pointed out to him. The basic editing convention on display here is that of "shot-reverse shot." It is most commonly used to film conversations or other interactions between two characters, as when we see someone speaking, and then the camera reverses to show another who is facing the speaker, listening or responding. It also works to show us what a character is looking at: we see someone looking, then a cut shows us what she sees. What this simple convention accomplishes, though, is really quite remarkable. It creates the impression that what we are seeing on screen is a closed-off world, one that stands apart from and independent of the world of the viewer.

A single shot, say, of a face looking in the direction of the audience, suggests an incomplete appearance. It is incomplete in two senses: one that might be called physical and the other metaphysical. On the one hand, what we see is an image, drawn from a world that goes beyond the boundaries of the screen, and we presume that there is always more that could have been included within those boundaries, that what we see is merely a selection from a wider range of possible objects. If we see an image of a person's face, we presume that face is attached to a body and that a wider shot would show us the entire person. If the image shows her standing on a street, we presume the street extends beyond where she stands, and that the frame could shift to show us more of the street or more of what surrounds the character. We could, of course, be wrong, since if she were standing on a set in a studio there might in fact be no more to the street than what we see. Still, in principle there could be more, and even if it were a set it could have been bigger, and so the image will always appear to be limited in the sense of being a selection. Any shot, also, could last longer than it does. It is limited both spatially and temporally, and that is the sense in which the incompleteness is physical: it presents us with an image of a physical reality, selected from (what seems to be) a spatio-temporal whole that extends indefinitely beyond the parameters of any particular shot. Insofar as each such shot is selective, insofar as each could have framed things differently or could have had a longer or shorter duration, they imply the independence of the world they present from the way it is presented on screen. At the same time, they also suggest the dependence of the image on that world from which it is drawn.

There is, on the other hand, something else missing from any shot which can never be included: the point of view from which it was shot, and, more abstractly, the agency responsible for making the selection. This absence is, we might say, metaphysical, insofar as the reality presented in the image cannot, in principle, include such elements. The camera itself, and the cameraperson, might appear in a mirror, of course, but what cannot appear within the frame is the perspective of the camera, from which the mirror itself is captured for the screen. This is true even if in a subsequent shot we see a camera, held by someone and pointed in what seems to be our direction, since of course that camera and that operator will not be the same as the camera and operator who is shooting *that* footage. While a part or a reflection of the objective body of the actual cameraperson can appear within the shot, what cannot appear is his or her subjectivity: his or her agency and point of view. What is always missing from any moving image is in fact a condition that makes that image possible, that a decision was made to point the camera in a specific direction and turn it on to record. This is, as noted in previous chapters, a general feature of appearances, that they are dependent realities, whose determining conditions may be implied by but do not themselves appear along with them. In the case of our own experience, appearances are dependent upon both us, as perceivers with our own subjective perspectives, and upon the world of which we and the appearances are a part, that provides the enabling conditions for the encounter we have with appearances. In the case of film, the analog to the perceiver is the camera and the decisions of the filmmaking team to point it as they do, and the analog to the world is the larger situation within which the filmmaking takes place. What never appears directly on screen are the conditions that make possible the activity of filmmaking.

It is precisely this missing dimension of the image that is masked when the frame cuts to a reverse shot. The second image seems to show us what would be seen from the perspective of the character in the first shot. In fact, what the person whose image appears in the first shot would see is the camera, but the second shot shows something else. In place of the camera and its operator, we see, say, another person, or something else we suppose that the first person sees, creating the impression that there is no camera at all, that what the image shows us is a situation unfolding on its own, independently, and not what in fact it is, the appearance of a situation, created by the filmmakers and actors, for the sake of the audience.

"Shot-reverse shot" is just one of many editing techniques employed commonly by filmmakers to imply (which is to say: to make it appear) that the situations and events depicted on screen are independent and autonomous, that they are not merely dependent realities, that they do not merely exist as products of artifice but that they have, as it were, a life of their own. Because the effect of these techniques is to give the impression that the events on the screen unfold smoothly, within a unified and internally consistent space and time, their use is usually characterized as "editing for continuity."

Editing for continuity is employed regularly within films that can be described as "realistic" and in the classical (or "Hollywood") style: they don't seem, strictly speaking, to be recordings of real events, but they don't call attention to the fact that they are artificial, either. They are in some ways obviously fictional, aimed at engaging the audience with an emotionally compelling story, but one that to work needs also to seem plausible, at least once we accept the conventions of the kind of story it is. They are neither strictly "realist" – in the sense of giving the impression that what they show us really happened – nor "artificial" – in the sense of calling attention directly to the artistry and technique of the filmmaking itself. They seem, rather, to put on display a scenario, set apart from the audience, that unfolds similarly enough to situations that audiences would be familiar with from everyday life. The upshot is that audiences can make sense of this scenario in roughly the same way as they make sense of events taking place in their own lives. They can respond to it emotionally as if it were, while recognizing clearly that it is not, a situation they are or can be directly involved in.

The apparent continuity and closure of the kind of situations that unfold ordinarily in classical cinema are quickly broken in the subsequent scene of *Breathless*. Michel drives his stolen car through the countryside, singing as he goes. He complains about a driver trying to pass him and then outlines out loud the plan he'd previously steeled himself for: "I try to collect the dough and then I ask Patricia, yes or no." He'll go to Paris, to sell his stolen car, collect some money he is owed, and find an American woman he'd met before and fallen for. He fiddles with the radio and then, breaking with the continuity of the film so far, he turns to look at the camera and addresses it (and us) directly: "if you don't like the shore, if you don't like the mountains, if you don't like the city, then get stuffed." The camera turns away from him next to face forward through the car's windshield, so that we can see two female hitchhikers in the distance along the right side of the road. He contemplates picking them up and then, as he approaches, complains that they are too ugly and passes them by. He opens up the glove compartment and is surprised to discover a loaded pistol. He points it out the windshield at cars passing in the other lane, shouting "pop, pop, pop," and then turns to his right and aims it out the passenger window, directly at the sun. This time, instead of his simulated sound effects we hear the sound of two loud gunshots.

In these brief moments, the film establishes that it will not maintain strictly the fiction of a closed-off fictional world. Michel addresses the camera (and by implication the audience) directly. A moment later we hear what is presumably not meant to be the actual sound of his gun shooting, but the sound that he imagines as he pretends to shoot the gun out of the window. The sound, in other words, is subjective, not something that a witness on the streets would hear, but something meant for the audience alone and meant to evoke the inner life of the character, perhaps akin to the moment at the beginning of the film when we hear what are presumably his private thoughts. He actually shoots the gun later; or, rather, the film later shows him pointing the gun at a policeman, and then we hear the same sound of repeated gunfire as the officer staggers and falls to the ground.

The impact of techniques like continuity editing, again, is to establish the sense that the story takes place in a spatio-temporally continuous and consistent world. If it weren't consistent, it wouldn't be *a* world. It wouldn't seem like what happened there was real. Shots edited for continuity make that world apparent, they show it to us. It may be a world in which things happen that couldn't happen in ours, as when we are watching a science fiction, fantasy or horror film. It may be a world in which things happen that might happen in the real world but wouldn't be likely, as in most mainstream films, in which the plot often hinges on coincidence, on things happening that, as we say, "only happen in the movies." Or it may be a world in which the things that happen are just like the kinds of things that happen in the real world. Yet in all of these cases the apparent world in which these things seem to happen is nevertheless a world apart. It is not a world we can enter into and interact with. It is, in that sense, closed off, seemingly separate and inaccessible.

The effect of Michel's address to the camera, and to the audience, is to disrupt that apparent closure. It does not disrupt it in fact, but in appearance. It is *as if* he is no longer in a world apart, unable to see us, as we see him. "Shot-reverse shot" edits create the impression that he doesn't see the camera, but that when he looks in the direction of the screen he is looking at something else in his presence. His address of the camera upsets that impression. We are reminded that it is only an impression, that in fact there is a camera present. Or, given that we aren't actually shown the camera, we may have the impression that what he sees and addresses is us, his audience, as we sit and watch his story unfold. In either case, it is only an impression, a way the image appears to us – as a moment's reflection would make obvious – because in fact what we are looking at is a recording drawn from a situation that is long past. Michel wasn't even actually there looking at anything. The event that produced the recording was in fact that of Jean-Paul Belmondo acting the part of Michel in a car driving down a country road in France, as shot on a Cameflex Eclair CM3 35mm camera by the cinematographer Raoul Coutard; and when Belmondo looks at the camera as it records, the moving image that results gives us the impression that Michel is looking at something. In this case, though, what he might seem to be looking at is someone in the car with him; but we have already seen that there is nobody there.

What creates the impression that Michel is looking at us is, in fact, not anything visual, but his voice. A shot of him looking at the camera would imply, like all the other shots so far, that he is looking at something in his presence, and even if the next cut didn't show us what it was, we might assume that what he saw was whatever he could see out of his window as he drove down the road. What creates the impression that he is speaking to us is that he seems to be speaking to someone, but the shots we have seen so far establish that there is no one there for him to address.

This is different from what takes place earlier in the sequence, when we see and hear Michel speaking out loud and singing to himself in the car. That doesn't seem to break with the continuity of the world that appears through the film, but seems rather to be part of that world. It is just something he does, another thing we learn about his character, as we've already learned that he is a thief and a jerk (from his rudeness to his accomplice). He is, additionally, a man who talks to himself while driving. The shots of him speaking to himself in the car showed him speaking out loud to no one in particular. The shot of him facing towards the screen gives the impression that he is speaking to us because it looks roughly like what we would see if he were looking at us and speaking.

In fact, what he is looking at is the camera, and what it looks like is what we would see if we were seated in the place of the camera. Since, however, the film has already established the impression of the absence of the camera and the closure of the world that is displaying on the screen, the effect of this shot accompanied by his voice is to disrupt that closure and create the impression that he sees through the screen and then speaks to us directly.

This apparent address to the audience is also very different from the voice we'd heard at the beginning of the film, when we saw that he was holding a newspaper in front of his face. In that case, the impression was of someone thinking to himself as if we overheard his thoughts. Voiceover is a familiar technique of classical cinema, that in no way disrupts the apparent continuity and closure of the world that is displayed through the images. That we can hear what seem to be the thoughts of characters on screen is no more mysterious than the fact that we can see what they are up to and what they are seeing, from a variety of perspectives that do not seem to require explanation. It is simply part of the artifice, part of the appearance, through which we are able to have the experience of the film. The subjective gunshot sounds are similar, even if the technique is less common, less familiar, and so slightly more jarring than voiceover. The sounds suggest, perhaps, what Michel hears imaginatively when he points the gun and says "pop, pop."

Film scholars distinguish between diegetic and non-diegetic uses of sound in cinema. "Diegesis" means story or narrative, and "diegetic sound" is defined as sound whose source is visible on screen or is otherwise indicated to originate from within the world depicted by the story. When Michel, driving, fiddles with the radio, we hear what sounds like switching stations, and then a song comes on that is presumably playing on his speakers. That is diegetic sound. So is everything else that he says out loud and hears all around him. The jazz soundtrack, by contrast, is "non-diegetic" sound. We don't have the impression that it is playing somewhere nearby on speakers in the sky, but that it is there only for us, that it is part of the art. It is simply a soundtrack. It affects our perception of what we see, it impacts the mood with which we watch the film, it made *Breathless* feel upbeat, modern, contemporary for its original audiences, but it doesn't belong to the world depicted therein. Voiceover and other narration, as well as the subjectively imagined sound of the gunshots, are other examples of the non-diegetic use of sound in this film. They are intended for the audience, they give it information, they modify its perceptions and emotional responses, they aren't part of the world of the story and don't appear to be audible to its characters.

If "diegetic" sound originates from the world of the story, and "non-diegetic" sound is intended only for the audience, this address to the audience by one of the characters in the story gives the appearance of disrupting the closure of the story world, and of blurring the lines between what is diegetic and non-diegetic. The voice seems to originate from the world of the story, but is intended by Michel for the audience.

In fact, however, the closure of the story world is merely apparent. It is an appearance accomplished by way of continuity editing. The effect of the address to the audience is to remind us that this closure is artificial, that it is not really a self-contained world we are witnessing on screen but a movie, a spectacle, something made to entertain. It is not a self-contained reality but a reality for an audience, and what does not appear within it are the conditions that bring it about, the filmmakers and their technology for capturing images from the world of the audience and their techniques for arranging them into a finished product.

The appearance of closure, that when we watch a movie we are observing the independent unfolding of events taking place in a world apart, is part of the appeal. It allows us to get caught up in the story without being involved in it, and to suspend our sense of disbelief, accepting it on its own terms. By breaking with that closure, even in small ways, such as by having a character address the audience directly, both in *Breathless* and more radically in several subsequent films, Godard pushes us to reflect upon our expectations, to think about what we get in the cinema. He breaks with the fictional closure of *Breathless* even more memorably through the liberal use of an editing technique for which this film has become famous: the jump cut, whose importance we will consider in the next chapter. The impact of such techniques is to remind audiences that they are watching a film, that it is merely a fiction.

Paradoxically, such reminders – that the film is just a film, that the scenario it depicts is not real but fictional – do not so much distract from its power as enhance it. Rather than make it feel fake, they lend it greater authenticity. Godard's debut film astonished audiences upon its first release, and still feels fresh today. It seemed (and still seems) alive and real in ways that most contemporary films, both in Hollywood and France (except a few of those inspired by the trend of New Wave cinema heralded by the works of filmmakers such as Godard and his friend François Truffaut), didn't (and don't). The reasons for this go beyond its novelty. They have to do, also, with the fact that its approach to its subject matter suggests a conception of reality more compelling than that implied by the purportedly "realistic" character of the classical style of cinema that *Breathless* (along with other films that it inspired and was inspired by) reacted against.

Cinema and reality

Godard's approach to creating authentic moving images – images that are both engaging and can awaken us to a reflection upon the ways in which we are shaped by images – was inspired directly by documentary filmmakers such as Jean Rouch. Jean Rouch, a French anthropologist and filmmaker, was dissatisfied with conventional approaches to capturing reality on film. Specifically, he considered conventional documentary filmmaking to be deceptive, and aimed to create an approach to making films that would overcome that deception (see Losada; also Aufderheide and Chanan). Documentaries purport to show something real, something true about the world, something that unlike fiction films is not merely performed for the camera, but that would have happened whether it happened to be recorded or not. Yet even where events are not explicitly staged, the situation displayed on screen is always, to some degree at least, impacted by the presence of the camera.

To adapt terminology from the philosophical tradition that culminates in Kantian philosophy, outlined in the preceding chapter, we might say the problem is that we never get at what a real situation is in-itself, but only ever how it appears for-the-camera. People who are being filmed tend to be aware of this fact, and even if they belong to a culture unaware of cinema they are at least aware of the presence of the cameraperson or of the documentary crew. The attitudes of filmmakers regarding the situations they record also have an inevitable impact on how they are portrayed. The presence of the camera and crew not only affects but is also literally a part of the reality it attempts to capture. The documentary deceives insofar as it conceals this.

One way of attempting to overcome this deception would be to minimize the impact of the camera's presence on the reality it documents. This is the method adopted by practitioners of documentary who labeled their approach "direct cinema." This approach is sometimes described as "fly on the wall" because the filmmakers attempt, as far as possible, to make themselves unobtrusive. They stand back from the situations they are filming, so that the people involved in those situations don't notice them; or, by being present all the time, they make themselves innocuous, so that the participants tend to forget they are even there.

The approach adopted by Rouch is different. Rather than pretend he isn't there as a part of the situation he is filming, he makes his presence obvious. He asks questions of the subjects in the documentary, for example; he allows them to react to their own images; he lets the movement of the camera and the cutting of the film call attention to itself, and doesn't attempt to create an artificial veneer of continuity and closure. What is more, in a film like *Moi un Noir* (1958), which had a very strong impact on the young Godard, Rouch even highlights the fact that the subjects of his documentaries are aware of the cinema. He shows that they consider how they appear on screen by comparing themselves with the characters and actors they have seen in other films. The effect is that the reality of the situation depicted on screen is very clearly not what would have happened if the camera weren't present. It is, rather, the reality of what happens in the presence of the camera, in a world where people have an understanding of themselves that is at least partially drawn from the cinema and from other media such as television. This interactive approach to documentary filmmaking has been described, derisively, by way of contrast with the "fly on the wall," as allowing the "fly in the soup," to suggest that it contaminates the realities it depicts. Rouch himself, however, called his approach "cinema vérité" (literally: "cinema truth") – a phrase inspired by the "Kino Pravda" of the Soviet filmmaker Dziga Vertov. The truth of the filmed situation, he insisted, is that it was filmed. It is inevitable. The camera is a part of the reality that unfolds on screen, and so the filmmaker should find ways to acknowledge this fact.

It should be noted in passing that filmmakers influenced by the traditions of "direct cinema" and "cinema vérité" have not always been consistent in their use of these phrases to contrast the observational with the participatory approach to making documentaries (Nichols, *Introduction to Documentary*; Chanan; Wintonick). Godard's film *Breathless*, while not itself a documentary, draws upon both in its creation of a distinctive fiction film, one that calls attention to its fictional status.

There are a number of insights into the relationship between film and life that Godard appears to have drawn from the cinema vérité approach to filmmaking. Each of these insights can be seen reflected in some of the central scenes and structures of the film *Breathless*. The first is the most obvious: that the reality that appears on screen is impacted by the presence of the camera. The second is that the film is itself a construct, that the way it is shot and arranged is the product of specific decisions on the part of the production team. In this case, Godard puts his stamp on the production by including himself at a pivotal juncture of the film.

A third insight is that plot is artificial. When another filmmaker insisted that movies should have a beginning, a middle, and an end, Godard is said to have responded: "Certainly... But not necessarily in that order" (Corliss). We might interpret this response to refer to the distinction between plot and narration. Plot is usually understood as a development. A sequence of actions occur in response to a problem, and these actions can create new problems. This sequence culminates in either the resolution of the problem or the creation of a new situation in which the problem has changed. The problem that gets the action started is the beginning, the middle is a point of crisis resulting from the response to the problem, and the end is the resolution of the problem. The narration would be the order and manner in which these events of the plot are presented. If that's all he meant, it is a fairly obvious point. In many films, after all, the order in which events are presented is not the same as the order in which they took place. Another possible interpretation would be that the plot itself need not begin at the beginning. In real life, it is not always clear when something has happened that changes the situation. The significance of events that call for action may not be clear from the moment they occur. In the case of *Breathless*, as we'll see, a standard description of the plot doesn't really clarify the significance of the events of the film for the characters involved, notably Michel and Patricia.

Another insight from the work of Jean Rouch that is reflected in *Breathless* is that not only does the presence of the camera impact the appearance of the characters on screen, so does the existence of the cinema impact their lives. In a world filled with images from television and cinema and advertisements, we all have our sense of ourselves affected. Moreover, not only actors but all of us, are performers. We learn how to act, how to present ourselves to others, not only by imitating those around us but also by imitating the performances of those whose images are larger than life. The individuals profiled in Jean Rouch's film *Moi un Noir* identified themselves with celebrities and screen stars, and interpreted their own "performances" in the documentary footage that Rouch asked them to narrate by comparing themselves to the images they remembered of fictional characters and famous personas. Likewise, the characters in *Breathless* compare themselves to literary and cinematic figures. The film not only draws upon the plot of a Hollywood film noir. Its characters very self-consciously model themselves after their film noir heroes. At the same time, by employing the techniques of documentary in their approach to filming *Breathless*, Godard and his cinematographer also manage to capture and highlight the blurred line between the actors and their performances, on the one hand, and their imitations of the performances of other actors. The film thus manages to encourage reflection on the extent to which life imitates art and art imitates life. Cinema is, after all, a part of reality. It offers one of the many ways through which we come to understand ourselves and by means of which reality, which includes us along with the many varieties of appearance, also appears to itself.

The impact of the camera

One scene in particular recalls the artificiality of what takes place in front of the camera. Patricia had been given an assignment to cover a press conference with the apparently famous (but fictional) novelist Parvulesco (played by the actually famous filmmaker Jean-Pierre Melville). Michel drops her off at Orly Airport. The cutting is quick once the interview begins. There is a close-up of a man raising a handheld movie camera to his face and shooting, and off-screen someone else asking a question about the title of his latest novel. Then a shot of the author complaining about the prudishness of the French. Then a photographer calls out to the author and takes his picture. Various other reporters compete to ask him questions about love, about sex, about the soul, about the relationships between men and women, about the difference between French and American women. His answers are silly snap judgments, of the sort that will appear later as profound sound bites filling profiles in newspapers and magazines, but they seem to be taken seriously, and are written down with solemnity, especially by Patricia, whom he ignores when she first asks him a question, about his greatest ambition in life. She then asks him if women have a role to play in contemporary society, and he says, lowering his own shades to look at her directly, "yes, if" (just like her) "they're charming and wear striped dresses and dark sunglasses." It is, once again, not really an answer to the question, but a flirtatious response to an absurd situation; yet she is, quite obviously, charmed by the response. She is struck, even more profoundly, when at the end of the interview he finally answers the question she had started out asking about his ultimate ambition: "To become immortal, and then die."

His responses are intercut with shots of cameras and recorders, and we sometimes see a microphone pressed directly to his mouth. What he says, we can't help but notice, is provoked by the presence of recorders, reporters, and cameras, something we might tend to forget when in other scenes we hear Jean Seberg (Patricia) and Jean-Paul Belmondo (Michel) speaking dialogue that Godard wrote for them, in the presence of an unseen camera. The answers given by the fictional novelist, played by a real filmmaker, in fact resemble the kind of responses Godard himself tends to give to reporters when they ask him about the meaning of his movies and for commentary on all things cultural. His pronouncements about them are no more or less enigmatic than anything in the films themselves. It is not simply that his work should speak for itself, but that he is already speaking as himself in the films, where his presence can be felt both directly and indirectly. The point of the participatory approach to filmmaking that inspired him is that cinema and life should not be held apart as if that will make films more objective. They are always already intermingled. As Godard has asserted on various occasions: cinema is life, and life is cinema.

The impact of the filmmaker

Godard in fact also has a notable cameo in the film, which occurs just before the interview with Parvulesco, when Michel drops Patricia at the New York Herald Tribune's Paris office to change her dress and pick up what she needs. He parks and she gets out. A man nearby is selling papers. After Michel buys one, a man crosses the road and requests another. Michel, in the car, opens his paper, and then the frame cuts to a close-up of the cover story, which shows his picture and proclaims that the police killer remains on the run. Next, a medium-shot of the other man, who is in fact Godard, looking intently at his paper and then looking at Michel. Michel, noticing he is observed, tries to hide his face behind his paper. We see another shot of Godard checking his paper and then another of Michel, then a wider shot as Patricia finally emerges from the office, wearing a new dress and then a sudden cut (a jump cut) and she is across the road showing her dress off with a flourish. She gets in and they drive away,

Figure 5.2 Godard's cameo.

and the frame shows Godard approaching two policemen, pointing out the picture on the paper and then pointing in the direction of the car. A darkened circular frame (an "iris") closes in around him to highlight the interaction and bring the scene to a close.

Notably, the immediate impact of this "directorial intervention" in the film is not so much to disrupt it as to get its plot back on track. It had been threatening, as it were, to become a film about ordinary moments, of the sort we might find in everyday life. Just before, there had been a very long scene in Patricia's apartment, lasting nearly a third of the entire running length of the film, in which practically nothing had happened. Or, rather, what had happened was life, a young man and woman hanging out and passing time, sorting out what it is they feel for each other, figuring out whether they can or ought to spend more time together, which is the kind of thing that happens between people every day, in the absence of the urgency to act that arises in the context of conventional Hollywood-style plots. The effect of Godard's intervention is to bring back this sense of urgency, because by seeing them together and putting the police on their trail, he leads the detectives to Patricia, who is then forced to decide whether she will betray Michel or become his accomplice in crime.

Reality has no plot

If we were to describe the plot of *Breathless* in classical terms it would sound fairly typical of the film noirs that inspired it. A criminal on the run falls in love with a woman, who later betrays him to the police. To describe it in acts, there is a first act that establishes Michel as a car thief, and his killing of a policeman is the inciting incident that gets the plot going. The second act depicts the rising action that follows as he is pursued by detectives while attempting to collect on a debt so he can flee the country. There's also a love interest, what is sometimes called the B-story, in which the hero (or anti-hero) becomes caught up in a romance, in this case with Patricia, whose fulfillment is tied to the success of the enterprise begun in the first act. If he manages to escape capture, presumably, she'll accompany him to Rome. The third act is the climax and resolution, in which the protagonist either manages to get away and get the girl or will die trying. In this case, since it is a film noir, the woman is a "femme fatale" whose betrayal of the protagonist will lead to his downfall.

If plot is what is artificially imposed by the filmmaker, as Godard suggests by including himself at a critical juncture to force its next development, we might consider what is authentic in the film to be found in the moments that break with plot structure. In fact, the description of its plot overlooks a critical fact about what happens in *Breathless*: that its seemingly pivotal plot moments were not considered very important at all by its main characters. Michel's plan was always just to get enough money to travel and then convince Patricia to go with him. The "inciting incident" (his killing of the policeman) had nothing to do with this. It is, for him, merely an annoying distraction. At most, as far as he is concerned, it adds some urgency to the need to convince Patricia to leave. He tells Patricia what he thinks their story should be when he shares a news story he'd read about a man who steals a load of money in order to impress a woman and when he runs out of cash he confesses and she accepts him and becomes his accomplice. The fact he is himself *both* a murderer and a thief doesn't figure into his description. He shot the policeman, as it appears, because he happened to have a gun and getting arrested for a stolen car would have upset his plans. He didn't plan on the shooting, and when it happens he doesn't take it very seriously. He still goes to Paris in hopes of collecting his dough, and still lingers dangerously in hopes of solidifying things with Patricia. He doesn't let his actions be determined by what appears from the outside to be the plot of his adventure. He goes about his plans regardless, and he only lets himself get shot in the end when it's clear she won't go with him. Even his death is not merely something that happens to him; he performs his death, an impossibly exaggerated stumble, as a final ploy to impress Patricia, and to live up (until the last breath) to his stated principles. As he'd told her in her apartment: between grief and nothing, he would choose nothing, because grief's stupid and disappointment is a compromise.

Likewise, Patricia doesn't seem to be heavily impacted by the elements that from the outside appear to be the plot. At first this is because she is ignorant. She can't help but notice the ease with which he switches cars, and so she must know she's hooked up with a thief. That doesn't seem to bother her much. She doesn't know until the detectives confront her, though, that Michel is wanted for killing a policeman. That seems to surprise her, but not to trouble her much. While she keeps the detective's number, she still helps Michel to get away so they can continue their day together. She even seems to be excited by the prospect of being an outlaw, and helps him steal a car out of a parking garage. The key question for her, at that point, is the one she'd posed to herself in his apartment: whether or not she loves him and whether she wants to continue to be with him. When she decides, later, it seems it is not primarily because of the detective's threat to cause troubles with her visa if she doesn't collaborate. She doesn't run away with Michel because she decides she doesn't love him. Or, as she puts it paradoxically, she discovers that she doesn't love him as a result of deciding to turn him in: "since I'm being mean to you, it proves I'm not in love with you." Godard's intervention didn't decide anything for her. At most what it did was give her a way out. By turning him in and then letting him know about it, she hoped to force him to flee, and then she could go back to her budding career as a reporter and begin her studies at the Sorbonne.

For both of them, the possibility of a love story, the question of what they are for each other, far eclipses the crime story that serves superficially, or from the outside, as the film's main plot. Yet even as they appear to be free to determine themselves, apart from the artificiality of the conventions imposed by the film's genre, their conception of themselves does not escape the influence of film and literary culture more broadly. Patricia tells him that she'd like them to be like Romeo and Juliet. We have seen that Michel imagines their romance to be comparable to one he'd read about in the papers. He is also shown looking at movie posters, and after escaping the detectives they duck into a Western in order to hide until nightfall. The most obvious reference, though, for Michel's conception of himself, is to be found in his fascination with Humphrey Bogart.

Art imitating life's imitation of art

While he never calls himself Bogart, his identification with the film star resembles that of the lead characters in Jean Rouch's documentary *Moi un Noir*. The main narrator of *Moi un Noir*, for example, calls himself Edward G. Robinson, an actor best known, like Bogart, for his roles playing tough guys and criminals. In *Moi un Noir*, this self-identification served to signal that the real-life subjects of Rouch's documentary were self-conscious of how they appeared on screen, and that their manner of expressing this self-consciousness was to compare themselves to and adopt some of the mannerisms of the screen heroes and sports stars they admired. Michel, also, as we have already seen from an early scene, wears a hat like that of Bogart, tilted like he tends to wear it. He smokes like Bogart as well and has the same casual way of rolling cigarettes and of grasping them between his index and middle finger. He adopts, like Bogart on screen with his co-stars, a casual nonchalance with Patricia that never fully masks how susceptible he is to her charms and how vulnerable he is around her. He shares, with Bogart's persona, the stoic acceptance of death's inevitability that André Bazin, writing for the *Cahiers du Cinema* just a few years before the appearance of *Breathless*, characterized as at the heart of his appeal ("The Death of Humphrey Bogart").

Michel also, as we've seen, rubs his thumb across his lips, in a gesture that appears to imitate Bogart directly. At least, that is how the gesture is usually interpreted on the basis of the film. It is a significant gesture in *Breathless*, and so it seems to call for an interpretation, given that he employs it several times in close-ups while looking directly at the camera or into a mirror. It is also the gesture that closes the film, as Patricia employs her own version of it in the final moments. Just after Michel dies, she looks straight into the camera, asks a question, and runs her thumbnail across her lips, first the top and then the bottom, counterclockwise, beginning on the left side. Then, still looking directly at the camera (or at us) she nearly smiles, then turns away suddenly as the frame fades to black, followed by the word "FIN" (or, the end), filling the screen, in white letters against black. If Michel copied the gesture from Bogart, she copies the gesture from Michel. As Michel has been influenced by Bogart, she has been influenced by Michel.

While many who have written about *Breathless* claim that Michel copies the gesture directly from Bogart, it is not (as far as I can tell) something that Humphrey Bogart the actor ever actually does in his films. If he ever does anything like it, it is at least not (as some have claimed when writing about its use in *Breathless*) a character-istic gesture of Bogart's screen persona. In his introduction to the English edition of the shooting script, critic Andrew Dudley claims (contrary to many who have written about *Breathless*) it is not actually from his performances but is an authentic, unstaged "tic" from Bogart's real life, that he presumably manages to suppress for the camera (*Breathless: Jean-Luc Godard* 13). Unfortunately, he doesn't provide a source for this claim, and it is not the place here to resolve the question of the origin of the gesture. The assumption that it's drawn from Bogart directly (either the man or the actor) may be nothing more than a cinematic "urban legend," like the myth that audiences fled in fear at the approach of the Lumière brothers' train. What is more interesting is its significance and impact within the film, since the question of whether it is drawn from Bogart directly is not something that can be settled on the basis of the film alone. The film can be appreciated and the gesture have its impact even for the viewer who either hasn't read about it or who doesn't possess the exhaustive familiarity with Humphrey Bogart's filmography and biography that would be required to arrive, without reading it first, at the idea that the gesture imitates Bogart. What is more interesting, then, is the question of why the gesture seems, so obviously, without any specific evidence, to signal Michel's self-conscious imitation of Bogart.

As we've seen, he does it when he first appears on screen in *Breathless*. At that point, it's not fully obvious what it might mean. It is, though, obvious that Michel aims to cultivate an image that is strikingly like that of a film noir protagonist or of a cinematic gangster. He wears his hat with the rim down, so it covers his eyes and is cocked slightly to the side. He blows smoke conspicuously, his cigarette hanging loosely from his lips, and he pulls it away casually before performing the gesture with his thumb. The gesture, at the very least, seems in its first appearance to be a part of Michel's cultivated look. It seems, in fact, to complete the look, a look centered on and given its casual air of seemingly impenetrable toughness by the slightly pursed and stoic lips.

It's in that look, centered on the deliberately expressionless lips, that Michel seems most clearly to imitate "Bogie." Rubbing his thumb across his lips is perhaps really just meant to emphasize that fact. The gesture itself, rubbing his thumb across his lips, if not exactly an imitation of anything that Bogart himself actually does, whether in films or in life, serves perhaps as a prompt, a tactile cue, to set his lips and attitude into an imitation of the Bogart screen persona. It is like the smiles that Patricia later "tries on" in her bathroom mirror, meant to put herself into the mood that her face expresses. In this case, it's not a mirror that allows him to reflect upon himself, to reg-ister and complete his intended expression, but the touch of his thumb, which provides immediate feedback as it runs back and forth across his sensitive lips.

The film doesn't merely suggest a connection, though; it uses the gesture to estab-lish directly a link between Belmondo, the actor, and Michel his character, on the one hand, and between Humphrey Bogart, the actor, and the Bogart screen persona, on the other. We've already considered the way the film reminds us that the portrayal of Michel is a performance, when Belmondo breaks with the so-called "fourth wall" and addresses the camera (and us) directly. In the gesture, then, Belmondo is performing Michel's attempt to imitate Bogart. That the gesture links Belmondo (as Michel) to Bogart is made clear the next time he makes it.

He'd gone to try and get his money from a friend. He leaves with a check, but no way to cash it, and doesn't yet realize he's been followed by detectives investigating the murder of the policeman. They just miss him as he crosses an underpass below a busy street. Emerging from the underpass, he finds himself in front of a movie theater and notices the French movie poster for *The Harder they Fall*, Bogart's final film before he succumbed to cancer in 1957 (just three years before the release of *Breathless*). The poster features the star in a tux, cigarette dangling from his lips, and Michel approaches, looking up at his face, and then mutters, in a deep gravelly voice, "Bogie." He steps over to the next marquee window, which features an array of publicity photos from the film. He looks closely at one of them, a portrait of Humphrey Bogart, then pulls his cigarette from his mouth and blows smoke. The frame cuts to a close-up of Bogart's photograph, cigarette smoke drifting past it. Cut again to Michel in close-up as he removes his sunglasses, the cigarette back in his mouth and dangling just like Bogart's, and blows another puff of smoke. Then back to the photo and then back to Michel, now without his glasses so we can see the adulation in his eyes. With his right hand, a cigarette held between his index and middle finger, he draws his thumb across his lips both ways and just as he does we hear the sound of someone walking by and whistling. The whistling stops when he pulls his thumb away and then he puts on his sunglasses and we cut to a wider shot that follows him as he walks away. The camera pauses on the darkened door of the theater in which are visible the reflections of men in the street, an iris closes in around and puts the focus on two of them to show that they are the inspectors on Michel's trail, looking around themselves frantically in every direction to indicate they have lost sight of him.

If the meaning of the gesture was unclear when Michel first performed it, in the opening scene of the film, he effectively defines it the second time. It is, we might say, an ostensive definition, in which a symbol is defined by pointing to its meaning or by offering an example. When Patricia asks Michel what he means when he tells her not to "make a face" ("C'est quoi, faire la tête?") he doesn't tell her what the French words mean in English but makes various faces in sequence: he opens his mouth wide, then closes it, then grins widely, then purses his lips and furrows his brows. The difficulty with ostensive definitions is that without contextual clues, it is hard to tell what is being exemplified or what exactly is being pointed out. Is "making a face" doing all of those movements in sequence, or only one of them, or merely something like them? In the case of rubbing his thumb across his lips, Michel doesn't literally point to the meaning of this gesture, but the editing shows that just before he makes the gesture he is looking intently at the image of Bogart, and the look on his face tells us that Bogart is important to him. The seemingly fortuitous whistling of a passer-by, that begins as he touches his thumb to his lips and ends as his thumb completes the circuit, draws special attention to the gesture, which already stands out as distinctive, thereby encouraging us to pay special attention. So we can't help but read the gesture as significant and as suggestive of some kind of link between Michel and Bogart. In this case, the context makes the link more specific, suggesting that what Michel signals to himself with this gesture, and what he aims to imitate, is not merely the expression of his mouth or the look on Bogart's face, but the seamless blend of private and public persona that Bogart appears to exemplify.

Actors and their roles

Before performing the gesture in front of Bogart's photo, he'd looked up at the poster, seeing Bogart in character as Eddie, the cynical sports writer from *The Harder They*

Fall (1956), a character who is only a slight variation from the character that Bogart had played in all of his films since he became a leading man and a star. Michel identifies that star persona by name: "Bogie." Then he looks at the photograph, an image drawn from the real-life Humphrey Bogart. It is not a still from the film but a posed photograph of the actor. He doesn't have his cigarette, as in the poster, but he still remains in character. He still has the same look, the expression, the gravitas that had made him famous. At this late stage in his career, in fact, the man Humphrey Bogart and the star persona "Bogie," had become fully integrated, at least in the public eye. It wasn't always so, as in his earliest films and stage performances he hadn't yet found the right blend of casual but cynical toughness, masking an underlying decency that made him so appealing as a leading man who never aimed to be a hero but always managed to pull off something heroic.

Humphrey Bogart's screen persona and public persona tended to reinforce one another. Who he seemed to be on screen appeared to be a version of the man himself, and he managed to exude the same easy self-confidence in his public appearances as he did in his performances. That is, perhaps, what defines a star rather than an actor who adapts to each part, that the star manages to portray on screen what we as the audience take to be an authentic and recognizable version of him or herself. It may, of course, not be authentic, but the star is the star in part because their performances and their public appearances and who they seem to be in their personal lives seem to reinforce one another. We care about the star's private life because it seems to be inseparable from the life of the characters we have come to care about on screen. We automatically accept and become invested in their cinematic portrayals when they mirror who we already take the star to be.

The vulnerability on Michel's face as he looks reverently at Bogart suggests that he isn't entirely the hardened tough guy he pretends and aspires to be. When he looks first at the poster and then at the photograph, and then makes the gesture, it suggests that

Figure 5.3 Michel admiring Bogart's photo.

what he wants to imitate is the seamless blend between who he is and how he appears that Bogart the man and the actor appeared to embody. He seems not to have fully become the character he pretends to be, and there are moments in the film when the cracks become apparent.

At the same time, even if Michel is just a vulnerable punk kid, playing at being a gangster, his imperfect performance of the role still has real consequences. He kills a policeman, Patricia gets pregnant – and what is noticeable is that he seems not to treat these with the seriousness they deserve. They are, for him, non-events. He doesn't, it seems, take them seriously because they are, for him, just the kind of things a character like him would do in the movies. Michel is living out a life pretending to be someone who isn't real, but his acts of pretending have real-life consequences, and by showing this *Breathless* suggests that cinema and life, appearance and reality, are not in fact so far apart. At the same time it makes clear that for Michel, his impact on others is not as important as his conception of himself.

Screening subjectivity, intersubjectivity, and objectivity

> Two persons, looking at each other in the eye, see not their eyes but their looks. (The reason why we get the color of a person's eyes wrong?)
> (Robert Bresson, Notes on the Cinematographer 23)

The difference between actors and the roles they play mirrors the more basic existential tension between who one is truly and how one appears to others. It also exemplifies the broader philosophical issue at the heart of this book, of sorting out the relationship between appearance and reality, between the way things seem and the way things are. We have seen that a comparison between how things seem and how they are is not possible when reality is conceived as something opposed to or outside of the realm of appearances entirely. We have no access whatsoever to how things truly are, when this is construed as something essentially other than how they appear. Yet there is no need to construe things in this way. Reality is just what appears, along with the conditions that make those appearances possible. We can access those conditions either directly insofar as they also appear, or indirectly, when we infer that what does appear could not have appeared except under certain conditions. When we construe things in this way, the difference between appearance and reality is not something we need to posit, but can be determined on the basis of appearances themselves. That things are not as they appear is something that itself appears. To recall a familiar example: a stick that appears bent in water will appear straight when you pull it out or run your hand along its length. Since it will seem to be the very same stick that seems bent in one circumstance and straight in another, it will also appear that its initial appearance as bent was deceptive. Of course, to discern that requires that the person perceiving the stick out of the water remembers how it looked when in the water, and that she is able to recognize it as the same stick. What is clear through such comparisons is that appearances are conditioned. How something appears depends both on the condition of its perceiver and on external conditions affecting its impact upon the perceiver.

Something similar can be said about the difference between actors and their roles. The difference is apparent when we compare how an actor behaves on stage or on screen with how he or she behaves off-screen. As we've noted, Bogart's appeal was due in part to the fact that, at least on the surface, his public persona and the persona he adopted on screen seemed to correspond to one another. For someone who knew of his public persona, her familiarity with Bogart the actor would affect her feelings about and interpretation of the character he played in this or that film. That is not to say that there was no discernible difference between Bogart the actor and the characters he played. The characters were varied, even if they tended to be variations on a theme. He also seemed gentler, perhaps, less hardened, in public, but there was at least a family resemblance between the various characters he played on screen, on the one hand, and his popular image, on the other. Of course, how he behaved off screen was not a transparent indication of who he truly was, but only of how he allowed himself to be seen in public. That does indicate something of what he is, but remains a conditioned appearance. That is inevitable. All appearances are conditioned.

Perhaps the only way to get closer to the truth of appearances is to acknowledge that they are conditioned. That is, as we have seen, the strategy adopted by documentarians working in the tradition of cinema vérité, and that Godard adapted for use in his fiction films. Rather than pretend to show audiences a situation as it really occurred, as if its being captured by the camera did not impact that situation in any way, cinema vérité shows clearly that the situation displayed on screen was affected by the presence of the camera, that the camera and the filmmaker are a part of that situation. By revealing the situation to be conditioned, cinema vérité aims to get closer to its truth than an approach that obscures the constructed character of its documentary images. Awareness of and inquiry into the conditions of an appearance has the potential to illuminate those appearances, both directly and indirectly by way of comparison with other appearances, even though we will never arrive at the unconditioned reality behind things.

The more basic distinction between the appearance and the reality of a person, between who she is and how she appears, may seem, however, to be less susceptible to illumination. It is not simply a matter of comparing how someone acts in one condition with how she acts in another. That is what we commonly do when we try to make sense of the behavior of another person. If someone is behaving strangely, or differently than we might expect them to, we may reflect on the circumstances motivating this behavior. Perhaps they are hungry, feeling stressed, afraid, or angry. The problem is that while some of the conditions motivating another's behavior may be apparent to an observer, what is critical for understanding them is not how their situation might be construed by another person, but how they construe it for themselves. The subjectivity of another person, how their situation appears to them from their own perspective, might seem to be something utterly inaccessible from the outside.

In fact, however, while I cannot share another person's perspective directly, the fact that her perspective differs from my own can be quite apparent from my own perspective. That is, after all, what it means to have another person appear to me. When I consider an object, like a book or a gun, it doesn't seem to be aware of me. It just is what it is. It doesn't have a perspective. I may adopt various attitudes towards it, but it will remain indifferent to me. To recognize someone as a person, by contrast, is to consider them as someone who has interests of their own and for whom things appear differently than they appear to me. That is, at least, how it seems. When I look into the eyes of another person, I don't just see their eyes as objects; I see that they seem to be looking back at me. I may see even more than that on their face. I can seem to see something of how they see me. They may seem to be judging me, for example, it may seem that I have made them angry, or they may seem to be taking an interest.

While faces are capable of expressing a wide range of attitudes, their actions and words can be even more expressive.

All of this, moreover, can be shown on screen. Characters in movies do not appear to be mere objects. They appear to be subjects, with interests and perspectives of their own. The close-up is effective in revealing a character's attitudes. The close-up of Michel, for example, as he looked at the portrait of Bogart, showed his admiration. The gesture with his thumb across his lips revealed his intent to emulate Bogart's stoicism, his apparent indifference in the face of death. At the same time, his need to repeat the gesture as an apparent reminder to himself indicates his awareness that he hasn't quite achieved it. While it is sometimes clear to an observer that who someone thinks they are differs from how they appear from outside, it can also be clear to that person that how they appear to others is different from what they consider themselves truly to be.

We externalize ourselves, appearing to one another *as* subjects, through facial expressions, bodily gestures, and words. While a facial expression has objective features, which can be discerned from the perspective of others, it does not function merely as an object. To perceive it as an expression is to interpret it as the external mark of a subjective comportment. Through such external marks, the subjective and intersubjective realities of lives can also be made to appear on screen. Much of what takes place in the film between Patricia and Michel can be understood as revealing the tensions in the intersubjective matrix that develops between them. He wants to be seen, by her and by others, in a certain way. His Bogartian mask, that he has to keep reminding himself to keep intact, is meant to communicate to others his lack of concern about anything apart from his immediate aims. Patricia is, on the one hand, put off by his casual disregard for the feelings of others. She can't live that way. On the other hand, he intrigues her. She feels that in his indifference he is free. In relation to him, she is well aware of his fascination with her. Sometimes his dogged persistence annoys her. Sometimes she finds it appealing. We will consider further in the next section some of the specific ways in which the film makes apparent these tensions in their responses to each other.

When one person encounters another, not only is it clear to each that how they seem to the other may be different than how they seem to themselves, but it can also be apparent to each of them that the same thing is clear to the other. It can be clear to me about another person, for example, both that she doesn't see herself as I see her, but also that she can see that I don't see her as she sees herself, and that she doesn't see me as I see myself. This complex matrix of intersubjectivity – what Hegel characterized as the "logic of recognition" – can become the basis for various misunderstandings and conflicts, such as when, as in the case of Patricia, it is clear to her both that he wants her to want to be with him, but resents or ignores the indications she has given that, while she finds him attractive and his impulsiveness appealing, she has more on her mind than going off on his adventure. Yet the fact that each of us can be aware of both how another sees herself and how the other considers that she is seen by others also makes possible genuine forms of mutual understanding and recognition. My very acknowledgment that there is more to the other than how she appears to me means that I do not reduce her to the status of an object, something whose behavior I can predict or control. My insistence that there is more to myself than how I appear to others, means I refuse to allow myself to be reduced to the status of an object and that I will want others to see that I am capable of seeing things differently. This very fact makes it possible for us to begin the effort to understand one another, to make sense of our selves by working through our differences. To be authentic is to own up to and take responsibility for the ways in which one's sense of oneself and one's presentation to others can be at odds with one another, and to commit to the effort of achieving a closer correspondence. We often think of authenticity as being "true to oneself," but construe this to mean being true only to how one thinks of oneself in opposition, or at least indifference, to how one thinks that others think of oneself. Yet how we appear to others is equally a part of who we are and neither side can be ignored if we aim for authenticity.

The subjective realities of Michel and Patricia, as well as the intersubjective reality that develops between them, become objective to the spectator. That Patricia is intrigued by but not caught up in Michel's obsessions, is something we can see. That Michel does not see Patricia as she sees herself, that he wants her to adopt his vision of their future but is unwilling or incapable of taking her own interests seriously, is all made apparent to the audience. Cinema has the capacity to render subjectivity objective. The mutual incomprehension of the characters on screen can be made apparent to and comprehended by the audience. Yet the film also calls attention to what we might describe as objective social realities to which both of them (as much as the audience) are subject. In particular, the film calls attention to the importance of the objective realities of commerce and economics, on the one hand, and of policing and the law, on the other. These are realms that impact the subjective aims of both Michel and Patricia, whether they wish to acknowledge or pay attention to them or not.

We have seen that Michel pays little attention to how others see him. He wears the mask, somewhat uneasily, of his film noir hero, Humphrey Bogart, and wishes to be seen as tough, implacable. His indifferent attitudes toward nearly everyone else and everything else are, we might say, a part of that mask. The exception is Patricia, but once again his vulnerability in relation to her is something he shared with Bogart, whose characters often had a weak spot for his leading ladies. Yet while he seems to have little concern for the power of the law that is closing in on him, Michel is clearly aware that he needs money to get away. It's not enough that he has friends in low places. It's not enough that he has a check in hand. He needs to find someone to cash it for him. He hopes to capture Patricia's imagination with his story of lovers on the run, but he knows that even their shared fantasy won't be enough. He needs money to realize his plans. Money, we might say, produces a nearly automatic recognition. I don't need to convince someone to want what I want. As long as I have money, I can pay them. The law, likewise, is indifferent to the question of Michel's attitudes. His subjectivity is irrelevant. His plans are unimportant. While he might have gone unnoticed if all he'd done was steal the occasional car, his killing of a policeman ensured that he would become a primary target. The fact that he hadn't planned to kill the cop, and that he didn't consider it important, makes little difference. He disrespects the authority of the law at his own peril. Patricia will turn out to have a greater respect for the power of the law to upset her own long-term plans, and this will be what leads to Michel's death.

Patricia understands that what she wants is something she can't get by herself. She needs to make connections at work in order to become a reporter. She needs to stay on the good side of the law, so that there will be no problems with her visa, which would cause problems for her plans to study at the university. Michel, by contrast, acts as if it is enough for him to decide in order for him to accomplish what he wants.

He seems frustrated, for example, that he can't automatically get the money he is owed for cars he had stolen. *Breathless* is able to make clear the extent to which the subjective perspectives of its main characters overlap and the extent to which they see things differently. It also makes clear that there are social realities to which both characters are subject.

Breathless tells a story that might seem to be straight out of Hollywood. It may seem, at first, to be nothing more than an entertaining fiction, disconnected from actual life. At the same time, it illustrates potently the impact of cinema upon everyday life. Michel's imitation of Bogart is just one of many examples. While the film is fictional, it also makes use of techniques drawn from the documentary style of cinema vérité, in order to remind audiences that the fiction is constructed. By emphasizing this, the film introduces the reality of the filmmaking process into the fiction of the film and manages to imbue its narration with a documentary feel. It enables, in other words, the conditions of the appearance to appear within the film. The story may be fictional, but in its structuring it reflects something of the truth of what we have characterized as "reality as a whole," or "the world."

Appearances are not what they seem to be. Human reality, reality as it appears, is likewise not what it seems initially to be. We seem to find ourselves in the world, confronted with realities that simply are what they are independently of how they appear to us to be. That appearance is, we might say, a fiction. In fact, these apparent realities are the product of a range of conditions, which do not themselves appear. They are produced by, on the one hand, the range of conditions responsible for producing the objects that appear to us, and, on the other, the conditions that shape how we perceive those objects. By calling our attention to the way in which cinematic appearances are constructed and also how those constructs impact the way that reality appears to us outside of the cinema, a film like *Breathless* draws upon and encourages a philosophical orientation in its audience. In the final chapter we will consider in some detail two of the most prominent techniques employed by Godard in order to at once entertain audiences and encourage reflection upon the significance of the realities he puts on display.

6 Film techniques and philosophy

Godard once proclaimed that "tracking shots are a question of morality" (Domarchi, Jean et al. 62). What he seems to have meant is that filmmakers have a responsibility to consider carefully the impact of specific techniques on how the content of moving images is interpreted by their audiences. How it is shown is essential to what is being shown, and to whether and how it is considered important. The very same event depicted on screen has a very different impact if it is shot with wide framing or in close-up, if the camera is handheld or steady, if movements traverse the screen or if the moving subject is kept at the center of the frame while the movement is followed on a dolly. A tracking shot, specifically, allows us to move along with the subject or subjects, so that we can witness their movements as if we were moving along with them. We don't share their perspective, but rather have a perspective upon them as their own horizons shift. It can offer an intimate and immobile window onto a subject in motion, an unchanging view upon them as they engage with and respond to a changing situation. There are, in fact, several tracking shots employed in the film *Breathless*, and later we'll consider the possible moral impact of a few of them.

The most memorable technique Godard employs in this film, however, is the "jump cut." Like Michel's direct address to the camera that we saw in the opening scene of the film, the jump cut violates the rules of classical continuity editing. It occurs either when several frames are removed from a single shot, so that there is an abrupt and inexplicable change, or when two different shots that are very similar in their framing but where something has changed its position are joined together one after the other. In standard continuity editing, such shots could be used in sequence, but there would need to be a "cutaway" between them: a shot from another point of view, or of something else, such as the face of another person noticing what happens in the first shot. The cutaway would mask the discontinuity, or make it seem as if time had passed between the two shots and as if the movement had happened in the intervening time. In a jump cut, there is no cutaway and no obvious shift in the framing. So the impression is of a single shot in which the framing remains roughly the same but the people within the frame suddenly shift from one location to the next. The effect is jarring.

Following his murder of the policeman, Michel arrived in Paris. He was out of money, having barely enough change to buy coffee and a paper (not enough change, apparently, to prevent him from stiffing his waitress for the coffee). He can't find Patricia at home so he visits the apartment of an old fling (Liliane Dreyfus), a former actress now working as a script girl at a TV studio, in hopes that she will lend him some money. First, though, he has to reconnect, to pretend he's come specifically to see her. He arrives as she's getting ready for work, and he asks what she's been up to,

Figure 6.1 Jump cut in Liliane's apartment.

and tells her he had been working on a film production in Italy. He is standing in front of her and then, abruptly, without warning or explanation, he is seated at her desk, as she leans over him. The framing has not noticeably altered, and the background remains the same, but a slice of time has been erased, and the discontinuity has not been masked by a cutaway or by a shot from another perspective, as continuity editing demands. While a careful inspection of the two shots (shown above) does show a slight difference in the framing – indicating that they were likely drawn from two separate camera takes – what stands out is the sudden difference in the position of the characters.

There are a few other jump cuts like this scattered throughout this scene in Liliane's apartment. He stands up, for example, starts to walk towards her and then is suddenly across the room, as if he'd disappeared and reappeared elsewhere within the frame. With apologies to Godard we might say in this context that if the tracking shot is a question of morality, the jump cut is a matter of metaphysics.

Metaphysics and the jump cut

At a very basic level, jump cuts remind viewers that they are watching a film. They break with the appearance of a single continuous action taking place on screen, and reveal that appearance to be the result of artifice. The appearance of continuous activity on screen results largely from two processes. First, there is the technological artifice of the cinema, which – at least in the age of analog film – projects still images in a sequence so rapid that the observer cannot discern the difference between frames and perceives them as a continuous movement. With digital recording and projection the technology is different, but the effect is largely the same. The second process that creates the appearance of continuous activity on screen is the technical artifice of editing, of ordering sequences or clips so as to avoid confusion regarding what is supposed to be taking place and when it is supposed to occur. Even where there are cuts, those cuts should be used to make clear the order and placement of events. If one shot shows someone entering a door, the next shot should show us the room they have just entered. If one shot shows someone speaking, the next shot should show someone listening. What happens, where it happens, and when it happens should all be clear.

Jump cuts interrupt the continuity of a single shot, rupturing the illusion created by the technological artifice of cinema. At the same time because unlike the majority of cuts in the continuity style they call attention to themselves, they call attention at the same time to the fact that the film is a product, that editing is the result of decisions on the part of the filmmakers. They thus signal the artificiality of the apparent continuity that is usually created through techniques of editing for continuity. If there are gaps, if the two shots don't match up precisely, that is because they are appearances, perhaps filmed on separate occasions. They remind the viewer that the world in which the film's narrated events are supposed to be taking place is not real but is a fictional construct. Its apparent continuity is the result of a deliberate strategy on the part of the filmmakers to create that appearance. At the same time, by allowing the constructed character of the image to show itself, the jump cut reveals the reality of its construction. The film shows itself to be a made thing, and thereby makes manifest the making.

Jump cuts signal the contrast between the world depicted in the cinematic moving image and that of the perceiver. They compress the duration of the film, without hiding the fact that something has been cut out. They thus give us a more clear sense of the difference between the timing of a given scene and the time it would have taken for the events it portrays to take place. They highlight the fact that the time and space in which the events on screen are supposed to be taking place is distinct from that of the world from which the audience member enters into the cinematic experience. The apparent pacing and spatial organization of situations and events taking place on screen are never strictly identical with that of the audience. Yet the contrast is obscured in films where cuts are designed to go unnoticed. When an audience member is caught up in the experience of a film she may still be aware dimly of time passing and of things going on around her in the theater and in the larger world outside. Yet such things are not the focus of her attention. To the extent that the film is effective, she will be absorbed in the rhythm and organization of the actions taking place on screen. Jump cuts interrupt that absorption. They reveal gaps in the world depicted on-screen. They call attention to the missing bits of time that are usually obscured by continuity editing.

Two separate shots, joined together by a cut, make sense only as a result of some kind of synthetic act on the part of the observer. While the shots might make sense on their own, the fact that they are joined in this way won't make sense unless there is some reason why and how they fit together. This doesn't need to be explicit, and making sense of a given cut doesn't always require much thought. Indeed the link might seem to be obvious. If there were a video containing clip after clip of yawning kittens, the link between the clips would be obvious. Each would consist of yet another example of a yawning kitten. A slightly less obvious kind of link can be found in the case of what Sergei Eisenstein called "conceptual montage," when images that on first glance contrast with one another are joined together by a cut, provoking audiences to think of the element or idea they have in common. The sharper the contrast, the more likely it is that bridging the gap will require some effort on the part of the viewer and that the linking theme will rise to the level of an explicit thought. A yawning kitten and then a yawning dog may seem too obvious to require attention. A shot of a kitten followed by a shot of a strong man may require a bit more effort and attention. The contrast between the shots provokes the question, however vaguely it may be formulated, regarding why the first shot was followed by the second. Perhaps the first shot suggests that the man is not as tough as he looks. A thought such as this, provoked by the cut, may even rise to the level of a hypothesis, one that can be confirmed or disconfirmed by what follows in the film.

The contrast between shots in the classical continuity style can seem to be much sharper than this one, and yet the link between them will still seem to be immediately evident. We see a close-up of a woman's face, looking at something, and then a shot of a car, two shots that seem to have nothing in common, and yet we know at once that she is looking at the car. In this case what links them is an action, unfolding in a common time and space. We grasp, apparently without giving it any thought, that the reason for the ordering of the shots is that the first one explains the other. The first shot shows that she is looking at something and the second shows what she sees. Our interest in the story leads us to interpret the second shot as a continuation of the first, as narratively linked to the first. The first shot, showing that she is looking at something, provokes the question what it is. The second shot gives the audience an answer.

Jump cuts tend to occur in the context of a scene where what is happening already makes sense. The cut to the second shot is not needed to explain what we are seeing in a first shot. It is not needed to provide context for a first shot in the content of a second shot, as when a first shot shows us someone startled by something she sees and the next shot shows what it is that has startled her. The second shot is, merely, an interrupted continuation of what began in the second shot. It doesn't add more context from the world represented in the film. If it does add context, the context it provides is from the world that produced the film, which is to say, from the world that includes both the audience and the filmmakers.

All edits tacitly signal the existence of an editor. Yet good editing, as is often said, is invisible. It doesn't call attention to itself. A jump cut, by that standard, is a bad cut, because it does call attention to itself. It calls attention to the fact that an edit occurred. It also calls attention to what was cut out, because unlike usual cuts which are constructive, creating from a series of disconnected shots the illusion that they belong to the same narrative space, the jump cut is destructive. It makes very clear that a slice of time has been cut out. By cutting out a bit of time from the shot the jump cut reminds us that the events that were filmed to create the shot took place in a different time than the time that is represented within the shot. The jump cut thus points to a reality outside of the world represented in the film. It points to the conditions that make the represented reality, the cinematic appearance, possible.

The jump cut calls attention both to the fact of a situation unfolding in its own way, a situation for which the camera merely happened to be present, and reminds us that our only access to that situation is by way of the specific bits of moving image shot by the cameraperson and selected for inclusion by the film's editor. By breaking with the illusion of a continuously unfolding event, the jump cut reminds us that what we are witnessing is not the event itself but a representation of that event. The event we seem to have been observing never in fact occurred. What did occur was a performance, and the recording of that performance by a camera, and the editing of the footage that resulted from that recording to produce a finished film. All of this now allows us to witness the representation of a series of fictional events, that would seem to be real events if they did not call such attention to their artificiality. The discontinuity of the jump cut may not be jarring enough in the moment to provoke reflection upon all of this, yet it interrupts our fascination with the image and provokes the question, at least in hindsight, of why the filmmakers chose to break with continuity in this way.

While jump cuts appear at various points throughout *Breathless*, they are not as ubiquitous as one might assume on the basis of the film's reputation. The film is shot with a handheld camera, something rarely done in mainstream films to that point, reflecting Godard's interest in documentary as much as fictional film. The film is, nevertheless, edited for the most part in a classical style, demonstrating that Godard and his editor are fully aware of and capable of employing the conventions of cinema that they occasionally violate. There are in fact more tracking shots than jump cuts throughout *Breathless* and the jump cuts are mostly clustered in a few different scenes, primarily scenes taking place in enclosed spaces, like cars and apartments. Their use is perhaps most notable in an early scene where Michel drives Patricia to an appointment with her colleague, and in a subsequent extended scene in which Michel attempts to woo her in her apartment. While jump cuts generally call attention to themselves, and remind the viewer that they are watching a film, and call attention to the difference between the representation and the conditions that produced it, different jump cuts can emphasize different things. To see what the prominent jump cuts in *Breathless* reveal, we need to consider some of them specifically.

Michel had been looking for Patricia and finally found her while she was out selling papers in the street. He told her he wanted to see her later, then he went to get his money from a friend. He found her later and tried to convince her to spend the night with him. He told her about a story he'd read in the paper about a bus driver who stole some money to impress a girl: when they'd spent the money, the bus driver told her it was stolen; she still stuck by him and stood lookout while they robbed some villas. Michel told her he thought that was sweet of her, but Patricia didn't seem to agree. She suddenly remembered she had an appointment and was about to look for a taxi when he offered her a ride. He walks off and then we cut to a close-up shot from behind Michel, showing just his head and his hat, and with his hands on the steering wheel of a different car, as he tells Patricia that the Ford she remembers him having from before was now in the garage for repairs.

The next shot shows just Patricia, shot closely from behind as she sits in the passenger's side of the car. We can see what she sees: the cars, the buildings, the pedestrians on sidewalks, all passing by in the background. We don't see Michel for the remainder of the drive, but we do hear his voice: "let me stay with you." She is looking away, and turns back to look at him. "I've got a headache." We hear his voice again, but he remains out of the shot: "We won't have sex. I just want to be with you." She shakes her head, "that's not it, Michel." They are passing an intersection, past two people standing on the corner. Suddenly, the background has changed. They are passing a parking lot. Her hands had been in her lap; now she is holding a mirror and fussing with her hair. She looks at him and then back at the mirror. Another jump cut. The background has changed, different cars, a different building, can all be seen in the distance beyond Patricia. She's no longer holding the mirror and she is looking in a different direction. She turns towards him: "why are you so sad?" She uses *vous*, the formal word for "you." He says, gruffly, "because I am." She tells him that's silly, and asks again "why are you so sad?" This time she says *tu*, the more intimate form of "you" and then asks which she should use, *tu* or *vous*. He tells her it makes no difference, then adds: "but I can't do without you" – addressing *her* with the familiar *"toi."* "You (*tu*) can very well," she tells him and he interrupts to point out an impressive passing car, and there is another jump cut. Two more jump cuts as she asks him about himself, and he orders her in a stern voice not to go see the man she is about to meet for lunch. Another and she's looking away, and he says, "woe is me! I love a girl with a pretty neck…" Again a sudden cut and she is looking at him, now they are somewhere else but his voice continues as if no time had passed, "…pretty breasts," cut and she is looking away, seeming to ignore him "a pretty voice," cut and she is looking back at him, "pretty wrists," now she is looking straight ahead, "a pretty forehead," cut again and she is looking to her right as they make a right turn, "and pretty knees …." No longer simply staring into the distance, she seems more attentive as she scans their surroundings and he continues, "but she's such a coward." She isn't paying attention to him, though, or to what he is saying anymore, but looks over at him quickly and tells him, urgently, pointing to the building on her right, "it's right here. Stop."

The next cut is not a jump cut. We get a new framing in which Patricia is no longer visible. The camera is higher up, facing down and over Michel's right shoulder as he tells her he needs to park and she tells him not to bother, then leans into the frame, kisses him on the cheek, and gets out of the car while he watches her leave. He tells her to get lost. Then, when she's gone, he adds: "Get lost. You make me want to puke." The word he uses is "dégueulasse" – and it really means something more like "lousy" or "rotten" or "disgusting." It's the word Parvulesco later uses to describe Chopin. We'll hear this word again at the end of the film. It is, in fact, the final word of the film.

There are ten jump cuts in total throughout the drive. The camera never changes its framing, facing Patricia from behind, but what might have been a single continuous shot is broken up, streamlined. The sound is continuous throughout, as if the time passing is irrelevant and the only thing that matters is their words. They could have shot and edited it differently, could have managed to compress the time it took to drive across town in another way, including the same dialogue but without using jump cuts that so obviously call attention to the editing but that also keep the focus on Patricia. For example, they could have cut between two perspectives: one in which the camera faced Patricia from behind and one which faced Michel from behind. We'd already seen the perspective on Michel in the very first shot in the car, and it would have been easy to alternate between shots, say, of Michel talking and Patricia listening and Patricia talking and Michel listening. That, or something like it, is what classical style would demand. In interviews, Godard has said that he chose to use jump cuts in *Breathless* just because it was his first feature film and was far too long and so he cut out bits to shorten it (Raskin). Even if that is true, it doesn't explain why he shortened it this way rather than by cutting out entire scenes or trimming shots while maintaining continuity. Whatever his reasons for considering jump cuts in the first place, the real question is why he chose to retain them in the finished product and what their impact is on how audiences make sense of it.

A given film technique can communicate a wide variety of different meanings, depending on how it is used. A close-up, for example, can be used to communicate the emotional state of a character. It can also be used to suggest his or her isolation from other characters. It can reveal information. Or it can mislead, or keep information hidden. It can only do any of these things because its primary function is to magnify the relative size of a specific object, and isolate that object from its context. This ensures that the audience will give the element that is magnified to fill the screen the attention it requires to convey what it should. A jump cut has two distinct primary functions, corresponding to one of the two different ways it can be created. It can either join two distinct shots into a longer quasi-continuous sequence, or it can shorten a single continuous shot, interrupting its continuity by removing a portion from within. It usually isn't obvious which method is employed, but each has distinctive merits.

The first method allows the filmmaker to combine pieces of separate shots, without obscuring the fact of their separation. Repeated takes of the same bit of dialogue or the same action, shot from the same camera position, can be cut up into the pieces that work and then combined into a choppy but effective unity. Of course, the same thing can be accomplished without the choppiness by varying the camera position between takes and combining shots with different framings, or by cutting away to something else in the middle of a take and then cutting back to the selected ending. So something else is needed to explain why a filmmaker would choose this first method besides the fact that it allows him or her to select the best pieces from multiple takes.

The second method allows the filmmaker to shorten a long take by cutting out the unnecessary bits. One might, once again, accomplish the same thing without the jump cuts by using cutaways or reverse shots. Of course, that wouldn't work if cutaways or reverse shots were never filmed and it was too late to go back and get them. So one reason to use jump cuts would be that there wasn't enough coverage to ensure a smoother edit in the classical continuity style. Godard himself suggested this as a reason he'd used jump cuts in *Breathless:* he'd been so eager to capture his subjects on film that he didn't stop to think how it would all fit together and then he picked the simplest solution of trimming the excess without regard for classical conventions. Yet there aren't jump cuts everywhere. They are mostly confined to a few scenes focused on establishing the significance of the uneasy relationship between Patricia and Michel. Moreover, the structure of the film doesn't feel like an afterthought, and, while his methods were unconventional he seems to have given them a great deal of thought. He and his cinematographer Coutard, for example, were very deliberate about shooting the film with a single handheld camera in a documentary style – similar to that employed by Jean Rouch while shooting *Moi un Noir* (1958) – a method that doesn't usually allow for multiple takes from different angles. As is well known, Godard often makes outrageous and provocative claims in interviews. His suggestion would imply that he was forced to include jump cuts in the film as a result of his incompetence or inexperience as a filmmaker. While many of his contemporaries thought as much upon the film's release, this doesn't explain why others found this break with the classical style so liberating and so fitting for the story he was telling or why the film has stood the test of time, and has come to be identified with the invention of a new style of filmmaking.

What stands out most in a jump cut is the suddenness of the breach: the unexpected, jarring, shift. Equally important is the fact that most of what is in the frame does not change. Only against a relatively stable and continuous background can a jump appear as a jump. What changes most notably in a jump cut is usually the position of the people in the foreground of the frame. Jump cuts nearly always include at least one prominent character, and while the position of his or her body may change somewhat, the framing of the background remains, roughly, the same. In the case of the jump cuts in the car, there were only slight changes in the position of Patricia's upper body, while the framing of the car remained the same. The background of the Paris streets also changes, but since we tend to be focused on Patricia, those changes don't feel as abrupt as the slighter changes in the position of her head, hands, and face. By focusing on Patricia, these jump cuts call attention to her performance, and to the fact that it is a performance. Because the shots do not show Michel, but only allow us to hear his voice as he addresses her, the shots allow us to focus on the way she casually resists his entreaties to enter into his fantasy of a romantic escape from the police.

The truth of the appearance, the truth of the film, is that it *is* a film, that it is a performance captured by the camera, produced for an audience. Patricia isn't really Patricia, and neither is Michel Michel. They are actors playing a part. Yet they are also real people, Jean Seberg and Jean-Paul Belmondo, performing for the camera, whose real performances are as real and taking place at the same time as the unperformed events that the camera also captures around them. The reality from which Godard pieces together the film is the reality of two actors improvising as they drive through Paris, with Godard and Coutard in the back of the car, reacting to one another and to circumstances around them as they speak out lines that Godard had likely scribbled out for them while seated in a café that very morning. Since the focus is always on Patricia, Michel's lines could be added in later. So the jump cuts in the car allow Godard to select those bits from Patricia's performance that both illustrate clearly what the scene needs to show and in which she manages to deliver his scripted lines with the same kind of naturalness as we see in the unstaged scenes taking place outside of the car. What appears in these shots, then, what calls attention to itself in this sequence, or what is made to appear by way of the jump cuts, is both the reality of an unfolding interaction between the actors and the director and the camera, and the fiction of a situation involving just the fictional characters they play.

The selection of just these bits of the performance, with a focus on Jean Seberg's performance of Patricia, allows us to see clearly the difference between Michel's already established desire to reconnect with her and draw her into his life, as a partner in his crimes, and her own plans to continue as she has, to work on her career. He didn't want to see her go and meet another man. He'd offered her a ride in hopes that she would change her mind. The camera, pointed at her throughout the ride, allows us to hear what he tells her but see her reaction. What we see and hear makes clear: she isn't going to change her mind. She never even really considered it. That's why Michel is disgusted. She got what she needed. He stole another car and drove her across town, and he's no closer to realizing his plan of convincing her to run away with him to Rome.

We see more than that, though. We see the streets of Paris passing by. If what we see and hear is Jean Seberg and Jean-Paul Belmondo acting for the camera, playing the parts of Michel and Patricia, what we see in the background on the streets is simply happening around them. Life unfiltered, unaware. For some of the other scenes, shot on the streets, the cinematographer Raoul Coutard hid in a covered cart, shooting film through a hidden hole while Godard pushed him around. That allowed him to avoid notice, so that people on the streets would not stare. Shooting from the back seat of the car has the same impact, but in that case there was no need to hide. Only Belmondo and Seberg, the actors, knew they were being filmed. So he could capture whatever was happening on the streets without a hint of artifice. That is, effectively, the documentary technique we characterized above as direct cinema. While the acting itself was not spontaneous, but performed for the camera, the jump cuts allow the audience to see the reality of the artifice, and allow Godard to pick and choose the essential bits from the performance of the actors. The jump cuts, effectively, work in the style of the documentary technique of cinema vérité, but used here in the service of creating a fictional film. Even while the scenario and the characters are fictional, the performance is real and the film documents it in pieces. So this sequence of shots in the car combines the spontaneous realism of direct cinema, capturing life as it happened on the streets of Paris, with the self-awareness or reflexivity of cinema vérité, reminding us that the performance is a performance and the film is a film.

The shots in the car also have the impact of a tracking shot, insofar as they stay focused on Patricia throughout the drive across the city. They allow us to see her reactions to Michel's attempts to convince her to drop her plans and stay with him. We see that they barely know each other, that she doesn't even know whether to address him as "vous" or "tu." We see that she doesn't share his fantasy of lovers on the run, that she has other things on her mind, but that he isn't interested in her plans. They also allow us to see what is going on in the streets as she passes, so that we see the contrast between her performance and the reality of what is happening around her. It is the jump cuts, though, that call attention to that performance, that remind us that what we are seeing is an actor in a car, with the cameraman seated behind her. It is only by calling attention to the artificiality of the situation in the car, that it is an actor performing for a camera, that the film calls attention to and makes apparent the contrast between this appearance and the spontaneous reality taking place around and beyond it that just happens to be captured by the camera.

By interrupting the continuity of the classical style of narrative film, the jump cut paradoxically at once manages to remind viewers that what they are watching is merely a film, and at the same time to heighten its realism. It does this, not by encouraging the absorption of viewers into the world of the film, but by calling attention to the distinction between the fiction of the images unfolding on screen and the reality of what was captured on camera to produce those images. Jump cuts do not function to help audiences make sense of a shot by contextualizing what takes place there in relation to the larger reality represented in the film. They, rather, contextualize that represented reality itself. They contextualize it in relation to the reality that produced that representation by reminding us, on the one hand, of the difference between that reality and that of the viewer, and, on the other hand, between that reality and the agencies responsible for its appearance.

Several jump cuts appear later in the lengthy sequence that takes place in Patricia's apartment. While the shots from within the car allowed the unfiltered reality of the streets of Paris to appear in the background as a contrast with the scripted performances, in the apartment sequence Godard and Coutard's approach to shooting long uninterrupted takes without concern for how they would be trimmed down later allowed for something authentic to emerge as a reluctant but real intimacy between the two actors. The sequence within the apartment allows for spontaneous and genuine moments to emerge from the performance, in the context of the artificial situation where two actors, a cameraman, and a director are confined for an extended period within a cramped single bedroom flat. The willingness to condense long takes using jump cuts, rather than standard continuity editing, gives the filmmakers the freedom to shoot the scenes like they would a documentary, without needing to worry much about setting up shots or asking the actors to perform multiple takes. They can use the bits of the performance that seem most genuine, or that capture most the mood and feel they are looking for, rather than the bits that fit into a continuous edit. This allows the extended sequence in the apartment to highlight the central theme of the film, which is that in spite of their coming together and sharing the same space, Patricia and Michel have very different perspectives and are having quite distinct experiences. The jump cuts also highlight the contrast between their situations and that of the audience.

By cutting out inessential bits of time, without hiding the fact that time has been compressed, the jump cuts in this scene remind us that even though the apartment scene occupies a relatively lengthy portion of the film from the perspective of the viewer, it would have occupied much more time for Michel and Patricia. Of course, because the cuts also call attention to the artificiality of the representation, they remind us that it must have taken even longer for the actors and the crew.

Michel had been following her around during her date with the reporter, and then snatched the key to her apartment when the concierge wasn't looking. When she went home, she found him lying in her bed. At first, she is annoyed. She'd rather be alone. They argue, they talk, they tease one another. He flirts, he becomes resentful. When she asks him why he'd come, he says he wants to sleep with her, that he loves her. She says she's not sure if she loves him back. This, effectively, becomes the question that the story will hinge on from here on out. In a conventional crime thriller the plot hinges on whether the criminals will be captured, and if there is a love story it is "the B-story," secondary to the main plot. In this film what happens is that the B-story becomes the main plot and everything else becomes secondary to it. He doesn't die, as we'll see, because the police catch up to him and shoot him. He lets himself be caught when she decides she doesn't love him and tells the inspectors where he's hiding.

Part of the problem, as this sequence in the apartment makes clear, is that their situations are completely different. They conceive of the implications and significance of love in very different ways, and so they are living out different stories. When she tells him she can't be sure if she loves him he asks her when she will know and she tells him "soon." He asks how long that is and when she refuses to specify, he complains: "A woman will never do in eight seconds what she'll gladly do eight days later. It's all the same, eight seconds or eight days." He is thumbing through a magazine that shows nude women posing. He adds: "why not eight centuries?" It's as if for him, the decision and the act were all that matters. He wants her to choose, without delay. Anything else is a half measure. Anything else is cowardice. Consequences be damned. To be free is to be bold, to act without consideration of the consequences. It is, as the movie poster Michel had seen reads, to "live dangerously until the end." Of course, that means that, at least until "the end," until the last breath, he always remains free to decide differently later.

For her, by contrast, it isn't merely a matter of decision. It is not about action, but passion. To go with him means giving up on a career she has begun, giving up on the prospects of education. Eight days, she says, might be enough, but not eight seconds. She could of course choose to sleep with him now, as in fact she does near the end of the scene. What she can't decide now is how she feels and what she wants. What she can't decide is a path for her future. That takes time. It involves a passionate commitment, with an acceptance of all that follows. She tells him she'd like them to be like Romeo and Juliet: overpowered by an enduring passion. "Oh, la la," he says, "that's just like a girl!" She clarifies: "Romeo," she says, "couldn't live without Juliet, but you can." He denies this – of course, he'll say anything to get her to sleep with him – and she replies "just like a guy!" The differences between them cannot, in fact, be reduced to the stereotypical gender difference between "a girl" and "a guy" since they are, in fact, living through very different situations and living out different stories.

His unwillingness to think beyond his present needs and desires is exemplified later, when she tells him she is pregnant, and that she thinks the child is his. He can't conceive of the long-term commitment that accepting this would imply. "You should have

Figure 6.2 Michel and Patricia.

been more careful," he tells her, and then goes to make another phone call about his money. When he's finished he crosses the bed and stumbles getting off. We see Patricia in a medium shot, doubled in the bathroom mirror, putting on perfume. He approaches and leans against her sink, smoking. He tells her a joke about a condemned man and then there is a jump cut. His hands are now enclosing her face, pulling her close. He tells her that up close she looks like a Martian, and there is another jump cut and he is looking away from her with his cigarette in his mouth, as she looks down, brushing her hair. "Some idea," he says, "having a kid!" She says that it isn't certain, but that she wanted to see what he would say about it. Another jump cut and he is pulling on the sleeves of her dress. He tells her to take off her clothing and when she refuses he tells her Americans are dumb, that they have bad taste. She never mentions her pregnancy again.

The jump cuts that punctuate this sequence allow Godard to maintain the same framing throughout, which allows us to see both Patricia and Michel as they stand next to each other, and to see clearly her facial expressions as she looks at herself in the mirror and as she reacts to Michel's words. The cuts, once again, remind us that what we're seeing is a performance for the camera, at the same time as they allow Godard to select from that performance the moments in which Patricia's reactions are most genuine. It's an important part of the larger scene within her apartment, even though it seems to consist of just more playful banter between them. It's here that Godard makes clear to the audience that it has become clear to her that he doesn't care much about her future, or about the impact of his actions on her, even if he is obsessed with her right now, and wants her to accompany him to Rome. It's also clear that she wants him to care, and that she feels for him the same kind of affection he feels for her.

So it doesn't come as a surprise when she sleeps with him, but it isn't a shock when she betrays him later, either. They'd talked about music, about art, about their pasts, and her ambitions. They'd played games. He'd shown himself to be vulnerable.

He'd looked at her with the same uncertain longing we'd seen when he gazed at Bogart's photo. He wasn't just a tough guy. He'd covered his head with the blanket when ashamed. He'd dropped the Bogart mask. They end up close under the blanket, and she tells him she can see herself in his eyes. Then the frame cuts to a shot of the bed from above. They are covered by sheets. He says: "this is Franco-American rapprochement." A jump cut and her face is out from under the sheet, and she says "we hide like happy elephants." Cut again and she is under the covers, he is rubbing his hand across her hip. He sits up. She is lying on her stomach. He covers her head with a sheet. Another jump cut and they are both under the sheets, moving together.

The frame cuts to the radio on the desk, which begins to play a jumpy whistling tune as the camera pans back to the bed showing more vigorous movement under the sheets, and then pans back to the radio as a hand reaches out from under the covers to shut it off. Then we get a close-up of Michel as Patricia announces, "so that's that" and crosses the bed towards the bathroom. They made love, but it doesn't mean she loves him. Sorting that out will still take time. The jump cuts in the bed, unlike the others, don't give us a window onto something real. They highlight its unimportance. Their making love is just passing time, no more nor less significant than their playful banter previously. The cuts show the passage of time. Patricia and Michel are, however, closer to each other following their "rapprochement." It is not until later, when the director intervenes by playing the man who points them out to the police, that their connection is tested, and Patricia is forced once again to decide whether a future with Michel is something she wants.

She decides it isn't. They'd been on the run until they could meet up with Michel's friends and arrange a pickup for his cash. Then they found themselves holed up hiding in the house of a friend. When they'd arrived a photographer was taking pictures of a model. Michel had asked Patricia why she didn't model, since the pay was good. She objected that models have to sleep around. Then he had his arm around her, he asked her what she was thinking. She wasn't sure. He asked whether she'd dumped her journalist friend and she said she had, but then he wonders why she'd spoken to him the previous night. "To make sure I didn't love him anymore," she replied. He complains that she complicates her own life. She turns away from him and the light goes out as the photographer and the model prepare to leave. He'd like it to be simple, and it would be if she simply followed him. It's not so simple for her. She will echo her words regarding the journalist the next day, when she announces to Michel that she had remained with him for the same reason: to discover whether or not she loved him.

They'd been having fun while on the run from the police. Now, clearly, they have nothing to say to one another. She puts on some music. He looks at a book. It's getting late and the frame cuts to a close-up of Patricia. "Sleeping's so sad," she says, smiling wistfully "we have to separ..." (*se sépar...*) and she hesitates, unsure how to complete the infinitive, so he completes it for her "...ate" (*...er*). It is a reminder of the language barrier that separates them, of so many failures of translation, that their thoughts are in different places, and that physical proximity, even sex, is not nearly enough to bridge the gap. At the same time, his completion of the word she begins suggests at least the possibility of a real "rapprochement." She repeats "se séparer," and then adds "you say 'sleep together' but you don't." They had made love, but they had not truly approached one another, and the distance between them is fully apparent, at least to her, and to us. She looks down and then at him. Then she looks directly at the camera, sadly, as it fades to black.

By the next morning, she had decided. He asks her to buy the paper and a bottle of milk, and when he isn't looking she takes the phone number of the inspector from her purse. When she goes out, she calls the inspector and tells him where he can find Michel, then she rushes back with the milk and the paper. When she arrives, she sets the paper down in front of him and puts the milk on the desk, and leans back against it, next to him. The camera has a long view of the room from overhead. He tells her that his friend Antonio is on the way with the money and puts his arm around her. "We're going to Italy, kid!" He starts to walk around the column at the center of the room, and then she tells him she can't go with him. There is a jump cut and he is suddenly around the column and facing her with his arms outstretched. "Sure you can. I'm taking you." He walks close to her but she pulls away, she places one leg up on a chair, and looks down. Another jump cut and she is looking at him. She tells him that she'd called the police and told them where he was.

Jump cuts, as we've seen, can remind us of the presence of the camera, making palpable that the film is a film. The appearance is an appearance, which is to say that it seems to be something it isn't. It seems to be the unfolding of a continuous series of events, when in fact the appearance of continuity is a construct, created by the joining together of discontinuous filmstrips. At the same time, because these interruptions of an action stand out from what happens on screen, without preventing us from making sense of it, they can serve also to comment upon the action, or to give it a rhythm or affect it wouldn't otherwise possess. The jump cuts in this scene seem to serve as punctuation, that puts emphasis on the moments of disruption between Patricia and Michel. The first jump cut comes when she tells him she won't go with him. He thinks she is concerned about practical matters like money. He can take care of that. The second jump cut comes as she makes clear it is more than that. She's called the police. There's no chance they'll work this out. They are on completely different tracks. He thinks she's bought into his plan, that she'll be his lover and co-conspirator as he flees the police. She, on the other hand, is ready to go back to the life and career that he'd interrupted when he came to meet her on the streets of Paris. She believes that by calling the police she can force him to flee on his own, and he will leave her alone. It also means she won't be charged as his accomplice and deported, which would disrupt her plans to study at the Sorbonne.

Cut to a medium shot of Patricia, still sitting on the arm of the chair, looking down. Michel is standing up facing her, his left arm on his hip and holding the milk in his other arm. He is visibly angry. "Are you crazy?" he yells, and puts his hand on her neck, pushing her back and then pulling away. She stands up and says "no, I'm fine," and walks away from him towards one of the studio lamps that the photographer had been using the night before. She turns it on and then shuts it off. "No, I'm not fine," and, as she begins to walk away from him, the camera begins to track her, keeping her at the center of the frame as she walks forward, "I don't want to go away with you now." "I knew it," he says. The camera remains facing her from the front as she continues walking around the room, leaving him behind.

Morality and the tracking shot

When Godard suggested that "tracking shots are a question of morality," it was in response to the question whether the unsettling feeling produced by Alain Resnais's film *Hiroshima mon amour* (1959) was due to its ethical themes or its aesthetic approach (Domarch, Jean et al. 62). He responded that they are the same thing. One cannot separate the subject matter of a shot from the evaluative interpretation implied by its manner of presentation. It is, moreover, a moral question whether to use a specific technique to show something or even whether to show it at all. He makes a similar point in the first episode of his extended visual essay on cinema and its impact, Histoire(s) du Cinema (1988). He calls attention to the apparent lack of technique in wartime newsreel footage. Cameras tended to maintain a respectful distance. Their images do not cater to mere curiosity. As an accompaniment to various clips depicting distorted images of destruction and death, we hear Godard's narrating voice: "no close-ups. Suffering is not a star. Nor is the burned down church or the bombed out countryside." While film techniques such as the close-up, shot-reverse shot, jump-cut, or tracking shots can each communicate a wide range of significances depending on their content, not every technique can be used to communicate every meaning, and, perhaps, some techniques should not be used at all in connection with certain subject matters. In any case, the felt significance and moral impact of a message will be shaped by the stylistic techniques used to deliver it. One cannot sharply differentiate between form and content, between the message of a film and the methods it employs.

While a given film technique does not automatically suggest a given meaning, certain techniques are more appropriate to the communication of certain senses. The jump cut, as we have seen, calls attention to itself. It also calls attention to the contrast between the representation of an action or situation on screen, and the actions or situation that produced that representation. If the action we see on screen is a woman walking across the room, its interruption by a jump cut calls attention to the activities of acting, filming, and editing that movement. The jump cut also calls attention to the difference between the duration of the representation and the supposed duration of the activities that were recorded to produce that representation.

Tracking shots call attention to themselves as well, but in a different way. By continuing, without interruption, they call attention to the duration of the shot itself, a duration that, we might say, must be endured by the audience. There is not, in the case of tracking shots, a contrast between the duration of the shot and the duration of the event that was recorded to produce that shot. A lengthy tracking shot signals that the events being filmed to produce that shot went on as long as the shot itself. If the shot is tracking an actor, they have to stay in character for the duration of the shot. If the shot moves from one action to the next, or from one actor or group of actors to another, all must be prepared to engage in a seemingly spontaneous action the moment they appear on screen. While a virtuosic tracking shot can serve to signal, at least to the savvy moviegoer, the choreographic effort it would have taken to produce it, it highlights the way in which those efforts culminate in the appearance of a coherent world, in which all of that effort remains hidden in the background. Tracking shots that follow a character as he or she moves about emphasize that character's belonging to a coherent world. To watch a tracking shot is to inhabit a moving perspective within the apparent world of the film, a moving perspective that follows the movements of a character within that world.

As the tracking shot that began with Patricia's confession continues, their words overlap. They are both speaking but not to each other. He considers what went wrong with them; she reflects upon her decision to turn him in. She says: "I don't know." He speaks out loud his realization of what the editing had already shown us: "I just talked about myself and you yourself." "I'm so stupid," she says, and he continues as if he no longer hears her: "You should've talked about me, and me, about you." They had been talking past one another, all along. He had envisioned one thing, a plan that included her but that never took her desires or her situation into account. Her uncertainty, her reluctance, would have been clear had he only been listening. She turns her head to look in his direction, speaking loudly, almost shouting: "I don't want to be in love with you. That's why I called the police." She is holding her hands together behind her back and then speaks more softly: "I stayed with you to make sure I was in love with you. Or that I wasn't." The framing has altered and now the camera no longer faces her but shows her in profile as she finishes the thought: "and since I'm being mean to you, it proves I'm not in love with you." She has completed her cycle around the room and is now back in front of the desk and they are both in the frame. He is listening now, and yells at her to repeat herself.

She repeats her last sentence as she begins to walk around the room again. The tracking shot continues without a break, and as she walks away from him they once again begin speaking as if the other were not present. "They say there's no happy love..." he begins, as she says "if I loved you ... It's too complicated!" He continues, now off-screen, "on the contrary, there's no unhappy love." She doesn't seem to hear or acknowledge his words, and as she reaches the column at the center of the room and begins to turn she says "I want people to let me be. I'm independent." He responds to that: "you think you are, you're not." She continues, "maybe you love me ... that's why I turned you in." "I'm better than you are," he says, which she follows with "Now you have no choice but to go." She has finished the circuit and is once again in front of the desk and standing next to him. "You're crazy!" he says. He pushes the back of her head: "that's a pathetic argument."

Now the camera stays on him, leaving her behind. He lights another cigarette and then tucks in his shirt as he begins to follow the same circuit around the room, but in the opposite direction. "You're like the girl who'll sleep with everyone except the one man who loves her, saying it's because she sleeps with everyone." He is buttoning up his shirt as we hear her voice addressing him from out of the frame: "why don't you go?" He shakes his head, throws his arms up in frustration. She adds: "I've slept with lots of men. Don't count on me." Although he has completed the circuit, and walked all the way around the room, he still remains alone in the frame. The camera is close to him and angled in such a way that she doesn't appear along with him as he had when the camera was tracking her while she passed where he stood. She speaks to him, more urgently, off-screen, "what are you waiting for?"

Given that they unfold in "real time" – because they have the same duration as the events they depict – tracking shots give us a clearer sense of the urgency involved in a situation than sequences put together using conventional editing. At the same time, when they highlight the experience of a single character, they allow us to see whether the sense of urgency we may feel corresponds to their experience. While the sense of urgency that Patricia and Michel feel may be different, we are reminded of the contrast between their subjective perspectives and what we might call the objective inevitability of the arrival of the police force. That has been a theme throughout the film. While the story emphasizes the contrasting perspectives and interests of Patricia and Michel, we are never allowed to forget that in the background there are detectives in pursuit, and that whatever plans they may have can be cut short.

The tracking shot comes to an end, abruptly. The frame cuts to a close-up of Patricia, and now he is off-screen as we hear him say: "no, I'm staying. I'm in bad shape. I prefer prison." Now she tells him he is crazy, and the camera pans away from her to frame his face in close-up. "Yes," he agrees.

If jump cuts disrupt the continuity of an action against a stable background, tracking shots serve to establish the continuity of a character's movements and actions as the background shifts. If jump cuts remind us of the presence of the camera by revealing the reality of the artifice, tracking shots immerse us within the fiction. As suggested above, if tracking shots do call attention to themselves it is only by way of their audacity, as when an extended shot follows the seamlessly continuous development of an elaborate series of actions involving a complex coordination of a host of actors and events, and an audience that is film-savvy wonders how they ever managed to pull it off. Those kinds of tracking shots – such as the opening shot of Orson Welles' film *Touch of Evil* (1958) – are astonishing because it is not possible in the context of a tracking shot to cut. As soon as there is a cut, the tracking shot is finished. Everything that appears within the shot had to be choreographed so as to unfold precisely as it appears, and the trick is to manage to make it all seem spontaneous and unstaged while keeping all of the direction and coordination of these elements out of view of the camera.

This shot, near the end of *Breathless*, isn't like one of those virtuoso tracking shots. It's much more modest, and doesn't call attention to itself in the way that jump cuts do. The shot followed her around the room twice and followed him around once more in the opposite direction. It would have been a fairly straightforward affair to shoot it. The smooth feel of the tracking shots in *Breathless* were achieved by having the cinematographer Raoul Coutard sit in a wheelchair operating the camera with Godard directing the performance while pushing him around. What this tracking shot accomplishes, however, is remarkable for its simplicity. We get a window onto Patricia's face as she traverses the room, caught up in her own thoughts, spoken out loud, and then a window onto Michel's face as he does the same. They are both speaking but they aren't really speaking to each other. They only respond directly to one another in the moments where their paths intersect, when they are shown within the frame together. So the tracking shot emphasizes their isolation, that while they inhabit the same space they are, as it were, in different worlds. Their perspectives hardly intersect, and this sequence establishes this both through its visuals, that isolate them from one another, and through the way that they speak over one another. This tracking shot highlights the fact that while their paths have intersected for a time, their situations and perspectives have been quite different.

This was hinted at previously in a number of ways, such as in the scene with the jump cuts, considered above, when Michel drove Patricia to her appointment with the journalist. We'd seen then, at least, that Patricia was not open to his advances if they got in the way of her own plans. She does clearly find him attractive and interesting, and when he breaks into her apartment she does eventually let their mutual attraction prevail, for a time. That she can't be fully drawn into his way of seeing things, however, is never more clear than in this sequence, when they are shown to speak over one another, and to occupy the same space while inhabiting very different perspectives that only partially overlap. Another recurring motif from the film, that emphasizes that in spite of their proximity they are living through very different situations and have different perspectives on the world that they share, are the many moments in the film where Michel says something in colloquial French that Patricia asks him to clarify. His clarifications always manage to leave something lost in translation. While they can ostensibly speak the same languages, in other words, what they mean by their words is not always the same. Just as the tracking shot indicates that their trajectories do not overlap, these moments suggest that their ways of making sense of the world differ, so that they do not really inhabit the same world. Perhaps the most poignant of these moments takes place in the very last scene.

Last breath: authenticity and death

In an interview with Yvonne Baby, for *Le Monde,* Godard pointed out that his friend François Truffaut supplied him the basic idea for *Breathless.* What he'd added was the idea of an attraction between an American woman and a French man whose existential attitudes were utterly different. "The American, Patricia, is on a psychological level, whereas the guy, Michel, is on a poetic level. They use words – the same words – but they don't have the same meaning." He adds that "things couldn't go well between them because he thinks about death all the time, while she never gives it a thought" (Baby 165–6). It's worth adding that she seems to give it some thought by the end. Michel, we might say, never changes throughout the film. He attempts throughout to live out an aesthetic ideal, perhaps best represented by his image of Bogart. Or, perhaps, by the slogan from the movie poster for *Ten Seconds to Hell* that he passes early in the film: *Vivre dangereusement jusqu'au bout!* – "Live dangerously until the end!" While he acts out that slogan as his final act, he lives it throughout. He starts out stealing a car and steals a few others throughout the film. He kills a policeman. He stays in Paris, in spite of the danger, not only in order to get cash but in hopes of winning over Patricia. Patricia, by contrast, tends to live much more cautiously. She has ambitions. She makes plans, to become a journalist, to pursue an education. She takes steps to see these plans to fruition, ignoring Michel's objections that she should be spending her time with him. While the time she did spend with Michel turned out to involve some risk, she gave up the adventure shortly after the detective had pointed out how it might impact her long-range objectives. Still, the consequence of her caution and of her decision to inform on Michel is that Michel dies in the street. His way of life, exemplified by his manner of death, did appear to affect her. Her confrontation with death may not lead her to live dangerously, like Michel, but, as will be clearer in what follows, it does seem to have led to a resolution on her part. It does appear, by the end, that she will no longer be someone who never gives a thought to death. Rather, she will be impressed by the fact that however carefully she plans for an open-ended future, death will always remain at the horizon. She will be struck by the finitude of human existence. She won't become obsessed with death. She will, perhaps, become impressed by the responsibility to live authentically, knowing that no endeavor carries with it the guarantee of completion and that each action she begins could be her last.

Michel had decided not to run, but he goes outside to warn his friend Berruti – who is just arriving with the money – that the police are on the way. Berruti hands him the money and offers him a gun. He refuses the gun, but as the inspectors arrive, Berruti tosses it at Michel's feet and he picks it up. He is shot by one of the policemen. That begins another long tracking shot, with Michel running down the street, careening back and forth as if he is drunk. The jazz score blasts with a pounding beat. Then we cut to a medium tracking shot of Patricia, running after him with a look of concern on her face. She puts her hand over her chest. Then we cut back to the tracking shot of Michel, who trips and falls when he looks behind him. He gets up, clutching at his back where the bloodstain on his shirt is spreading. He continues to run down the street, and it seems he can barely stand up, but he continues, in what seems to be a parody of an exaggerated death in a Hollywood film. He is running towards an intersection and, as he reaches the crossing lane, just before he reaches the traffic of the intersecting street, he falls forward, seemingly onto his face, and then his legs fly up behind him. The camera continues to get closer even as he no longer moves.

Patricia reaches him, with the police car following closely behind her. Then we get a shot from above him as he lies down on the street, now on his back, with his arms spread out. He is still wearing his sunglasses, and a cloud of cigarette smoke billows from his mouth. The feet of three policemen and those of Patricia enter the frame, so that they surround his dying body. We see her in close-up, her hand covering her face. She is breathing heavily, and lets her hand fall. Then we see his face in close-up, lying on the brick street. He is looking up and to the right, at her. He opens his mouth wide, makes a grimacing smile, then purses his lips: the sequence of expressions he had displayed when she had asked him before what he'd meant by "making a face."

She looks at him, upset, and then we see him again. He says: "makes me want to puke." Then he covers his face with his hand and presses his own eyes shut, his head rolling to the side. He is, presumably, dead. She asks the policemen what he'd said. One of the policemen answers: "He said you make him want to puke." The word he used was "dégueulasse," which is slang for something disgusting, or for someone whose behavior is repellant. While "makes him want to puke" is a loose translation of the word, the policeman mistranslates the phrase as a whole, though we can't know whether or not this was deliberate. The policeman said he was referring to her. In fact what he'd said is "c'est vraiment dégueulasse" – "it (or this) is truly disgusting" – and the policeman told her he'd said "que vous êtes vraiment une dégueulasse" – "that you are a truly disgusting person." Michel could have been speaking of life as a whole, of the situation he's in, being shot in the streets, or betrayed by Patricia. Regardless of what he meant, she didn't understand, because the word he'd used was unfamiliar.

So she asked, like she'd asked Michel so many times before, to clarify the meaning of an unfamiliar word. She looks directly at the camera, and raises her thumb to the side of her lips and asks: "qu-est-ce que c'est 'dégueulasse'" – "what does that mean: 'puke'"? It is as if she is asking us. Without waiting for a response, she runs her thumbnail across her lip and then traces her lower lip in the other direction. Her face is blank for a moment then becomes resolute, with a hint of a smile, as she turns away from the camera and the frame fades to black and in bold white letters the word "FIN" (the end) appears on the screen.

She posed the final question to us: what is disgusting? Her turn towards the camera resembles the moment from the beginning of the film when Michel addressed the audience. There, too, his words seemed to assess the audience directly, passing judgment on those (of us) who can't enjoy life as it presents itself: "if you don't like the shore, if you don't like the mountains, if you don't like the city, then get stuffed." In this final scene, she is asking a question, but her question, addressed to the audience, appears to be not just meant to ascertain the meaning of a French word she doesn't understand, which also happens to be the final word of the film. Rather, for this shot at the end of the film to have its full impact, the question presumes we know the meaning of the term, and asks us to consider what in the scenario that has been presented to us we would describe by that term. He'd said "this" is disgusting.

Figure 6.3 Qu-est-ce que c'est 'dégueulasse'?

What do we think that "this" is? The policeman seemed to think he meant Patricia. Do we consider Patricia disgusting, for having turned on Michel? Or is he the disgusting one, for stealing with impunity and killing without remorse? Or is the world he inhabits disgusting because there is little room in it for spontaneity, for living authentically, for breaking free from the kind of conventional career path that Patricia was unwilling to escape? The moment one steps out of line and tries to live freely, perhaps like they do in the movies, he is, as it were, "shot down in the streets" by the powers that be. Perhaps that is our "reality," a material and social reality defined by laws and conventions we can never fully escape regardless of the distinctness of our perspectives. Perhaps that is what is disgusting. Godard's film, unlike the more conventional films that he draws upon and emulates, specifically addresses its audience, posing to them the question of how they respond to the characters and scenario presented therein. Just as Michel is shaped by his response to Bogart and to cinematic portrayals of gangster lifestyles, we are also impacted by the cinema, and presumably also by this film in particular. It is not simply an appearance, an escapist fantasy divorced from our reality. It is part of our reality, and Godard, through this film, seeks to acknowledge that fact.

The tracking shot from the studio emphasized that while Michel and Patricia inhabit the same space, they live and think in it differently. They find themselves in different situations, and their situations define what is uniquely possible for each of them. The jump cuts, and this final shot, in which Patricia seems to address us directly, reminds us that we have our own perspective on their situation, that our own perspective is also just a perspective and that what we consider to be Michel's and Patricia's perspective are in fact only how their perspectives appear to us. As with words from different languages, there is always the possibility here of misinterpretation. There also remains the possibility of an authentic but novel translation. We might consider, in closing, Patricia's final gesture, which followed her last word, and ask whether it represents a misinterpretation or an authentic response to the life of Michel, who has just drawn his last breath.

After she asks what is "disgusting" (dégueulasse), she traces the outline of her lips with her painted thumbnail. Above the upper lip, first, and then below the lower lip in reverse. It's not, exactly, the same gesture as Michel's. He'd rubbed his thumb across his lips, while she merely grazes with her nail their outer edges, where they meet with the skin of her face. Where he followed the gesture by adopting an expressionless pose with his lips, just like that of Bogart, she completed the gesture with what was almost a smile. Even if she drew the gesture from Michel, it is clear that it means something different on her lips. She, likely, has no idea about the connection it has for him with Bogart. It signals, for her, a connection to Michel; unlike Michel, however, whose use of the gesture appears to express his desire to imitate the toughness of Bogart, the star, Patricia takes up the gesture and makes it her own. She doesn't simply want to imitate Michel, though there is something she clearly admires in his carefree spontaneity. The gesture, perhaps, expresses her desire to live for herself, authentically, to not allow herself to be defined by another's trajectory.

Michel's death, perhaps, had served as a reminder that one cannot be defined by another's path. Our lives are finite, and the possibilities they afford us are our own. We find ourselves, always, not simply in "the world" but in a situation, in the world as we have become capable of perceiving it. We see and hear only what we are able to make sense of, and consider possible only those actions we can conceive of and carry out. Yet we almost always deceive ourselves in our sense that there is always more time. There is, as it were, around the corner from all possibility the fact that will close off all possibilities, the moment of our death, after which, as far as we can know, there is no longer a world for us. We always act as if it won't come yet. When death does come to others, we treat it as an accident, something that happens to them, as if it were merely bad luck, as if death did not belong essentially to the living. When Michel was faced with death, however, he didn't simply let it happen to him. He took it on. He'd been shot in the back, and yet he chose to run, not so much to get away since he'd already given up on that but to put himself, a dying free man, on display, in defiance of the police and in front of Patricia. Then, after he had fallen down with an exaggerated tumble at the end of the road, he'd waited to die until Patricia arrived and he could speak his final words, a bold (but ambiguous) pronouncement on her, or on his situation, or on existence itself, that it is, truly, nauseating: "c'est vraiment dégueulasse."

If the film opens on Michel, and if he seems to be its protagonist, by the end of the film the focus has shifted to Patricia, and through her to us, the audience. The real plot of the film, the real event it puts on display, is not that of a petty criminal who kills a cop and goes on the run, but of the impact he has on an American student in Paris, an everyday person, presumably, like us. The film thus poses the question of the impact of films like this one upon us. She had appealed to Michel because he detected in her some of the same kind of spontaneity and independence to which he aspired. Still, she liked her routines, and, unlike him, didn't simply live for the present, but considered the impact of her actions on her future. Her question what is "disgusting" might be read as her refusal to accept the interpretation of the policeman that Michel considered her actions to be disgusting. He had, after all, looked at her with fondness in the end. He'd suggested indirectly that she not wear a sad face at his death. His death reminded her, perhaps, that whatever time she had left, and even if she had a long future ahead, she had to make it her own. Human reality is finite and, just as

Godard's films use devices like the jump cuts to remind us that the film is a dependent reality, we must, if we are to be authentic, find ways to remind ourselves that whatever freedom we possess must be carried out in the face of a finitude we cannot surpass. So she used her own version of his gesture to turn her own upset reaction into a hopeful (half) smile, determined perhaps, if not to live dangerously, like him, to live fully and boldly, authentically, until her last breath.

Conclusion

When, in *Breathless*, Patricia comes home to find Michel napping in her bed, she asks what he's doing in her apartment. "The Claridge was booked up," he explains, "so I came here." She tells him he's crazy and frowns. "Don't make such a face," he tells her, in French, "it doesn't suit you." She doesn't understand and asks what it means to "make a face." He shows her, opening his mouth wide, then frowning, then grinning widely, then pursing his lips and squeezing his eyebrows. The camera cuts to show her standing in the bathroom, gazing at herself in the mirror. She opens her mouth wide, then grins, frowns, and looks at herself, pleased. "It suits me just fine," she says and then turns back to Michel with a satisfied look.

We can't see ourselves directly. We can't see whether the face we make suits us, without some way of seeing our face. We don't perceive the impression we make on others. We need a mirror.

This is true not only of our physical appearance, but of our appearance in general, of our impact on others and on the world. We can't see ourselves by ourselves. There is something missing from every perspective: the position from which that perspective is observed. Our own presence is absent from the world as it presents itself to us. We see what lies outside and around us. We cannot see how we are seen. We don't appear to ourselves, except indirectly, except insofar as our appearance is reflected back to us through our impact on the world around us and, especially, through the ways that other people respond to our presence. While physical mirrors are objects through which we can see how we look, other people can tell us even more about the impression we make. Other people thus function as mirrors through whom it can become apparent to us how we appear from outside.

Michel saw a version of himself in the characters played by Humphrey Bogart on screen. He even tried to mirror himself upon that image. His oft-repeated gesture of rubbing his thumb across his lips, shows him attempting to model his expression and mood on the implacable mask he associated with "Bogie." He was "making a face," suited to the appearance he hoped to present to others, based on an appearance that had been cultivated by a famous actor across several films. When Patricia copies his gesture in the end, it signals that she has seen something in Michel that draws out a latent potential in herself, that of taking her own finitude seriously, of reflecting in her choices the recognition that each act might be her last.

Films do more than provide role models. They mirror for us broadly what we take the world to be like. Not only can we not see ourselves by ourselves, but we also cannot become fully clear about the way we see the world without some point of comparison or contrast. Films can provide that. By providing an appearance that can be compared with our own perspectives, films allow us to see that what we see is not the way things are but how they appear to us. Films allow us to critically evaluate our conceptions, to understand ourselves. Reflecting on cinema can be a part of what Socrates called "the examined life."

The primary subject matter of cinema is reality as it appears to us, reality on a human scale. Films tell us stories about other people, and at the same time teach us about ourselves. Films show us the world we inhabit, and thereby show us how people have shaped that world through their activities. Films also, at the same time, shape the ideas and attitudes of their audiences, influencing them in subtle and incalculable ways to remake the world according to the images they are presented. While films can function as mirrors, there is no guarantee the image they present us is undistorted. Good film criticism is vital to ensure that such distortions do not go unnoticed.

Cinema, from its beginnings, and even in its simplest forms, possessed the power to grip audiences with the impression that they were seeing something real, which they knew to be merely an image. It is, in other words, an appearance. When watching a movie, it seems as if the actions and events we observe taking place on screen are unfolding autonomously. It seems as though they would be taking place even if we weren't observing them and that they are not taking place in the place from which we observe them.

Not only, then, can film provide a mirror that allows us to reflect upon the specific ideas we may have about the world, it also offers a mirror through which our situation with respect to reality as a whole becomes apparent. Because our relationship to the images on screen is analogous to our relationship to appearances in general, film has the potential to illuminate the contrast between reality and appearance with which philosophy begins. Just as audiences in cinema are given a particular perspective on the world that appears through the film, we are also only ever afforded a finite and specific grasp upon the world as a whole. That the film is manifestly a dependent reality, a product of conditions that do not directly appear within the film, can serve to heighten our awareness of the ways in which what we consider to be real is also the result of an interaction between conditions outside of us and conditions internal to us.

Cinema is metaphysically interesting because it presents us with an appearance of reality that we know to be an appearance. So it allows us to step back and reflect upon what we consider reality to be like. Unlike the appearances we encounter in our everyday life, the appearance generated through cinema is manifestly an appearance. It is clearly not the autonomous world it appears to be, but an artifact, that appears as a result of the artistry of cinema.

Realist films aim to show us real people in real situations, whose lives are often quite different from those of the audience. Through such exposure, viewers are able to expand their conception of the situations that people can face and what they are capable of. They may manage to discover some of the limits of their preconceptions, and to see that people who initially seemed to be foreign to them are not so different in their concerns. Films whose primary aim is to entertain may not seem to be real, but are often realistic enough that their audiences can suspend disbelief. They may not reveal what reality is like, but rather what their audiences might like it to be. They are entertaining, not only because they engage the emotions of the audience, but also because they offer a vicarious experience of events they might not otherwise encounter. They can thus serve as a mirror that reflects the desires and ideals of their audience. While the scenarios they present may be unreal, they may also manage to reveal to audiences the limits of their imagination, their sense of what might be possible and desirable. Finally, films that are explicitly reflective can provoke ideas, leading their audiences to ask questions about the reality that presents itself through cinema, or to consider the nature of cinema itself and of why we find it fascinating.

All films have the potential to show us something about who we are, what we care about, and what we take to be real. Some of the best films challenge our understanding of ourselves, provoking us to rethink our values, and to revise our account of reality. While going to the cinema may sometimes seem like no more than an entertaining way to pass the time, this book was written in the hopes that some of its readers will consider the ways in which films provoke reflection upon questions regarding the nature of human experience, our obligations to others, questions of interpretation, and considerations regarding the impact and importance of art.

Suggested films

Readers interested in pursuing the idea that films naturally invoke philosophical reflection – on themes such as reality, knowledge, art, and ethics – may wish to examine some of the following films.

Metaphysics – on appearance and reality

Solaris, *directed by Andrei Tarkovsky*, 1972
A psychologist is recruited to travel to a space station surrounding an enigmatic planet when its crew begin to doubt their own sanity. When he is visited by the double of his dead wife, he has to decide whether he prefers emotional truths to scientific facts.

The Taste of Cherry, *directed by Abbas Kiarostami*, 1997
A man drives around the outskirts of Tehran, searching for someone who would be willing to bury him if he decides to commit suicide. In addition to concerns about the morality of assisting in suicide, the enigmatic ending of the film poses the question whether it even makes sense to ask about a film "what really happened?" if it doesn't appear in the film.

Koyaanisqatsi, *directed by Godfrey Reggio*, 1982
This film, composed entirely of images and sounds, without dialogue, presents us with an unsettling depiction of the reality of life in the modern industrialized world.

Vertigo, *directed by Alfred Hitchcock, 1958*
A former detective with a fear of heights falls in love with the woman he is recruited to spy on. Unable to save her when she leaps to her death, he is rescued from depression when he finds another woman who looks just like his lost lover and attempts to remake her in the image of the original. The film troubles the relation between image and original, appearance and reality, performance and actor.

Epistemology – on perspective and knowledge

Stalker, *directed by Andrei Tarkovsky*, 1979
An apocalyptic wasteland known as the Zone harbors a secret room where it is rumored that one's deepest wishes come true. An illegal guide known as the Stalker leads a writer and a scientist on a perilous journey, that tests the merits of their quite different ways of knowing against the guide's faith in the power of the Zone.

Rashomon, *directed by Akira Kurosawa, 1950*
While waiting out a downpour beneath a ruined city gate, a priest and a woodcutter reflect on the events of the past few days. A woman was raped, and her husband, a samurai, was killed. Through a series of contradictory flashbacks, the film highlights the elusive character of knowledge.

Total Recall, *directed by Paul Verhoeven, 1990*
A bored construction worker from the future dreams of going to Mars. He pays a company called Rekall to implant in him the memories of having been on Mars and saving the planet as a secret double agent. Unexpectedly it turns out (or seems) that he had in fact already been on Mars as a secret agent, and his memories had been suppressed. What is he supposed to believe?

Blow Up, *directed by Michelangelo Antonioni, 1966*
A fashion photographer captures an ambiguous image that he thinks may be evidence of a murder. The film poses the question of what counts as photographic proof, and how to differentiate between perception and interpretation.

The Conversation, *directed by Francis Ford Coppola, 1974*
A surveillance expert records a conversation that he worries may have motivated his client to assassinate a young couple. This homage to *Blow Up* puts the focus on the difficulties involved in gathering evidence from sound recording, and the moral responsibilities one has when one's work is used to commit a crime.

Embrace of the Serpent, *directed by Ciro Guerra, 2015*
The Amazonian shaman Karamakate guides two separate white explorers through the jungle in search of the yakruna, a sacred plant, once as a young man and once when he is much older and has forgotten many of his traditional ways. Based on the travel diaries of a German and American explorer, the film depicts and evokes ways of life and ways of experiencing the world that are very different from those familiar to those who live in industrial societies in the modern world.

Aesthetics – on art and beauty

The Five Obstructions, *directed by Lars von Trier and Jørgen Leth, 2004*
The inventive Danish filmmaker Lars von Trier challenges his former mentor Jørgen Leth to remake his experimental short film "The Perfect Human," under a series of progressively more challenging constraints. This documentary highlights the nature of the artistic process, questioning whether it is possible or desirable for the artist to maintain an aesthetic distance from the subject matters she explores.

Certified Copy, *directed by Abbas Kiarostami, 2011*
A writer on a book tour promoting a monograph that celebrates the value of artistic copies over their originals, finds his theories about art and life put to the test when a romantic encounter with a beautiful stranger morphs into an improvised attempt at reconciliation between estranged spouses.

Videodrome, directed by David Cronenberg, 1983
A television executive in search of new content begins broadcasting a show that features torture and porn. He begins to suspect that the graphic violence is not faked. The idea that extreme content on cable television and video has an impact on our psyches is made literal when the bodies of consumers are transformed, literally developing orifices that ingest videotapes.

Andrei Rublev, directed by Andrei Tarkovsky, 1966
An artistic exploration of the intellectual and spiritual development of the famous Russian icon artist, Andrei Rublev.

In the Mood for Love, directed by Wong Kar-Wai, 2000
Two young couples move into adjacent apartments, and the husband from one couple and the wife from the other begin to suspect that their respective spouses are having an affair with each other. As they consider how to address this, they begin to develop feelings for one another. The film is moody, enigmatic, and stylish.

Ethics – on morality and the question of how to live

The Sacrifice, directed by Andrei Tarkovsky, 1986
At the dawn of a terrible war, an aging actor comes to believe that he can stop it and save his family if he performs a single act that will appear as the act of a madman, and that he will never be able to explain to them.

The Decalogue, directed by Krysztof Kieślowski, 1988
A series of short films, made originally for Polish television, each based on one of the ten commandments of the Bible. They do not preach adherence to these rules, but each one suggests in subtle ways that each commandment contains insights that cannot be lightly dismissed.

Do the Right Thing, directed by Spike Lee, 1989
Racial tensions mount when the Italian owner of a pizza joint in Brooklyn refuses to replace the pictures of famous Italians on his wall with photographs of black actors. When police intervention leads to a black casualty, the young employee of the restaurant is forced to take sides.

Sex, Lies, and Videotape, directed by Steven Soderbergh, 1989
The sudden visit by an old friend exposes the lies preserving a marriage intact. The film examines the ethics of the camera, as well as the connection between honesty and taking responsibility for the impact of our activity.

Glossary

Aesthetics   one of the core traditional areas of philosophical inquiry, focused on the value and significance of art and of related concepts such as beauty. (See also *Metaphysics*; *Epistemology*; and *Ethics*.)

Ambiguity   given that we experience situations from an inescapably finite perspective, any true account of them will acknowledge that they would or could be experienced differently from another perspective. The existentialist philosophers Jean-Paul Sartre and Simone de Beauvoir emphasized that even our own perspective on ourselves is ambiguous since we vacillate between two distinct and incompatible ways of making sense of ourselves: as free subjects, conscious of and capable of acting upon a world outside of us; and as objects, acted upon and determined by forces and conditions outside of our control. (See also *Existentialism*.)

Analytic Philosophy   a philosophical tradition that developed in the early decades of the twentieth century, which emphasized the clarification of philosophical concepts by relating them, on the one hand, to ordinary language and experience and, on the other, to scientific theories and methods. (Contrast with *Continental Philosophy*.)

Appearance   the way things seem; often opposed to the way things are. Kant characterized appearance as the "phenomena," which he contrasted with the "noumena" or the "thing-in-itself." Philosophy is often motivated by the desire to get beyond appearances; yet arguably the lesson to be drawn from the history of philosophy is that the only realities we can arrive at and comprehend are those that appear. (See also *Thing-in-Itself*.)

Aristotle (384–322 BCE)   ancient Greek philosopher who studied with Plato at his Academy before going on to develop his own school, known as the Lyceum. His work, covering a wide range of topics from natural science and logic to ethics and metaphysics, was enormously influential throughout the middle ages. (See also *Plato*.)

Auteur Theory   film is a highly collaborative process. Unlike novelists or painters, filmmakers don't work alone. This is especially true of the films made in the heyday of the American studio system. Yet French cinephiles, some writing about film in Bazin's *Cahiers du Cinema*, noticed that a few directors working in the Hollywood studio system seemed to have made their mark on a body of work. Even as they worked in different genres, or with different studios, their films were recognizably their own. These filmmakers were dubbed *auteurs* (or authors), and critics became interested in tracing the continuities of their stylistic and thematic concerns across their body of work. (See also *French New Wave*; *Bazin, André*.)

Authenticity "Be true to yourself!" has become a cliché, more often used to sell products than at urging genuine self-discovery, and yet various philosophers have considered the ideal of authenticity as a call to freedom and responsibility. Heidegger, and Sartre following him, recognized how easy it is to consider oneself as merely one of many, a member of the crowd, subject, like the rest, to forces beyond one's control. The awareness of death as our "ownmost possibility" calls us to take responsibility for our situation by reminding us that the life into which we are thrown is nevertheless our own, that no one else can live it for us. (See also *Existentialism; Sartre, Jean-Paul.*)

Bacon, Francis (1561–1626) an English philosopher, scientist and statesman, who served as legal counsel to Queen Elizabeth and was knighted by King James I. His most important philosophical contribution was his *Novum Organum*, in which he argued that Aristotelian logic was unable to discover new facts regarding the operations of nature. He argued for its replacement with an inductive and experimental approach to logic that is a precursor to what is now described as the "scientific method."

Bazin, André (1918–1958) co-founder of *Cahiers du Cinema*, a highly influential journal of film criticism, to which many of the filmmakers associated with the French New Wave contributed. In his two-volume work *What is Cinema?* he championed Realism, an approach to making films that delivers the impression that what is seen on screen is a record of real events. (See also *Cahiers du Cinema; French New Wave;* Realism.)

Belmondo, Jean-Paul (b. 1933) an amateur boxer become actor, Belmondo had appeared in a few roles on stage and in short films when he was selected by Jean-Luc Godard to star in his debut feature film, *Breathless*. His performance in the film established his international stardom, and he appeared in several films by directors such as Francois Truffaut, Vittorio de Sica, and Jean-Pierre Melville.

Berkeley, George (1685–1753) born in Ireland, he is, along with John Locke and David Hume, one of the three most famous and influential empiricist philosophers. He is most well known for his defense of idealism (the view that everything that exists is either a mind or depends upon a mind for its existence), and his correlative insistence that matter does not exist independently of the minds that are aware of it. (See also *Empiricism; Hume, David.*)

Bogart, Humphrey (1899–1957) got his start on the stage and played small parts in films until his breakout role in Warner Brothers' *Petrified Forest*. He played a number of roles, primarily in gangster films, until the 1940s when he starred in some of his most memorable films including *The Big Sleep*, *Casablanca*, and *The Maltese Falcon*.

Boyle, Robert (1627–1691) born in Ireland, Boyle was an experimental chemist who is perhaps most famous for the law named after him, which states that when the temperature is held constant, the pressure exerted by a specific quantity of gas is inversely proportional to its volume.

Cahiers du Cinema a French film magazine founded in 1951 by André Bazin. Several of the young cinephiles who became the leading filmmakers of the French New Wave – Godard and Truffaut – got their start writing for this journal. (See also *Bazin, André;* French New Wave.)

Cavell, Stanley (1926–2018) an American philosopher, trained in the Anglo-American (or Analytic) tradition of philosophy, but whose work was informed and provoked by thinkers in the so-called Continental tradition of phenomeno-logical and existential philosophy. He was among the first major American philos-ophers to engage significantly with film, and devoted several books to teasing out the philosophical relevance of classical cinema. He is considered, along with Gilles Deleuze, to be one of the major inspirations for the film-philosophy approach to cinema. (See also *Analytic Philosophy*; *Continental Philosophy*; *Deleuze, Gilles*; and *Film-Philosophy*.)

Cinema Vérité inspired by the Soviet filmmaker Dziga Vertov's "kino pravda," cin-ema vérité endorses an approach to making films that makes explicit the involve-ment of the filmmaker and crew in the situation that is captured on screen. It was initially intended to contrast with Direct Cinema, but the movements are often confused, and the terms are sometimes used interchangeably, even by their practi-tioners. (See also *Direct Cinema*; *Kino Pravda*.)

Classical Style an approach to constructing films that places formal techniques of cinema (such as framing and editing) entirely in the service of telling an emotion-ally compelling story. When it is effective, such techniques do not call attention to themselves but rather call attention to characters, plot, and setting. The classical style is associated with the golden age of Hollywood, but is evident in mainstream works of cinema from around the world.

Conceptual Montage (also known as Dialectical Montage) the Soviet filmmaker Sergei Eisenstein coined this phrase to describe the way that contrasting images, edited in sequence, can provoke audiences to generate the concept that links them. (See also *Eisenstein, Sergei*.)

Continental Philosophy along with analytic philosophy, continental philosophy is one of the two major philosophical traditions to emerge in the twentieth century. Named for the fact that some of its major figures are from continental Europe (especially Germany and France) it is, nevertheless, a global philosophical move-ment. Some of the schools of thought that are associated with continental phi-losophy include phenomenology and existentialism, hermeneutics, critical theory, structuralism and post-structuralism, deconstruction, and so-called postmodern-ism. (See also *Analytic Philosophy*; *Phenomenology*; *Existentialism*.)

Continuity Editing ("Hollywood style") the approach to filmmaking in which editing techniques (and other stylistic features) are meant to be "invisible" in the sense that they do not call attention to themselves but rather put emphasis on the meaning-ful moments of a developing narrative that they link together. Familiar techniques employed within this approach include cutting on action and shot-reverse-shot.

De Beauvoir, Simone (1908–1986) prolific French writer and activist whose most influential work is *The Second Sex* (1949), a detailed biological, psychological, historical, and experiential study of femininity. A long-time collaborator with Jean-Paul Sartre, she wrote the *Ethics of Ambiguity* to explore the ethical implica-tions of existential philosophy. (See also *Sartre, Jean-Paul*; *Existentialism*.)

Deleuze, Gilles (1925–1995) French philosopher whose two-volume work on *Cinema* aimed to trace a shift in the kind of thinking that cinema gives rise to, from a pre-war thinking that subordinates time to movement, and that tries to make sense of action as having a determinate and closed structure and significance, to a thinking that is open to time itself in its flux and its open-ended and varying significance. His detailed analysis of cinematic images in terms of the mode of thinking that enables audiences to make sense of them has proved to be enormously influential.

Along with Stanley Cavell, Deleuze is considered one of the major influences of film-philosophy, which considers film not only as an object of philosophical investigation but as capable of contributing to philosophical thought. (See also *Cavell, Stanley* and *Film-Philosophy*.)

Democritus (b. circa 460 BCE) an ancient Greek philosopher, known primarily for his view that the apparent diversity of the world is produced by different arrangements of indestructible atoms.

Descartes, René (1596–1650) a French philosopher who made important contributions to mathematics, and was influential in the development of the methods of modern science. He argued that our knowledge of the external world is rooted in and dependent upon our awareness of ourselves and of the contents of our own consciousness. (See also *Rationalism*.)

Diegetic Sound Sound that has its apparent source in elements that belong to the story-world of a film, such as ordinary dialogue, ambient noises, and music emanating from a radio that is visible on screen (or implied off-screen). (Contrast with *Non-Diegetic Sound*.)

Direct cinema sometimes described as a "fly on the wall" approach to filmmaking, direct cinema is primarily used in documentary, and eschews the use of external commentary and talking heads interviews. Practitioners attempt to minimize interaction between the filmmakers and the situations being filmed so that those situations unfold nearly as if there had been no camera present, or at least give the impression that there had been no camera present. Often confused with cinema vérité. (See also *Cinema Vérité*.)

Duchamp, Marcel (1887–1968) French artist who began as a painter working in the style of cubism, and who gradually moved towards a more conceptual approach to art. He is most famous for his cubist painting *Nude Descending a Staircase*, which anticipates cinema in its depiction of segmented motion, and for his *Fountain*, a signed urinal which challenges traditional conceptions of what art is and ought to be. (Note: in his recent book *Stranger Than We Can Imagine: Making Sense of the Twentieth Century*, John Higgs argues that *Fountain* is falsely attributed to Duchamp, and that credit should be given to his friend and collaborator Elsa von Freytag-Loringhaven.)

Edison, Thomas (1847–1931) American inventor and businessman, who developed an early motion picture camera with his collaborator William K.L. Dickson, which he patented as the "kinetograph," whose moving images could be viewed through a "peep hole" in a viewer called the "kinetoscope." His kinetoscope inspired the development of a camera by his rivals the Lumière brothers that would both shoot images and project them onto a screen. He also pioneered the creation of one of the first indoor film sets, known as the "Black Maria," which allowed filmmakers to achieve precise control of interior lighting. (See also *Lumière Brothers*.)

Editing the act of joining together individual filmed sequences so as to produce a continuous display. To put emphasis on the significance or felt impact of such joined sequences, editing is sometimes described as "montage."

Eisenstein, Sergei (1898–1948) an influential Soviet filmmaker and film theorist who developed the theory of conceptual montage. His most influential films include *Battleship Potemkin*, *Strike*, *October*, and *Alexander Nevsky*.

Empiricism a branch of epistemology, committed to the view that sense experience alone can produce and generate knowledge, and that reason plays at most the auxiliary role of comparing, grouping, and differentiating between ideas that are originally derived from experience. Prominent empiricists include John Locke, David Hume, and George Berkeley. (See also *Rationalism*; *Locke, John*; *Hume, David*; and *Berkeley, George*.)

Epistemology　the branch of philosophy concerned with the nature and extent of knowledge. (See also *Metaphysics*, *Ethics*, and *Aesthetics*.)

Ethics　one of the core traditional areas of philosophical investigation, focused on the question of how we ought to live, and on notions such as good and evil, right and wrong, justice and injustice. (See also *Metaphysics*, *Epistemology*, and *Aesthetics*.)

Existentialism　a philosophical movement characterized primarily by the insistence that there is no human essence, that what it means to be human is something that human beings themselves determine, in the course of history, through their actions. Unlike other beings that are what they are as a result of either their nature or the function built into them by their designer, for human beings "existence precedes essence." While it was first labeled as "existentialism" in the twentieth century, and associated with thinkers such as Martin Heidegger, Jean-Paul Sartre, Simone de Beauvoir, and Albert Camus, existentialist themes can be traced back to the nineteenth century in the works of thinkers such as Søren Kierkegaard and Friedrich Nietzsche. (See also *Sartre, Jean-Paul*; *De Beauvoir, Simone*; *Nietzsche, Friedrich*.)

Film-Philosophy　an influential approach to thinking about the relationship between film and philosophy, that emphasizes the ways in which film is not merely an object for philosophical investigation or a source of handy philosophical illustrations, but has the potential to be philosophical in its own right.

French New Wave　in the late 1950s and 1960s, a group of young cinephiles, some of whom were critics for the film journal *Cahiers du Cinema*, began to make their own films. Champions of the independence of style and vision they discerned in the work of some of the filmmakers working within the Hollywood studio system, they aspired to become *auteurs* themselves, and created several highly original films that were influential throughout the world. François Truffaut, Jean-Luc Godard, Claude Chabrol, Jacques Rivette, and Eric Rohmer are some of the major figures; others associated with the movement include Agnès Varda, Jacques Demy, Louis Malle, and Alain Resnais. (See also *Godard, Jean-Luc*.)

Galilei, Galileo (1564–1642)　an Italian mathematician, astronomer, and physicist who was a powerful proponent for the use of mathematics in the study of the natural world. His controversial defense of the heliocentric worldview of Copernicus led to his trial before the Inquisition.

Godard, Jean-Luc (b. 1930)　a French-Swiss film critic and filmmaker and passionate cinephile, who was critical of mainstream French filmmaking, and sought with his contemporaries to develop an alternative approach to filmmaking, that was at once more personal and more capable of exploring ideas. Their new approach, heralded by early successes such as Truffaut's *The 400 Blows* (1959) and Godard's *Breathless* (1960), became known as the "French New Wave." (See also *French New Wave*.)

Hegel, G.W.F. (1770–1834)　a German philosopher working in the post-Kantian German Idealist tradition who held that finite realities can only be and be understood in relation to the other finite realities upon which they depend. He characterized the one absolute reality, that conditions and contains within itself the being of any finite entities, as *Geist* or Spirit. He held that Spirit not only exists, but also becomes progressively more aware of itself and its own activities in the course of history, through the activities of the self-conscious beings it gives rise to. (See also *Kant, Immanuel*.)

Hume, David (1711–1776) a British empiricist philosopher who argued that our understanding of ourselves could not be modeled upon the concepts through which we make sense of the world of objects. He went further to insist that when we trace the concepts (such as that of substance or of causal connection) through which we make sense of the external world to their origins within our sense experience we find that they turn out to be much less clear and self-evident than they seem to be initially.

James, William (1842–1910) an American philosopher and psychologist who was an early advocate of pragmatism. (See also *Pragmatism*; *Pierce, Charles Sanders*.)

Kant, Immanuel (1704–1824) German philosopher who argued that we cannot know what reality is like independent of our experience but we can determine what it must be like in order that we can have experience of it. Given that the lawlike regularities we discover in the natural world are, at least in part, a product of our own ordering activity, we cannot reasonably hold that they apply to us. So, he held, it is possible to think of ourselves as free – and thus leave room for a moral view of the world to make sense – even as we insist that the external world, as we experience it, is determined. He is most well known for his *Critique of Pure Reason*, the *Groundwork for the Metaphysics of Morals*, and the *Critique of Judgement*, in which he develops a highly influential analysis of the nature of aesthetic judgments.

Kino Pravda Kino Pravda (Russian for "Cinema Truth") was the name that Dziga Vertov gave to a series of short documentaries aimed at providing an unstaged and unscripted investigation of various topics from everyday life. It was also the slogan for his masterwork, *Man with a Movie Camera* (1929), that not only aims to show a wide range of facets of life in a Russian city, but also to show how the camera interacts with the reality it records. The slogan was an influence on the subsequent development in France of the cinema vérité approach to documentary filmmaking. (See also *Cinema Vérité*.)

Lumière Brothers Auguste (1862–1954) and Louis (1864–1948) – the two brothers worked in their father's photography studio before being introduced to motion pictures. They developed a camera that could also project its images onto a screen, and achieved some success displaying their motion pictures before they decided that there was no real future for their invention. They withdrew from the film business, but continued to innovate in the field of color photography.

Marx, Karl (1818–1883) a German philosopher who was influenced by progressive interpreters of Hegel to examine and criticize what he considered to be the real forces of history, namely the conflicts that arise within its economic system. His studies, developed in a long-time collaboration with Friedrich Engels, of the dialectic of history from an economic perspective inspired the rise of communist parties and political systems in various parts of the world.

Méliès, George (1861–1938) he had already been a magician when Méliès attended a demonstration of the Lumière brothers' cinematograph. He became fascinated by the medium and became an early innovator in the use of cinematic special effects to create fantastic and magical stories. His 1902 adaptation of Jules Verne's novel *A Trip to the Moon* was a highly acclaimed international success. (See also *Lumière Brothers*.)

Melville, Jean-Pierre (1917–1973)   filmmaker who was part of the French resistance to Nazi occupation during the Second World War. Known primarily for his film noir crime dramas, he was a major influence to the younger filmmakers who contributed to the French New Wave. He plays a minor role in Jean-Luc Godard's *Breathless*. (See *French New Wave*; and *Godard, Jean-Luc*.)

Metaphysics   one of the core traditional areas of philosophical investigation, focused on the nature of reality, the relation between appearance and reality, whether there is an ultimate reality (such as God), the question whether there are different kinds of reality (such as mental and physical realities), and if so how they relate to each other. (See *Epistemology*; *Ethics*; and *Aesthetics*.)

Mulvey, Laura (b. 1941)   British film theorist who is perhaps best known for her essay "Visual Pleasure and the Narrative Cinema," in which she argued that mainstream narrative fiction films cater to the "male gaze," by depicting male protagonists in such a way that audiences identify with them, and female characters in ways that suggest they are "to be looked at."

Muybridge, Edward (1830–1904)   British photographer and inventor, who made an essential contribution to the history of cinema by developing techniques to take rapid sequential photographs of movement. He also developed a device (the "zoopraxiscope") that allowed such images to be seen in rapid sequence, making it possible to view an appearance of the original movement.

Necessary Condition   a first condition is said to be necessary for a second, if the second will never occur in the absence of the first. So, for example, a fuel source is necessary for fire. Necessary conditions are contrasted with sufficient conditions. A fuel source is not sufficient for fire, since there would also need to be some way of igniting the fuel source and enabling it to burn. (See also *Sufficient Condition*.)

Nietzsche, Friedrich (1844–1900)   German philologist and philosopher who is known for his critical analysis of various dogmas of philosophy and popular thought, such as the idea that historical events have a univocal significance, that history amounts to progress, that there are transcendent or a priori moral values, and that the truth of ideas is more important than their practical impact.

Non-diegetic Sound   Sound that accompanies a film and that helps shape the viewer's experience of the film but that does not appear to originate from a source that would be audible to someone belonging to the world depicted in the film. Common examples of non-diegetic sound include the musical soundtrack and voiceover narration. (Contrast with *Diegetic Sound*.)

Ordinary Language Philosophy   sometimes called "Oxford Philosophy" it is an approach to solving philosophical problems by way of careful consideration of the meaning of the terms in which those problems are formulated.

Parmenides (b. circa 514 BCE)   pre-Socratic philosopher whose only surviving work, *On Nature*, distinguishes between the way of opinion, which follows appearances, and the way of truth, which, following reason, arrives at the insight that what truly is can never not be, so that change is merely an illusion.

Paul, R.W. (1869–1943)   a British inventor and pioneer of cinema, he developed a device for projecting images upon a wall at nearly the same time as the Lumière brothers had developed their own. He also developed his own camera and created a number of films, including *The Countryman and the Cinematograph* (1901). (See also *Lumière Brothers*.)

Phenomenology   a philosophical methodology that involves careful attention to the structural dimensions of "lived experience." While he has important precursors, Edmund Husserl is credited with the explicit formulation of the method. Other influential phenomenologists include Martin Heidegger, Emmanuel Levinas, Maurice Merleau-Ponty, and Jean-Paul Sartre. (See also *Continental Philosophy*, *Sartre, Jean-Paul.*)

Philosophy   literally meaning "love of wisdom," the Greek term *philosophia* was used by Plato to contrast the non-dogmatic and open-ended pursuit of insight regarding fundamental values and ideas with the teachings of so-called "sophists" who considered themselves already to possess wisdom. Philosophy examines basic assumptions underlying human practices and theories, assumptions regarding what is real, what can be known, what is of value, and how we should act, as well as assumptions regarding the proper character of philosophical investigation itself. (See also *Metaphysics*; *Epistemology*; *Ethics*; and *Aesthetics*.)

Philosophy through Film (Film and Philosophy, Philosophy and Popular Culture)   films and other popular media such as television can offer powerful and vivid illustrations of philosophical themes, and can be used to illustrate some of the importance and complexity of these themes.

Pierce, Charles Sanders (1839–1914)   An American philosopher considered to be the originator of the philosophical school of pragmatism. His thoughts on the nature of signs, both linguistic and non-linguistic, were a major influence on Gilles Deleuze's account of cinematic signs in his two volume work on cinema. (See also Pragmatism; James, William; Deleuze, Gilles).

Plato (circa 428–348 BCE)   influenced by Socrates to pursue a life of philosophy, his works provide a powerful portrait of Socrates as he engages his fellow Athenians in dialogue. Plato founded the Academy, and was Aristotle's teacher. (See also *Aristotle*; *Socrates*.)

Plato's Theory of the Forms   Plato's name is widely associated with the so-called Theory of the Forms, according to which the changing perceptible realities we experience depend upon and participate in unchanging intelligible essences (or forms). While Plato has his characters discuss such a theory, he also has them raise objections to this theory. We can say that Plato reflected seriously upon the question whether our capacity to make sense of our experience requires us to posit the existence of truths (or realities) that transcend experience and make it possible.

Pragmatism   a philosophical method that developed in North America in the late nineteenth century. Charles Sanders Pierce is credited with formulating the method explicitly, and William James with establishing its importance within academic philosophy. The core of the method is to clarify concepts and resolve philosophical problems by appeal to the difference it would make in practice to conceive things in one way or another.

Rationalism   an approach to philosophy committed to the view that sensory experience is unreliable, and that reason alone can yield knowledge. Major rationalist thinkers include René Descartes, Benedict Spinoza, and Gottfried Wilhelm Leibniz. (See also *Descartes, Renè*; *Spinoza, Benedict*; and *Leibniz, Gottfried Wilhelm.*)

Realism   in the arts, such as literature, painting and film realism refers to a style that attempts to render subjects naturally and truthfully, so that depictions resemble closely the things they depict; in philosophy it is the thesis that concepts refer to real things, and that these exist entirely independently of the concepts that refer to them. Plato's theory of the forms is considered to be realist, for example, because it holds that forms exist and that when we think about them we are thinking about something that would be what it was regardless of how we think about it.

Rouch, Jean (1917–2004)   pioneering French filmmaker and anthropologist who played a central role in the development and influence of the cinema vérité approach to documentary filmmaking. He is most known for his films *Moi, Un Noir* (1958), and *Chronique d'un Été* (1961), in which he employs his ethnographic approach to filmmaking to examine social life in his contemporary France.

Skepticism   the philosophical position that knowledge is not possible. Ancient proponents of skepticism considered it to be a way of life that could alleviate the anxiety that comes from uncertainty.

Seberg, Jean (1938–1979)   an American actress who established herself as a star in France with her performance in Godard's *Breathless*, following a few less promising roles in American films. (See also *Godard, Jean-Luc*.)

Socrates (circa 470–399 BCE)   what is known about Socrates comes from the writings of others, since he himself apparently never wrote anything down. He is the main interlocutor in many Platonic dialogues, and is depicted as a powerful thinker who was more interested in challenging others to push past their own preconceptions than in developing and defending a body of doctrines of his own. His most characteristic teaching is that the most important thing one can learn is the extent of one's own ignorance. He held that this insight should not lead to despair but towards a commitment to work with others to acquire wisdom. He called this pursuit of wisdom "philosophy." (See also *Plato*.)

Spinoza, Baruch (1632–1677)   a Dutch philosopher who was excommunicated from the Jewish faith for his purportedly heretical ideas. His most famous and influential work is the *Ethics*, in which he argues that there is only one reality, which we may choose to call either God or nature, but there is nothing supernatural about it. All things, including human beings, are merely localized manifestations of this one reality, whose characteristics depend upon the causal relationships they sustain with all other realities. We are free only to the extent that we understand and accept the interdependence of all things. (See also *Rationalism*.)

Stoicism   named after the open market or porch (*stoa*) in Athens where the original stoics used to gather and discuss ideas, it is a school of philosophy focused on living well by cultivating virtue. The emphasis of stoic practice is living according to nature, which means accepting the fact that much of what happens in the world is out of one's personal control. Better to focus on what one can control: one's thoughts and attitudes.

Sufficient Condition   a first condition is said to be sufficient for a second if whenever the first condition obtains, the second one will. In a room with plenty of oxygen, striking a dry match is sufficient to start a small fire; it isn't necessary, since small fires can be started in many other ways. (See also *Necessary Condition*.)

Thales (b. circa 624 BCE)   an early pre-Socratic philosopher and mathematician from Miletus, who is known for his attempt to explain natural phenomena in terms of the capacity for material substances to undergo change, rather than in mythological terms.

The Good   many things are good, but most of them are only relatively good, good for something but not intrinsically good, irrespective of context. In several of his dialogues, Plato explores the idea that to consider anything good is to have some inkling of an absolute good, which he calls the idea (or form) of the Good.

Thing-in-Itself   the term Immanuel Kant employed to refer to the way things are, independent of how we experience them. He argued that while reason leads us to speculate on ideas such as the cosmos, the soul, and God – none of which could ever be experienced directly – we can never know anything about such things as they are in themselves. We can't even say that they do or don't exist.

Vertov, Dziga (1896–1954)   a pioneering Soviet filmmaker, who aimed to expose directly through film the complexities of everyday life. He coined the term "Kino Pravda" (or "Cinema Truth") for an early series of documentaries, and is most well known for his *Man with a Movie Camera* (1929), a complex experimental documentary portrait of life in the Soviet Union, that also manages to depict and examine the nature of the filmmaking process. (See also *Kino Pravda*.)

Wittgenstein, Ludwig (1889–1951)   an influential Austrian philosopher whose early *Tractatus Logico-Philosophicus* holds that we cannot think or express anything that cannot be unambiguously pictured. In his later work, he argues that language is more complicated, and that meaning is essentially bound up with use and with context.

Bibliography

Works cited and suggested readings

As noted in the preface, this book was written with the aim that a reader interested in film or in philosophy could follow the arguments without having any specific prior knowledge of either subject. What follows is a list of additional readings, including every text referenced in the book, for those interested in pursuing any of these topics further.

Primary philosophical texts

Anselm. *Monologion and Proslogion, with the Replies of Gaunilo and Anselm*, trans. Thomas Williams. Hackett Publishing Co., 1996.

Aristotle. *Metaphysics*, trans. C.D.C. Reeve. Hackett Publishing Co., 2016.

Aristotle. *The Nicomachean Ethics*, trans. Joe Sachs. Focus Philosophical Library, 2002.

Aristotle. *Prior Analytics*, trans. Robin Smith. Hackett Publishing Co., 1989.

Ayer, A.J. *Language, Truth, and Logic*. Dover Publications, 1952.

Berkeley, George. *A Treatise Concerning the Principles of Human Knowledge*. Hackett Publishing Co., 1982.

Carroll, Robert and Stephen Prickett (eds). *The Bible: Authorized King James Version*. Oxford University Press, 2008.

Descartes. *Discourse on Method and Meditations on First Philosophy*, trans. Donald A. Cress. Hackett Publishing Co., 1999.

Gettier, Edmund. "Is Justified True Belief Knowledge?" *Analysis*, 23(6), 1963, 121–123.

Heidegger, Martin. *Being and Time*, trans. John Macquarrie and Edward Robinson. Harper Perennial Modern Classics, 2008.

Hegel, G.W.F. *Aesthetics: Lectures on Fine Art*, vols. I & II, trans. T.M. Knox. Oxford University Press, 1975.

Hegel, G.W.F. *Hegel's The Philosophy of Right*, trans. Alan White. Focus Publishing, 2002.

Hegel, G.W.F. *Phenomenology of Spirit*, trans. A.V. Miller. Oxford University Press, 1977.

Hume, David. *An Enquiry Concerning Human Understanding*. Hackett Publishing Co., 1993.

James, William. *Pragmatism and Other Writings*. Penguin Classics, 2000.

Kant, Immanuel. *Critique of Pure Reason*, trans. Paul Guyer and Allen Wood. Cambridge University Press, 1998.

Locke, John. *An Essay Concerning Human Understanding*. Hackett Publishing Co., 1996.

Merleau-Ponty, Maurice. "The Film and the New Psychology," trans. Hubert L. Dreyfus and Patricia Allen Dreyfus. *The Continental Philosophy of Film Reader*. Bloomsbury Academic, 2018.

Nietzsche, Friedrich. *Basic Writings of Nietzsche*, trans. Walter Kaufmann. Modern Library, 2011.

Nietzsche, Friedrich. *The Gay Science*, trans. Josefine Nauckhoff. Cambridge University Press, 2001.

Nietzsche, Friedrich. *The Portable Nietzsche*, trans. Walter Kaufmann. Penguin Books, 1977.

Peirce, Charles Sanders. "How to Make Our Ideas Clear." *Philosophical Writings of Peirce.* Dover Publications, 1955.

Plato. *The Apology of Socrates* in *Five Dialogues*, trans. G.M.A. Grube, rev. John M. Cooper. Hackett Publishing Co., 2002.

Plato. *Meno* in *Five Dialogues*, trans. G.M.A. Grube, rev. John M. Cooper. Hackett Publishing Co., 2002.

Plato. *The Republic of Plato*, trans. Allan Bloom. Basic Books, 1991.

Plato. *Theaetetus*, trans. Joe Sachs. Focus Philosophical Library, 2004.

Ryle, Gilbert. *The Concept of Mind*. University of Chicago Press, 2000.

Sartre, Jean-Paul. *Being and Nothingness*. Washington Square Press, 1993.

Spinoza, Baruch. *The Essential Spinoza: Ethics and Related Writings*, trans. Samuel Shirley. Hackett Publishing Co., 2006.

Wittgenstein, Ludwig. *Philosophical Investigations*, trans. G.E.M. Anscombe. Macmillan Publishing, 1958.

Wittgenstein, Ludwig. *Tractatus Logico-Philosophicus*, trans. D.F. Pears and B.F. McGuiness. Routledge, 1974.

On philosophy and the history of philosophy

Adamson, Peter. *Classical Philosophy: A History of Philosophy Without Any Gaps*, Vol. 1. Oxford University Press, 2014.

Adamson, Peter. *The History of Philosophy Without Any Gaps Podcast*. Dec. 21, 2010–present, https://historyofphilosophy.net/. Accessed October 22, 2018.

Adamson, Peter. *Philosophy in the Hellenistic and Roman Worlds: A History of Philosophy without Any Gaps*, Vol. 2. Oxford University Press, 2015.

Adamson, Peter. *Philosophy in the Islamic World: A History of Philosophy Without Any Gaps*, Vol. 3. Oxford University Press, 2016.

Baggini, Julian and Peter S. Fosl. *The Philosopher's Toolkit: A Compendium of Philosophical Concepts and Methods*. Wiley-Blackwell, 2010.

Beauvoir, Simone de. *The Ethics of Ambiguity*. Open Road Media, 2018.

Collingwood, R.G. *An Essay on Philosophical Method*. Thoemmes Press, 1995.

Craig, Edward. *The Shorter Routledge Encyclopedia of Philosophy*. Routledge, 2005.

Deleuze, Gilles and Guattari, Félix. *What is Philosophy?* Columbia University Press, 1994.

Goldin, Owen and Patricia Kilroe. *Human Life and the Natural World: Readings in the History of Western Philosophy*. Broadview Press, 1997.

Goldstein, Rebecca Newberger. *Plato at the Googleplex: Why Philosophy Won't Go Away*. Pantheon Books, 2014.

Hadot, Pierre. *Philosophy as a Way of Life: Spiritual Exercises from Socrates to Foucault.* Wiley-Blackwell, 1995.

Kenny, Anthony. *A New History of Western Philosophy: In Four Parts*. Oxford University Press, 2010.

Lawhead, William F. *The Voyage of Discovery: A Historical Introduction to Philosophy,* 4th ed. Cengage, 2014.

Melchert, Norman. *The Great Conversation: A Historical Introduction to Philosophy,* 7th ed. Oxford University Press, 2014.

Mumford, Stephen. *Metaphysics: A Very Short Introduction*. Oxford University Press, 2012.

Nagel, Thomas. *The View from Nowhere*. Oxford University Press, 1986.

Russon, John. *Bearing Witness to Epiphany: Persons, Things, and the Nature of Erotic Life.* Suny Press, 2009.

Russon, John. *Sites of Exposure: Art, Politics, and the Nature of Experience.* Indiana University Press, 2017.

Sellars, Wilfred. *Science, Perception, and Reality.* Ridgeview Pub. Co., 1991.

Shapin, Steven. *The Scientific Revolution.* University of Chicago Press, 1996.

Smith, Justin E. *The Philosopher: A History in Six Types.* Princeton University Press, 2016.

On film history and theory

Andrew, Dudley. *What Cinema Is!* Wiley-Blackwell, 2010.

Arnheim, Rudolf. *Film as Art.* University of California Press, 2006.

Baudry, Jean-Louis, "Ideological Effects of the Basic Cinematographic Apparatus." Film Quarterly, 28(2), 39–47.

Bazin, André. *What Is Cinema?*, Volumes 1 and 2, trans. Hugh Grey. University of California Press, 1967 and 1971.

Bordwell, David. *Narration in the Fiction Film.* Routledge, 1987.

Bordwell, David, Kristen Thompson, and Janet Staiger. *The Classical Hollywood Cinema: Film Style and Mode of Production to 1960.* Columbia University Press, 1985.

Bordwell, David, Kristen Thompson, and Jeff Smith. *Film Art: An Introduction.* McGraw Hill Education, 2016.

Branigan, Edward and Warren Buckland. *The Routledge Encyclopedia of Film Theory.* Routledge, 2015.

Chion, Michel. *The Voice in Cinema*, trans. Claudia Gorbman. Columbia University Press, 1999.

Corrigan, Timothy and Patricia White. *The Film Experience: An Introduction*, 3rd ed. Bedford-St. Martins, 2012.

Cousins, Mark. *The Story of Film.* Pavillon, 2011.

Elsaesser, Thomas and Malte Hagener. *Film Theory: An Introduction through the Senses.* Routledge, 2015.

Eisenstein, Sergei. *Film Form: Essays in Film Theory*, trans. Jay Leyda. Harvest Books, 1969.

Gaudette, Emily. "'Black Panther' Targeted by Alt-Right Trolls Who Also Tried to Tank 'Last Jedi'." Newsweek. February 2, 2018. https://www.newsweek.com/black-panther-reviews-fanboys-rotten-tomatoes-boycott-798445. Accessed July 1, 2018.

Goldman, William. *Adventures in the Screen Trade: A Personal View of Hollywood* (reissue ed.). Grand Central Publishing, 1989.

Hayward, Susan. *Cinema Studies: The Key Concepts.* Routledge, 2013.

Higgs, John. *Stranger Than We Can Imagine: An Alternative History of the Twentieth Century.* Soft Skull Press, 2015.

Kirsner, Scott. *Inventing the Movies: Hollywood's Epic Battle Between Invention and the Status Quo from Thomas Edison to Steve Jobs.* CinemaTech Books, 2008.

Koeze, Ella, Walt Hickey, Rachel Dottle, and Gus Wezerak. "The Next Bechdel Test." *FiveThirtyEight*, Dec. 21, 2017, https://projects.fivethirtyeight.com/next-bechdel/. Accessed October 22, 2018.

Krakauer, Siegfried. *Theory of Film: The Redemption of Physical Reality.* Oxford University Press, 1960.

Mulvey, Laura. "Visual Pleasure and Narrative Cinema." *Film Theory and Criticism*, ed. Leo Braudy and Marshall Cohen. Oxford University Press, 2009.

Münsterberg, Hugo. *Hugo Munsterberg on Film: The Photoplay: A Psychological Study and Other Writings.* Routledge, 2001.

Nichols, Bill. *Engaging Cinema: An Introduction to Film Studies.* W.W. Norton & Co., 2010.

Nowell-Smith, Geoffrey. *The Oxford History of World Cinema.* Oxford University Press, 1999.

Perkins, V.F. *Film as Film: Understanding and Judging Movies*. De Capo Press, 1993.

Sklar, Robert. *A World History of Film*. Harry N. Abrams, Inc., 2001.

Small, Edward. *Direct Theory: Experimental Film and Video as a Major Genre*. Southern Illinois University Press, 1995.

Smith, Stacy L., Marc Choueiti, & Katherine Pieper. "Inclusion in the Director's Chair: Gender, Race, & Age of Directors across 1100 Films from 2007-2017," Annenberg Inclusion Initiative, January 2018. http://assets.uscannenberg.org/docs/inclusion-in-the-directors-chair-2007-2017.pdf Accessed October 1, 2018.

Tarkovsky, Andrei. *Sculpting in Time*, trans. Kitty Hunter-Blair. University of Texas Press, 2006.

White, Patricia. "Feminism and Film." *Oxford Guide to Film Studies*. Oxford University Press, 1998.

Wiegman, Robyn. "Race, Ethnicity, and Film." *Oxford Guide to Film Studies*. Oxford University Press, 1998.

Philosophy of film, philosophy through film, and film-philosophy

Andersen, Nathan. *Shadow Philosophy: Plato's Cave and Cinema*. Routledge, 2014.

Carel, Havi, and Greg Tuck. *New Takes in Film-Philosophy*. Palgrave Macmillan, 2011.

Carroll, Nöel. "Narration." *The Routledge Companion to Philosophy and Film*. Routledge, 2008.

Carroll, Nöel. *The Philosophy of Motion Pictures*. Blackwell, 2008.

Cavell, Stanley. *Contesting Tears: The Hollywood Melodrama of the Unknown Woman*. University of Chicago Press, 1996.

Cavell, Stanley. *Pursuits of Happiness: The Hollywood Comedy of Remarriage*. Harvard University Press, 1984.

Cavell, Stanley. *The World Viewed: Reflections on the Ontology of Film*. Harvard University Press, 1979.

Deamer, David. *Deleuze's Cinema Books: Three Introductions to the Taxonomy of Images*. Edinburgh University Press, 2016.

Deleuze, Gilles. *Cinema 1 & 2*, trans. Hugh Tomlinson & Barbara Habberjam. University of Minnesota Press, 1986 & 1989.

Falzon, Christopher. *Philosophy Goes to the Movies*. Routledge, 2007.

Herzogenrath, Bernd. *Film as Philosophy*. Minnesota University Press, 2017.

Kahn, Paul. *Finding Ourselves at the Movies: Philosophy for a New Generation*. Columbia University Press, 2013.

Litch, Mary. *Philosophy through Film*. Routledge, 2010.

Mulhall, Stephen. *On Film*. Routledge, 2008.

Plantinga, Carl and Greg Smith, (eds). *Passionate Views: Film, Cognition, and Emotion*. John Hopkins University Press, 1999.

Sinnerbrink, Robert. *Cinematic Ethics: Exploring Ethical Experience through Film*. Routledge, 2015.

Sinnerbrink, Robert. *New Philosophies of Film: Thinking Images*. Continuum, 2011.

Smith, Murray, and Thomas E. Wartenberg. *Thinking through Cinema: Film as Philosophy*. Blackwell, 2006.

Thomson-Jones, Kathryn. *Aesthetics and Film*. Continuum, 2008.

Vaughan, Hunter. *Where Film Meets Philosophy: Godard, Resnais, and Experiments in Cinematic Thinking*. Columbia University Press, 2013.

Wartenberg, Thomas E. *Thinking on Screen: Film as Philosophy*. Routledge, 2007.

Yacavone, Daniel. *Film Worlds: A Philosophical Aesthetics of Cinema*. Columbia University Press, 2015.

On *Arrival of the Train*

Bottomore, Stephen. "The Panicking Audience?: Early Cinema and the 'Train Effect.'" *Historical Journal of Film, Radio and Television*, 19(2), 1999.

Gunning, Tom. "An Aesthetic of Astonishment: Early Film and the (In)Credulous Spectator." *Viewing Positions: Ways of Seeing Film*, ed. Linda Williams. Rutgers University Press, 1994.

Loiperdinger, Martin and Bernd Elzer. "Lumiere's Arrival of the Train: Cinema's Founding Myth." *The Moving Image*, 4(1), Spring 2004: 89–118.

Lumiére, August and Louis. "Arrival of a Train (1895)" in *The Movies Begin, Vol. 2: The European Pioneers*. Kino Lorber Films, 2002.

Paul, R.W. "The Countryman and the Cinematograph (1901)" in *The Movies Begin, Vol. 2: The European Pioneers*. Kino Lorber Films, 2002.'

On Godard, *Breathless,* and Cinema Verité

Andrew, Dudley. *Breathless: Jean-Luc Godard, Director*. Rutgers Film in Print Series, Rutgers University Press, 1988.

Andrew, Geoff. "Abbas Kiarostami." *The Guardian*. April 28, 2005. https://www.theguardian.com/film/2005/apr/28/hayfilmfestival2005.guardianhayfestival. Accessed December 1, 2017.

Aufderheide, Patricia. "Cinema Verité". *Documentary Film: A Very Short Introduction*, 44–55. Oxford: Oxford University Press, 2007.

Baby, Yvonne. "Interview with Yvonne Baby." *Breathless: Jean-Luc Godard, Director*, ed. and trans. Dudley Andrew. Rutgers Film in Print Series, Rutgers University Press, 1988.

Bazin, André. "The Death of Humphrey Bogart." *Cahiers du Cinéma, The 1950s: Neorealism, Hollywood, New Wave*, ed. Jim Hillier. Harvard University Press, 1986.

Brody, Richard. *Everything Is Cinema: The Working Life of Jean-Luc Godard*. Henry Holt & Co., 2008.

Bresson, Robert. *Notes on the Cinematographer*. Green Integer, 1997.

Chanan, Michael. "Truth Games." *The Politics of Documentary*. British Film Institute, 2007.

Conley, Tom and T. Jefferson Kline. (eds) *A Companion to Jean-Luc Godard*. Wiley-Blackwell, 2014.

Corliss, Richard. "Cinema: Over Easy" in *Time*, 118(11), Sept. 14., 1981

Domarchi, Jean, Jacques Doniol-Valcroze, Jean-Luc Godard, Pierre Kast, Jacques Rivette and Eric Rohmer, 'Hiroshima, notre amour', Cahiers du cinéma, 97, 1959. *Cahiers du Cinema, The 1950's: Neo-Realism, Hollywood, the New Wave*, ed. Jim Hillier, trans. Liz Heron. British Film Institute, 1985.

Frodon, Jean-Michel. "From Pen to Camera: Another Critic." *Companion to Jean-Luc Godard*, ed. Tom Conly and T. Jefferson Kline. Wiley Blackwell, 2014.

Godard, Jean-Luc. *Godard on Godard*, ed. and trans. Tom Milne. Da Capo Press, 1986.

Godard, Jean Luc. *Histoire(s) du Cinema*. Olive Films, 2011.

Godard, Jean-Luc. *Breathless (Blu-ray + DVD)*. Criterion Collection, 2014.

Losada, Matt. "Jean Rouch." *Senses of Cinema*, 57, December 2010, http://sensesofcinema.com/2010/great-directors/jean-rouch/. Accessed August 15, 2018.

Monaco, James. *The New Wave: Truffaut, Godard, Chabrol, Rohmer, Rivette*. Oxford University Press, 1977.

Nichols, Bill. "The Observational Mode." *Introduction to Documentary*, second edition, 172–179. Bloomington: Indiana University Press, 2010.

Nichols, Bill. "The Participatory Mode." *Introduction to Documentary*, second edition, 179–194. Bloomington: Indiana University Press, 2010.

Nichols, Bill. *Representing Reality: Issues and Concepts in Documentary*. Indiana University Press, 1991.

Raskin, Richard. "Five Explanations for the Jump Cuts in Godard's *Breathless.* " *p.o.v. filmditskrift: a Danish Journal of Film Studies*, December 6, 1988, https://pov.imv.au.dk/Issue_06/section_1/artc10.html. Accessed April 15, 2017.

Usher, Phillip John. "*À bout de souffle*: Trials in New Coherences." *A Companion to Jean-Luc Godard,* ed. Tom Conley. Wiley-Blackwell, 2014.

Wintonick, Peter. *Cinéma Vérité: Defining the Moment* (VHS). Montréal, Québec: National Film Board of Canada, 1999.

Index

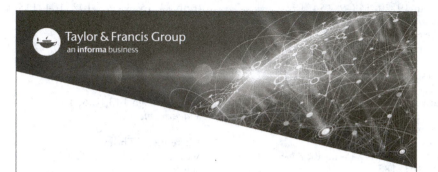

Taylor & Francis eBooks

www.taylorfrancis.com

A single destination for eBooks from Taylor & Francis
with increased functionality and an improved user
experience to meet the needs of our customers.

90,000+ eBooks of award-winning academic content in
Humanities, Social Science, Science, Technology, Engineering,
and Medical written by a global network of editors and authors.

TAYLOR & FRANCIS EBOOKS OFFERS:

A streamlined
experience for
our library
customers

A single point
of discovery
for all of our
eBook content

Improved
search and
discovery of
content at both
book and
chapter level

REQUEST A FREE TRIAL
support@taylorfrancis.com

Routledge
Taylor & Francis Group

CRC Press
Taylor & Francis Group